LEGACY OF DEBT

CORRUPTION OF REAL MONEY (PART II)

FIRST EDITION

MARCO CHU KWAN CHING

This publication is designed to provide competent and reliable information regarding the subject matter covered. However, it is sold with the understanding that the author and the publisher are not engaged in rendering legal, financial, or other professional advice. Law and practices often vary from state to state and if legal or other expert assistance is required, the service or a professional should be sought. The author and publisher specifically disclaim any liability that is incurred from the use or application of the content of this book.

Photo on U.S. National Debt Clock by Matthew Bisanz appears with the permission under GNU Free Documentation License.

"To my Dear Wife Carrie"

Acknowledgements

Where do I begin thanking all the people who helped to make this book possible? This book represents one of my most dedicated missions of my life.

I would like to express my gratitude to my parents, Angela Tsang and Tony Chu, for their encouragement. I would like to give special thanks to Mike Maloney who started me on the road to invest in precious metals; and to Peter Schiff for his unparalleled economic insights; Ron Paul for his diligent politics lectures. I would like to thank Daniel Wilson for proofreading my book; I especially like to thank my grandparents, as my childhood with them is instrumental in bringing this book to fruition.

Contents

Introduction

Part I: Legacy of Debt

Part II: How to Restore The Global Prosperity?

Constitution of U.S. Article I

No State shall coin money; emit bills of credit; make anything but Gold and Silver coin a tender in payment of debt.

Introduction

Why did I write this book?

There is an idiom saying that *money* does not grow on trees. But our modern banking system creates money far faster than trees can grow. For us to maintain the level of prosperity we have, our government must be in twice as much debt when they leave office than when they come in, or the whole thing will collapse.

This book is the 2nd book of the Corruption of Real Money series. It is a journey on debts in the global economy. It is also my warning to millennials. Through reading this book, you will have essential knowledge that can help you to weather or potentially prosper through the age of debt. By studying the evolution of debt-based economy through the lens of history, you will understand how the nature of the global economy changed. This is part of the reason I believe baby-boomers' financial advice is impractical day by day. Along your journey on the *Legacy of Debt*, you will understand the origin of credit bubbles threatening the global stability.

The subject of debt is the single most complex yet important subject in the global economy. It can be so intimidating that it is difficult to understand everything in this book in one go. But don't worry as this book is designed in a way that is easy to understand.

With great knowledge comes great responsibility. I think it is crucial for everyone, especially the young generation, to understand the implication of debts in our global economy. Millennials are our future. They will drive our future economy. That is why I want to share my knowledge through this book – *Legacy of Debt*.

Questions on Debt

There is an interesting question from Mike Maloney – The Founder of GoldSilver.com. And the question is:

Q: Imagine you borrowed the first dollar (**Green / Currency**) into existence, and that's the only dollar that exists on the planet. But you promised to pay back the principal dollar (**Red / Debt**) with another dollar as interest (**Red / Debt**), where do you get the second dollar from?

Figure 1: The economy has one dollar and owes two

A: The answer is that you have to borrow the second dollar (**Green / Currency**) into existence. Like the first dollar in Figure 1, this newly created dollar in Figure 2 must pay back a principal (**Red / Debt**) with interest (**Red/Debt**). So now we have two dollars in our economy, but we owe four dollars.

Figure 2: The economy has two dollar and owe four

Q: If this system continues, can we pay back our debt?

A: A Smart reader like you will properly figure out there will never be enough currency to pay the debt. There is always more debt in the system than there is currency in existence to pay debt.

Figure 3: Can we pay back our debt?

Q: What will happen if we stop borrowing?

A: Currency and debt cancel out each other. If we stopped borrowing, there will be no new currency (**Green / Currency**) created to pay back the portion of the debt (**Red / Debt**).

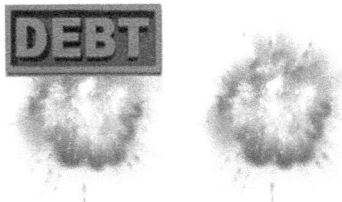

Figure 4: Debt and Currency cancel out each other

To put this into perspective, if we pay off the principal only on all the debt (i.e loans and bonds) (**Red / Debt**) that exists in our entire currency supply in the world, our whole currency supply (**Green /Currency**) will just varnish, leaving us only with debt.

Figure 5: When our currency supply extinguishes…

Q: What will happen if our entire currency supply is extinguished?
A: The world suffers a deflationary spiral.

So, as for now, do you understand why we have to go deeper into debt every year to keep the economy going? We will go into the part on deflation later.

The Concept of Values

When a builder takes lumber and creates a house, he is producing something valuable out of something less valuable. In the process, values are created. When a real estate agent takes a house and sells it in the market, his talents and time make a transaction happen. In the process, values are created. When Steve Jobs and Steve Wozniak invented the Apple II personal computer in a garage, they revolutionized the personal computer industry. In the process, a massive amount of values were created. When you are working 9-to-5 as a white collar, you are also creating values. Creating values are what drives our economy to grow. It is your blood, sweat, labor, time and invention that create values.

But how do we quantify values?

How many apples can you buy with your daily salary?

That is when the invention of money comes into play. Money is the bloodline of a civilized society; it is an instrument by which a product is sold or bought.

Basically, everything else requires a certain amount of effort to produce to create value, except one thing – money. When we create money, we have created an instrument of value, which has no value on its own. It is just as expensive or inexpensive to print a $20 note as it is to print the $1.

Now let's pause for a moment. Can you sense the problem? Is it possible for an instrument of value not to have value on its own? If these instruments of value can be created at will, what does this mean for the real value you and I deliver to the economy?

Some thoughts on Standard of Living

Besides the concept of value, I want to share with you my perspective on the quality of life and standard of living.

If you are a millennial, your parents might have told you how little they earned back when they were young.

In 1960, the average median income in U.S. was $5,600 USD.

Does an annual income of $5,600 USD sound appealing to you?

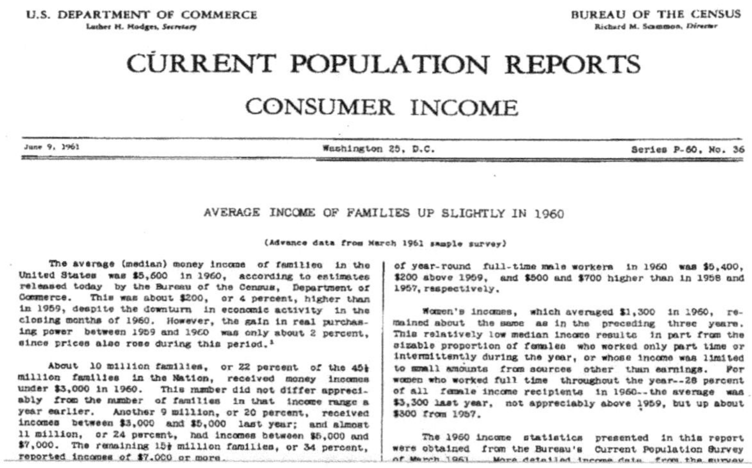

U.S. DEPARTMENT OF COMMERCE   BUREAU OF THE CENSUS
Luther H. Hodges, Secretary   Richard M. Scammon, Director

CURRENT POPULATION REPORTS
CONSUMER INCOME

| June 9, 1961 | Washington 25, D.C. | Series P-60, No. 36 |

AVERAGE INCOME OF FAMILIES UP SLIGHTLY IN 1960

(Advance data from March 1961 sample survey)

The average (median) money income of families in the United States was $5,600 in 1960, according to estimates released today by the Bureau of the Census, Department of Commerce. This was about $200, or 4 percent, higher than in 1959, despite the downturn in economic activity in the closing months of 1960. However, the gain in real purchasing power between 1959 and 1960 was only about 2 percent, since prices also rose during this period.[1]

About 10 million families, or 22 percent of the 45½ million families in the Nation, received money incomes under $3,000 in 1960. This number did not differ appreciably from the number of families in that income range a year earlier. Another 9 million, or 20 percent, received incomes between $3,000 and $5,000 last year; and almost 11 million, or 24 percent, had incomes between $5,000 and $7,000. The remaining 15½ million families, or 34 percent, reported incomes of $7,000 or more.

of year-round full-time male workers in 1960 was $5,400, $200 above 1959, and $500 and $700 higher than in 1958 and 1957, respectively.

Women's incomes, which averaged $1,300 in 1960, remained about the same as in the preceding three years. This relatively low median income results in part from the sizable proportion of females who worked only part time or intermittently during the year, or whose income was limited to small amounts from sources other than earnings. For women who worked full time throughout the year--28 percent of all female income recipients in 1960--the average was $3,300 last year, not appreciably above 1959, but up about $300 from 1957.

The 1960 income statistics presented in this report were obtained from the Bureau's Current Population Survey of March 1961. More detailed income data from the survey

Figure 6: US Income in 1971

Source: http://www2.census.gov/prod2/popscan/p60-085.pdf

Probably not.

Today, if you are a blue or white collar, you might be earn $78,000 USD per year, and $5,600 USD cannot meet the living wage – the income you need survive.

So, on paper, you might see yourself richer.

But the standard of living doesn't *quite* match the numbers?

Something isn't right….

Before discovering what went wrong, let us put on our detective hat and find out.

Since home ownership is the most important indicator in defining the standard of living, I will pick U.S. home affordability as an example.

I encourage you to do this exercise by using statistics in your country.

Median Home Values: Unadjusted

	2000	1990	1980	1970	1960	1950	1940
United States	$119,600	$79,100	$47,200	$17,000	$11,900	$7,354	$2,938
Alabama	$85,100	$53,700	$33,900	$12,200	$8,600	$4,473	$1,610
Alaska	$144,200	$94,400	$76,300	$22,700	$9,100	$3,477	NA
Arizona	$121,300	$80,100	$54,800	$16,300	$11,100	$5,935	$1,400
Arkansas	$72,800	$46,300	$31,100	$10,500	$6,700	$4,087	$1,100
California	$211,500	$195,500	$84,500	$23,100	$15,100	$9,564	$3,527
Colorado	$166,600	$82,700	$64,100	$17,300	$12,300	$7,151	$2,091
Connecticut	$166,900	$177,800	$65,600	$25,500	$16,700	$11,862	$4,615
Delaware	$130,400	$100,100	$44,400	$17,100	$12,400	$9,079	$4,159
Dist. of Columbia	$157,200	$123,900	$68,800	$21,300	$15,400	$14,498	$7,568
Florida	$105,500	$77,100	$45,100	$15,000	$11,800	$6,612	$2,218
Georgia	$111,200	$71,300	$36,900	$14,600	$9,500	$5,235	$1,957
Hawaii	$272,700	$245,300	$118,100	$35,100	$20,900	$12,283	NA
Idaho	$106,300	$58,200	$45,600	$14,100	$10,600	$5,852	$1,600
Illinois	$130,800	$80,900	$52,800	$19,800	$14,700	$8,646	$3,277
Indiana	$94,300	$53,900	$37,200	$13,800	$10,200	$6,226	$2,406
Iowa	$82,500	$45,900	$40,600	$13,900	$9,900	$6,320	$2,253
Kansas	$83,500	$52,200	$37,800	$12,100	$9,300	$5,462	$1,733
Kentucky	$86,700	$50,500	$34,200	$12,600	$8,800	$5,283	$2,074
Louisiana	$85,000	$58,500	$43,000	$14,600	$10,700	$5,141	$1,414
Maine	$98,700	$87,400	$37,900	$12,800	$8,800	$4,856	$2,008
Maryland	$146,000	$116,500	$58,300	$18,700	$11,900	$8,033	$3,031
Massachusetts	$185,700	$162,800	$48,400	$20,600	$13,800	$9,144	$3,837
Michigan	$115,600	$60,600	$39,000	$17,500	$12,000	$7,496	$2,863
Minnesota	$122,400	$74,000	$53,100	$18,000	$12,800	$7,806	$3,024
Mississippi	$71,400	$45,600	$31,400	$11,200	$7,900	$4,159	$1,189
Missouri	$89,900	$59,800	$36,700	$14,400	$10,900	$6,399	$2,392
Montana	$99,500	$56,600	$46,500	$14,000	$10,900	$5,797	$1,651
Nebraska	$88,000	$50,400	$38,000	$12,400	$9,400	$5,918	$2,156
Nevada	$142,000	$95,700	$68,700	$22,400	$15,200	$8,859	$1,987
New Hampshire	$133,300	$129,400	$48,000	$16,400	$10,700	$6,199	$2,505
New Jersey	$170,800	$162,300	$60,200	$23,400	$15,600	$10,408	$4,528
New Mexico	$108,100	$70,100	$45,300	$13,000	$10,700	$5,697	$656
New York	$148,700	$131,600	$45,600	$22,500	$15,300	$10,152	$4,389
North Carolina	$108,300	$65,800	$36,000	$12,800	$8,000	$4,901	$1,802
North Dakota	$74,400	$50,800	$43,900	$13,000	$9,800	$5,396	$1,626
Ohio	$103,700	$63,500	$44,900	$17,600	$13,400	$8,304	$3,415
Oklahoma	$70,700	$48,100	$35,600	$11,100	$7,900	$5,228	$1,293
Oregon	$152,100	$67,100	$56,900	$15,400	$10,500	$6,846	$2,343
Pennsylvania	$97,000	$69,700	$39,100	$13,600	$10,200	$6,992	$3,205
Rhode Island	$133,000	$133,500	$46,800	$18,200	$12,300	$9,767	$3,848
South Carolina	$94,900	$61,100	$35,100	$13,000	$7,500	$5,112	$2,145
South Dakota	$79,600	$45,200	$36,600	$11,400	$8,800	$5,410	$1,618
Tennessee	$93,000	$58,400	$35,600	$12,500	$8,300	$5,268	$1,826
Texas	$82,500	$59,600	$39,100	$12,000	$8,800	$5,805	$1,693
Utah	$146,100	$68,900	$57,300	$16,800	$12,600	$7,409	$2,320
Vermont	$111,500	$95,500	$42,200	$16,400	$9,700	$6,277	$2,836
Virginia	$125,400	$91,000	$48,000	$17,100	$10,800	$6,581	$2,633
Washington	$168,300	$93,400	$59,900	$18,500	$11,700	$7,169	$2,359
West Virginia	$72,800	$47,900	$38,500	$11,300	$7,600	$5,473	$2,350
Wisconsin	$112,200	$62,500	$48,600	$17,300	$12,600	$7,927	$3,232
Wyoming	$96,600	$61,600	$59,800	$15,300	$12,300	$6,811	$2,174

NA: Not Available
Source: U.S. Census Bureau

Table 1: Median Home Value

Source: U.S. Census Bureau

Above is a chart extracted from the U.S. Census Bureau website showing the home price of different states in U.S. between 1940 and 2000. These are non-inflation adjusted data.

[**Note**: Remember to use non-inflation adjusted data as they are measured at their nominal value of the dollar the year that the census was being taken.]

If we take Texas as an example, a single medium price home in Texas in 1960 was about $8,800 USD, which was about 1.57 times the nominal wages in 1960.

Yes. The price of a medium home in Texas is 1.57 times the average nominal wage in 1960!

So, $5600 USD in 1960 was actually a lot of money.

Table A.--NUMBER OF FAMILIES BY FAMILY INCOME, FOR THE UNITED STATES: 1960

Family income	Number of families
Total............................	45,435,000
Under $1,000............................	2,285,000
$1,000 to $1,999........................	3,613,000
$2,000 to $2,999........................	3,970,000
$3,000 to $3,999........................	4,456,000
$4,000 to $4,999........................	4,773,000
$5,000 to $5,999........................	5,839,000
$6,000 to $6,999........................	4,889,000
$7,000 to $7,999........................	3,973,000
$8,000 to $9,999........................	5,135,000
$10,000 to $14,999......................	4,795,000
$15,000 and over........................	1,707,000

Figure 7: Average Income of family in 1960
Source: U.S.Bureau of the Census; Series P-60, No 36

And another table shows it is not a minority group of people with such huge affordability.

26% of the U.S. families in 1960 had the purchasing power to afford a medium price home in Texas with their annual household income with little to no mortgage!

I know these facts are like fantasy in 2016. Particularly, you are born in the 80s, you might think I am lying.

But the fact speaks for itself.

In the past, the normal things were men went to work and the women stayed home and raised kids. Now, both parents, must work a lot harder to have the same quality of life and have the same standard of living. This is becoming our new normal.

Would you not agree?

Real GDP per capita refers to the prosperity of a country by the population – inflation adjusted. According to government, statistics, between 1960 and 2015, real GDP per capita, raised by about 3 times.

Is government, statistics, always telling the truth?

Who is this Book for?

The entire world is facing a debt-driven disaster the scale of which has never seen before in human history. As I am writing, indicators are suggesting disastrous events are unfolding. This book is mainly written for individuals who want to understand the essence of the global debt-based economy system and protect themselves from it; it is also a receipt that world leaders can adopt to restore the global imbalance, reduce income polarity and lock in decades of prosperity for the present generation.

There are ways out of this crisis but time is of the essence.

If you are picking up this book, you might fall into one or more of these categories:

1. People puzzled by why most countries are in debt and who owes the debts,

2. Investors puzzled about the financial market,

3. Students who want to understand the fundamental of economics and how contents in traditional economic textbook are invalid in the modern economy,

4. People who want to learn more about how their retirement plans could get wiped out,

5. Anyone who wants to learn about the past and the future of China's economy,

6. People who want to study about credit bubbles around the world,

7. People who want to learn about Foreign Exchange Reserve,

8. Australians puzzled about the Australian Real Estate Bubble,

9. Anyone interested in European Economy,

10. Anyone interested in derivatives and shadow banking,

11. Investors who wish to understand the illusion of financial markets,

12. People who want to learn the truth how the world gets out of the Great Depression,

13. Politicians who want to restore global prosperity,

14. Creative people enthusiastic about how to restore global prosperity,

15. People who like to criticize my book.

Part One: The first part of the book is divided into eight chapters. The first three chapters of the book are simple but inspiring stories about how our economy used to grow; you will realize why and how everything is slowly transformed with debts and fiat currency. Then, we will look at how debts reshaped our world and the law of economics, which is contrary to how our economy used to grow traditionally.

In chapter four, I will slowly guide you through how the legacy of debt is threatening your retirement account. I will also talk about the current entitlement wagon and its relationship with the history of social security.

Chapter five mainly focuses on Chinese monetary history.

Chapter six is the core of the book. It aims to demystify the role of U.S. trade imbalance, the size of the foreign exchange market and its implications, the future of Australian Real Estate Bubble, the cause of global imbalance, and what drives economic growth today.

Chapter seven will discuss the European Debt crisis, the policy responses and the flaws in Euro.

Chapter eight will discuss a bigger threat – derivatives. We will look at the size of the derivatives market and the rise of shadow banking. You will gain insights about the derivative holdings of the top six largest financial holding companies in U.S. and how they will affect your wealth.

Although the material in these chapters seemed independent at first sight, they are highly correlated through the chain of debts. You will appreciate it much more when you finish reading Part I.

Part Two: The second part of the book is about how to restore global prosperity. However, to understand the solution proposed in Part II, it is a prerequisite to read Part I.

In this part of the book, I have evidenced how and why there is a golden bullet and a small window of opportunity that governments and central banks around the world can use to shrink the global imbalance, reduce poverty and potentially lock in decades of economic growth. This golden bullet had been proven to work and lifted the world out of the Great Depression.

PART I

LEGACY OF DEBT

Chapter 1

Our Clock is Ticking...

"If you put the Federal Government in charge of the Sahara Desert, in five years, there'd be a shortage of sand."

-Milton Friedman

"New York City, such an incredible place for Christmas vacation!" I exclaimed as we were descending from the magnificent New York skyline. The famous Statue of Liberty was towering on the Liberty Island, waving a welcome gesture. The Empire State Building, an iconic architecture in Midtown Manhattan, topped out among the sea of skyscrapers.

Ladies and gentlemen, welcome to John. F Kennedy International Airport, the local time is 6:00 am and the temperature is 25°C.I'd like to thank you for joining us on this trip, and we are looking forward to seeing you on board again soon. Have a nice day!

"Grandad must be waiting for us in the pick-up area for a looooog time," Crystal complained while waiting for me to offload the luggage from the overhead bin.

"Come on Princess Diana. Don't tell me that you are just going to sit there with your iPhone," I replied while busy offloading our luggage.

1

Crystal is my sister, and she is twelve. She is a typical, adorable Asian girl with big black eyes and long black hair down to her waist. Despite her princess attitude, she is a bright one for her age. Even at twelve, she already has her own investments. And she keeps telling me about her crazy ambitions that she will do in the not too distant future.

That is my sister.

A refreshing breeze awakened us all as we make our way inside the airport. We felt ecstatic the moment we landed.

Thinking about New York.

Thinking about Grandad. We have not seen him for a long time since he was invited to work as a consultant for the World Bank in Washington DC; we miss him a lot.

Grandad's stories on economy inspired us ever since we were little.

The Clock is Ticking?

"If the American people ever allow private banks to control the issue of their currency, first by inflation, then by deflation, the banks and corporations that will grow up around them will deprive the people of all property until their children wake up homeless on the continent their Fathers conquered..."

-Thomas Jefferson

Grandad was touring us around the city as we made our way to Time Square. Suddenly, something caught the corner of my eyes on the sidewall of a building, facing W. 44th Street. It was a billboard-sized running seven-segment display with multiple LEDs per segment. The numbers on top were flickering as if it was a time bomb. On the top, it said:

OUR NATIONAL DEBT
18,002,136,607,567
THE NATIONAL DEBT CLOCK

Figure 1.1: U.S. National Debt Clock

"Grandad, did you see that?" I asked excitedly, as if I just made a huge discovery. Crystal irresistibly took a photo with her beloved iPhone.

The three of us paused and we raised our heads.

Pedestrians were passing by, uninvolved.

A white collar was too busy listening to a financial broadcast.

The recession is over. We are looking at potentially the first major improvement really since the recession began. The economy is improving, and we are creating jobs…

"What is national debt?" Crystal and I were confused.

"I am glad you asked," Grandad smiled. "Most people pass by daily, busy with their lives. They would rather listen to what the mainstream media says, than actually find out what is really going on in the global economy. The sad truth is that the information on the billboard closely lingers to their financial life."

Before Grandad could continue, a sudden phone call interrupted our conversation.

Grandad took the call. Crystal and I kept glancing at the billboard. This clock. What could national debt possibly mean? The two of us couldn't take our eyes off the rapidly flickering digits of the seven-segment display. If the numbers represent the U.S. national debt, then who are the rich lenders behind these debts? Why is U.S. borrowing at this startling rate?

Dozens of questions run in our minds.

"Alright kids," Grandad returned his head and gave us a wink. "Let's make our way to one of the most sensational places listed in Michelin for lunch."

Crystal and I exchanged glances and smiled.

Grandad's wink signaled that he had stories to tell.

National Debt Talk

The open space of Per Se had a striking view of Columbus Circle and Central Park. This sensational restaurant had notable Michelin 3-Star Awards. Grandma reserved a table with excellent views.

"How was the trip?" Grandma asked.

"Longest flight I have ever had. 16 hours and 59 minutes," Crystal responded, flipping the menu, and irresistibly took out her iPhone.

"It was fantastic. More important is how are you after moving to New York City?" I smiled, while giving Crystal a kick from under the table.

I hoped she would get my hint to put that thing away.

"New York City is such a fantastic place. The people are nice." Grandma continued.

Crystal narrowed her eyes at me.

"Why don't you two order something to eat. The food here is sensational." Grandad's eyes looked fascinated.

"I love the oyster and pearls." Crystal flashed Grandad a big grin as her stomach growled.

"Excellent choice," Grandad grinned back." You do look at the menu after all."

Everyone laughed.

Suddenly, the volume of a news broadcast from a wall-mounted TV caught our attention.

It was FOX NEWS.

***

"The National Debt passed $18 trillion dollars this week. And it is estimated to close at $2 trillion by the time President Obama leaves office since the election in 2008. The Debt has soared 70%, despite tax increases from all over the place on everything," the host gave an introduction.

"Look. I just got my tax bill and paid a lot more money. But the debt keeps going up. What is going on?" the host continued.

"Well, let me say to you what my sainted mother said this year," the guest responded. "If you got tax trouble, you ain't got trouble. I think it is a good thing for us who make a lot of money."

"Yes. But I am talking about the debt hitting $18 trillion this week, by the way, the press ignored it… more tax money is coming to Washington so the debt should be going down." The host directed him back to the main subject.

"It should be. We have seen taxes rise - whether it is Medicare or an additional 5% on the highest income earner. The reality is that this money is just simply going out at the back door. It is going to defense, and it is going to entitlement and social welfare programs. We are a government out of control in every sense of the term…" The guest explained.

Suddenly, we all smelled something delicious. We just realized all the dishes had arrived. The discussion was too exciting for us to lose focus.

"… the real number is close to 60% for those who are receiving more in federal support than those who are paying into the system. It is an extraordinary $18 trillion dollar, and it got to stop!" The guest continued.

"It has to stop, or this whole financial thing is going to collapse in this country."

"Both parties will not acknowledge we are looking at a debt level now that is surpassing our GDP."

"I know," the host agreed

"And when we get to that stage you are in the company of risk."

***

The interview ended. Our curiosity didn't.

"Grandad, what is national debt? Why does the host say, he paid more tax, but the debt keeps on going up? " Crystal and I began our starter questions.

Grandad didn't respond to our question directly. He took out a dollar bill and handed it over to me.

"Free money?" I asked suspiciously.

"It could be if you still remember what I taught you about debt," Grandad smiled.

"Imagine you borrowed the first dollar, (**Green /Currency**) into existence, and that's the only dollar that exists on the planet, but you promised to pay back the principal dollar (**Red / Debt**) with another dollar as interest (**Red /Debt**); where do you get the second dollar from?"

Figure 1.2: The economy has one dollar and owes two

"You just can't get it. There is only one dollar existing in the system." Crystal was puzzled.

"Umm... you borrow it too?" I responded skeptically.

"That is right. You borrow the second dollar into existence. At the beginning, the economy has one dollar and owes two. And after you borrowed the second dollar into existence to pay back the interest of the first dollar, the economy has two dollars and owes four. "

Figure 1.3: The economy has two dollar and owe four

"By definition of this economic model, debt can NEVER be paid down." I continued "There is always more debt in the economy than money (currency)."

"Do you understand now why the host says the more tax he pays, the national debt keeps going up?" Grandad asked, enjoying his oyster.

"Huh? Do you mean this is actually happening?" Crystal was astonished.

"Of course. This is just an overly simplified model to explain the debt based monetary system. And it is happening every second every day, even during this moment when I am enjoying this oyster," Grandad coughed.

"But everyone is talking about reducing the debt level. It has hit –" I paused.

I suddenly forgot the exact figure.

"$18 trillion." Grandad added.

"Yes. $18 trillion!" I exclaimed too loudly and realized that everyone in the restaurant was looking at me.

"But how much is $18 trillion?"

How much is $18 Trillion?

So how much is $18 trillion? I know it is an astronomical number. Since this figure will constantly reappear throughout the rest of the book, I think it is worth getting our arms around the concept.

First, we all know what a $100 note is. We have all seen it, earned it, spent it or invested it somehow in our lives. We all know what a millionaire is from the *"Who Wants to be a Millionaire?"* game show.

If you have a stack of $1000 notes about 4 inches high, then I have to congratulate you.

You are a millionaire.

How about a billion dollars? It is roughly a stack of $1000 notes equal to 358 inches high. It is a little bit taller than the Statue of Liberty.

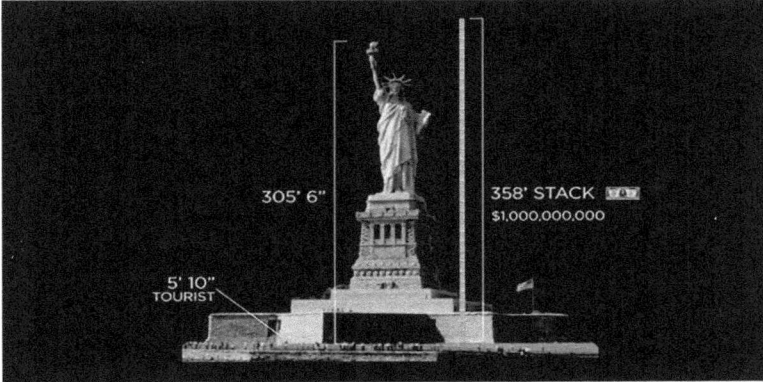

Figure 1.4: How much is a Billion

Bill Gates and Carlos Slim are billionaires of our times. If you ever wondered what it feels like to earn stacks of $1,000 notes taller than the wonders of the world, please give these people a call.

Now, how much is a trillion?

In numeric perspective, a trillion is, followed by twelve zeros.

THOUSAND = 1,000
MILLION = 1,000,000
BILLION = 1,000,000,000
TRILLION = 1,000,000,000,000

But what does it look like?

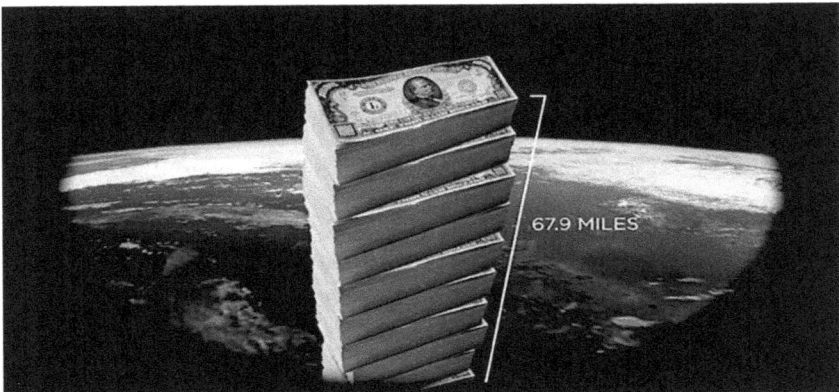

Figure 1.5: How much is a Trillion

Well, it is 67.9 miles high. This height is a little bit more than the height of Karmen line – the boundary between the earth's atmosphere and outer space.

This height is the physical size of $1 trillion dollars.

[Note: If you think a trillion is not enough, in August 2013, Japan's national debt exceeded 1 Quadrillion Yen for the first time. Stacks of $1000 Yen notes wrapping around Earth 2.7 times.]

What is the Difference between Debts and Currency today?

"Grandad, I feel so confused now. What is the difference between debt and currency?" Crystal asked.

Yes. My sister may ask some intelligent questions - sometimes.

"It seems it is very difficult to distinguish the difference between a dollar bill and a dollar denominated debt." Grandad glanced at the $1 bill he shown us earlier. "Most countries hold our nation's debts, and they call them currency reserve. In reality, they are not currency reserve. They are in fact IOUs from U.S. government."

Grandad had a taste of his oyster and then continued.

"Before 1971, there was a very precise definition of debt and money (currency). Money was gold, and debt was the obligation to repay the money. Now a dollar is only worth another dollar. There is no difference between a dollar and a dollar-denominated debt. They are IOUs and derivatives of IOUs."

Then we recalled the debt clock we saw on our way to *Per Se*.

"Why would the rest of the world buy U.S. national debt?" Crystal asked eagerly.

Why Would the Rest of the World Buy U.S. National Debt?

"Would you buy debt from your brother?" Grandad smiled.

"Of course not! I don't even know if he will ever pay me back," Crystal laughed. "But can debts really be sold?"

"Certainly, debts are bought and sold every day in the world. Imagine if you buy a house, you put 20% down as down payment and take out a mortgage equal to 80% of the home value with a bank. A mortgage is a form of debt, and you have to pay interest on it. So, it is also a type of cash flow for your bank. Mortgages are banks' assets. These mortgages are bought, sold, stripped and securitized in the *secondary mortgage market*."

"*Secondary mortgage market*?" I frowned, as this is the first time I heard this term.

"*Secondary Mortgage market* is the market where mortgage loans are bought and sold between mortgage originator (e.g., your bank), the mortgage aggregators and investors," Grandad continued.

"Just like any other investments?" Crystal asked.

"Good on you. A step forward to opening an investment bank," I teased.

Crystal stuck her tongue out.

"So do you two understand now why the world buys U.S. national debt?" Grandad asked.

"Yes. U.S. debts are like investments to the rest of the world that are backed by U.S. government," Crystal responded.

"And buying debts from U.S. is another way to say U.S. is borrowing from the rest of the world. U.S. debts are financial assets. They pay interest to creditors." I added.

"What constitutes U.S. national debts?"

What Constitutes U.S. National Debts?

"There are two components of U.S. national debts. They are *debts held by the public* and the *debts held by government account or intra-government debts*. And these two types of debts are classified into marketable debts and non-marketable debts."

"Let me guess. Marketable debts are debts packaged to be sold."

"Yes and No. Marketable debts are securities like Treasury Bonds, bills and notes. Governments from around the world, as well as investors, buy these debts. On the other hand, Non-marketable debts are debts in government trust funds like Social Security Trust Fund. In cases where a government runs big deficits on their Social Security Trust Fund, the government might issue debt to the public to fund their deficit account. In orders words, the government can exchange one type of debt for another."

"So the governments can just issue their debts to raise capital to fund other debts," Crystal concluded.

"Exactly."

Debt Ceiling Talk

"Grandad, is there some limit to govern how much U.S. debt can reach? $18 trillion national debt to me seemed very unrealistic," I asked.

"Ironically this is the debt level U.S. owed today," Grandad coughed. "And it is called the debt ceiling."

"A debt ceiling?"

"Yes. The debt ceiling is a limitation on federal government's ability to manage and finance government operations," Grandad replied.

"But if such ceiling really exists, how did the debt level reach $18 trillion? What is the history of this debt ceiling? And why is it constantly being breached?"

"Before 1917, there was no debt ceiling. It is Congress who authorized each bond issued by the U.S. Treasury. However, during WWI, Congress created the debt ceiling with *Second Liberty Bond Act of 1917*. This act allows Treasury to issue bonds and take on debts without the need of Congress approval. This arrangement is allowed to happen as long as the debts incurred fell below the debt ceiling they created. Back then, each debt had their own debt limit. It is not until 1939 when the first limit was set for the total accumulated debt."

"What is *Second Liberty Bond Act*?" Crystal asked.

"It is a type of war bond to raise capital for U.S. to support allies in WWI. It is a type of financial securities to raise capital."

The four of us had food then Grandad continued.

"The debt ceiling has constantly increased since its implementation. In fact, depending on who is doing the research, the U.S. debt ceiling increased at least 90 times in the 20th century."

"90 times? Buy why?" I was astonished.

"In 2013, the government proposed that the debt ceiling needed to be raised by $700 billion otherwise all financial operations would come to a halt. GDP would contract. All the social security contracts would default. A recession would follow."

"But does that mean the U.S. government depends on continuous borrowing to fund its operation? It does not make sense. You taught me before how an economy should grow – the rise and fall of Great Britain, the roaring 20s, and the Great Depression, etc."

"I am glad you remembered," Grandad smiled, wrinkles spread across his face. "What is the economy condition between now and then?"

"Umm….."

"Come on, you know it. I gave that to you as a birthday present when you were little."

"We are no longer under Gold standard!"

"You are right. When the world was still under the Gold Standard, there was still a debt ceiling. However, the pace was quite steady. After President Nixon had taken the U.S. dollar off the Gold Standard, the dollar became the reserve currency; then, the debt ceiling began to accelerate at an incredible pace. The end of sound money means the government now manages our economy. Credit growth drives economic growth. The Federal Reserve (The Fed)'s monetary policies and the fractional reserve banking system create an unlimited amount of credit. And the government makes sure the credit must expand."

"Grandad, do you mean our economy is no longer a capitalist economy? And, instead, it is now driven by credit growth managed by the government?"

"Precisely."

"But can the debt ceiling continue to expand indefinitely?"

"Yes and no. There is no simple answer. You see this coin?" Grandad handed over a one-dollar Amercian Silver Eagle to us suddenly and asked. "How many sides does it have?"

"Huh?" I was puzzled by Grandad.

"Head and tail," Crystal joined in.

"Take a second guess," Grandad smiled.

"The head, the tail and the r-ree" I stammered.

"That is correct. Not everything is black and white, yes and no, right and wrong. Even coins has reeded edges. If you understand what we talked about before, you will realize our existing economy can never allow us to pay off our debt. We must go deeper into debt to pay off the existing debt. The result is there is never enough currency to pay the debt. There is always more debt in the system than there is currency in existence to pay the debt.

Figure 1.6: Can we pay back our debts?

Currency and debt cancel each other out. If we stopped borrowing, there would be no new currency (Green) created to pay back the portion of the debt (Red).

And if we pay off the principal only on all the debt (i.e. loans and bonds) (Red) that exists in our entire currency supply in the world, our whole currency supply (Green) will just vanish, just leaving us with debt. The whole world will enter a deflationary spiral."

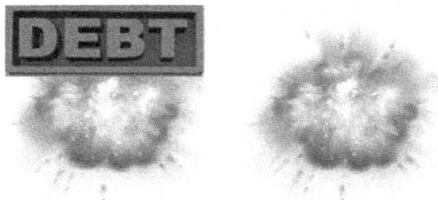

Figure 1.7: Debt Collapse

"What about the other side of the coin?"

"People on the other side of the coin insist that the debt ceiling can expand indefinitely like this did for almost a century. And they are right too!"

Grandad makes sense; both can be right, and both can be true. Even of very different opinions.

"What about the people who stand on the reel?"

"The people who stand on the reel will observe. The debt ceiling may continue to expand indefinitely. The national debt may hit one quadrillion. The debt clock we saw on our way may flicker for another 100 years. Who knows? The debt ceiling is just one important indicator to keep the debt of our economy in check. The real question should be what if one day the government can no longer grow the economy by more debts? What if your generation cannot pay back the interest of your country's national debt? What if the world has a debt level multiple times of its global GDP level? What if your children incur a world of debt even before their birth? And that is why there is an emergency going on."

Why is there an Emergency?

The national debt in 1901 was $1 billion; it stayed there until WWI. After WWI, national debt jumped to $25 billion, because of one war.

1918 – 1942, on the eve of WWII, it went from $52 - $49 billion.

1942 – 1952, it went from $72 billion to $265 billion.

1962 – 1970, it went from $303 billion to 383 billion

1971 – 1976, it went from $409 billion - $631 billion

1976 – 1990, it went from $631 billion - $2 trillion

1990 – 2015, it went from $2 trillion - $18 trillion

By 2012, it was growing at an average of around $2 billion per day!

This amount is what U.S. owes today. However, to whom?

Do you know right now if every American got together and we sold every building on every square inch of American soil for the total amount it is worth, U.S. citizens would have to pay back the value of America and two more? No wonder Milton Friedman once said, if you put the Federal Government in charge of the Sahara Desert, in five years, there'd be a shortage of sand.

Chapter 2

A Story of the Isle of Prawn

Grandad liked to tell me interesting stories when I was 12 years old. It was his way of helping me to understand complex economic concepts in an easy and fun way. While the subject of debt is serious and complex, I too, wish to approach it with simplicity and humor – just the way my Granddad would have wanted it. One of the storybooks that particularly interested me is a comic, called "How an economy grows and why it doesn't?" by Irwin Schiff. I strongly suggest you read it. It is a masterpiece. This chapter is a story, influenced by the economic concepts in his comics. It will be a fun read. Before understanding the complex economy we have today, let's go back to the simple economy before debt existed.

Welcome to the Isle of Prawn

Once upon a time, there was a remote island, called the *Isle of Prawn*. On the island lived five people - Amy, Bill, Crystal, David, and Eva. This island was a rough place to live with no luxuries. No iPhone. No Internet. No Wi-Fi. No shopping. No tools. Also, food options on the island were rare. The only thing on the menu was *King Size Prawns*. This is why this island is famously called the *Isle of Prawn*.

Fortunately, there is an abundant population of *King Size Prawns*. These homogenous *King Size Prawns* have top protein levels. They are large enough to feed an adult for the entire day.

However, there is one problem – they have to use their bare hands to catch these prawns.

Trust me. These prawns are hard to catch. On average, they can only catch one *King Size Prawn* per day.

"Ouch!" Bill shrieked when a prawn stuck him – *again*.

So, working for food is extremely time consuming and *painful*. What is caught is consumed that day. There is nothing **saved** for a rainy day, and nothing left to lend. This economy is a **debt-free economy**.

One lonely night, feeling exhausted after battling with the hostile prawns, Crystal gazed upon the twinkling little stars and began to re-think her life.

How am I going to improve my standard of living? What if I managed to catch two King Size Prawns per day instead of one? Then I would have one day of free time to pursue my other interests. But how…

After a whole night of struggling, suddenly a glimpse of hope appeared.

Crystal smiled to herself.

She had an idea.

An idea that was about to transform the entire economy of the *Isle of Prawn*.

The next morning, instead of catching prawn in the water like her four buddies, Crystal was busy making a prawn-catching device – A Net.

"Crystal! What are you doing?" David asked suspiciously.

"I am making a net to transform the economy of the *Isle of Prawn*," Crystal replied.

"I am going to transform the economy of the *Isle of Prawn*." Bill mimicked her girly voice, laughing.

"If you fail, don't come to us for an extra prawn." Amy tried to keep a straight face, but laughed too.

After a whole day of hard work, taking risks, and under consuming, Crystal finally completed her first tool.

The next day, the four began their 9-to-5 prawn-catching career, once again. While everyone was busy battling and getting stuck by the King Size Prawns, Crystal was testing her net.

"Ouch! Ouch! Ouch!" The other four shrieked again and again as they battled for their meal.

A sudden splash of water drew everyone's attention as Crystal raised her new device from the water.

All of the four Islanders looked at her, dumbfounded.

Crystal painlessly caught two prawns in her net.

With the invention of the net, Crystal's economy had become revolutionized. Instead of catching one prawn per day, Crystal could now catch two prawns per day. She is one prawn per day wealthier than all her buddies. Instead of consuming everything that is produced, the economy of the *Isle of Prawn* is now growing by one prawn per day – which is huge.

***

TAKE AWAY

So, even with a small-scale economy, the fundamental principles of economics are the same. An entrepreneur creates something of value to benefit him/her, and in the process, it grows the economy.

Do you see any involvement of government or central banks?

For an economy to function, it does not really need government and central banks. And we will explore this later as the size of the Isle of Prawn's economy grows. Anything that exists must have its value.

So, what would you do next if you were Crystal?

The Birth of Debt

One month has passed since Crystal became a prawn tycoon. She is now sitting on a pile of prawns, gazing at her hard-working buddies and thinking about her next move.

"Crystal, please share some of your prawns! You cannot eat them all, anyway," David pleaded.

"Yes, share your wealth. Share that magic tool of yours," Amy suggested.

Crystal waved her ponytail back at them and walked away.

Why would I give you something for nothing? I took the risk to build this device. Weren't you guys laughing at me before?

"Why don't you try to build a net?" Crystal shook her head and asked.

"N-No way, I don't know how to make a net. What if I fail to make it? I will starve to death tonight," Amy replied.

"Ho-how about if you give me a prawn, and I will start making the net tomorrow. Afterward, I will repay you your prawn," David stammered.

You must be kidding me! How do I know whether you'll just take my prawn and take a day off? More importantly, how do I know you will succeed in making nets? If you fail, then I will lose my prawns for nothing.

Crystal ignored them. David's idea did not appeal to her.

Suddenly, Bill returned from his prawn hunting and joined the conversation.

"Let's make a deal. For every prawn you loan us, I will repay two," Bill suggested.

Crystal paused for a moment.

If I loan a prawn to Bill, for every prawn I loan, I will get two back. That is a 100% return. I never need to get into the water again.

The financial idea of loans (debt) is born.

***

TAKE AWAY

By loaning a prawn to Bill and getting back two per loan, Crystal is profiting from her savings. Crystal is a creditor. And Bill is a debtor. The risk that Crystal takes enables not only her, but also the entire *Isle of Prawn* to expand its economic size.

Crystal must be very careful who she lends to. If David and Amy take out a prawn loan from Crystal just to have one day of leisure or do nothing, then this is a *bad debt*. Bad debts destroy wealth in our economy.

Instead of helping an economy to grow, bad debts shrink an economy. Can you relate this with the social welfare we have today?

We will talk about this in the chapters ahead.

On the other hand, if Bill takes out a loan from Crystal and made nets, he will not only benefit himself by catching more prawns per day, but he can also lend his nets to others. Either way, it will help the size of the *Isle of Prawn*'s economy to expand, which is a *good debt*. The bottom line is that any debts that will lead to the catching of more prawns on the *Isle of Prawn* are a form of good debt.

So, in today's economy, is any debt that leads to more money (currency) a form of good debt?

Not necessarily.

The answer lies in money.

Please read on.

The Birth of The Government

The size of the *Isle of Prawn* grew to an unprecedented level of prosperity, thanks to the talented capitalist - Crystal. The invention of the concepts of debts and loans had increased the potential to expand the size of the economy. Now, the island has at least a year of prawn supply. Everyone finally has time to pursue other interests.

As the size of the population increases on the island, so too does the complexity between people. There was no rule of law. Conflicts were usually settled with stones and fists. Thefts were not uncommon. Also, intruders from other islands were threatening the lives of others in the *Isle of Prawn*.

So, one day, all the people from the island came together and formed a committee - a committee with the **sole** responsibility to ensure fairness, impose laws and regulations for everyone to follow, and to defend the Island by providing security.

They called it THE GOVERNMENT.

For THE GOVERNMENT to operate, it needs finance. That is why everyone on the island agrees to pay an annual prawn tax from his or her income. All the prawns sent to THE GOVERNMENT will be put in a special vault to fund the government's expenditures.

THE GOVERNMENT is formed by a committee of a selected few people. They call it the Senate. Everyone is worried about putting too much power in the hands of a few. So a constitution was drafted to define and restrict certain powers of the government, and the rest of the power is reserved for the people living on the island.

All government employees understand that their jobs exist because THE GOVERNMENT taxes producers – those whose jobs bring in more prawns to the island. If it were not for the producers, government jobs would not exist. That is why the people working in THE GOVERNMENT are commonly known as public servants.

Everyone in the senate carefully checks all government expenditures; this is because everyone on the island knows that government spending is from the taxes. Hence, voting for whoever sits in the senate is decided by taxpayers only.

The Business of Debts

As the population grows, a wave of fear from theft hit the island. Also, bad loans from debtors made everyone feel insecure about loaning prawns to each another.

The brilliant mind of J.P.Hurgan foresaw an opportunity of a lifetime. He thinks that, by pooling everyone's prawns and keeping them in a highly secured vault, guarded by the toughest citizens on the island, people can eliminate the risk of leaving all their prawns at home and losing them to theft. With all the deposits centralized at his hand, people will no longer need to door-knock their neighbor for loans. Instead, they can just come to one person - J.P.Hurgan!

This will save everyone a lot of time.

So, J.P.Hurgan only has to filter out which loans to approve using his genius mind. This procedure can minimize bad loans that could destroy wealth in the *Isle of Prawn*.

For that reason, he created THE PRAWN BANK.

THE PRAWN BANK is basically a business on **debts**.

Islanders deposit their prawns into J.P.Hurgan's vault and receive interest.

The prawns that depositors receive as interest are based on the interest rate *–depositors' saving interest rate*. Depositors may withdraw their deposits only after a period of time if they are to earn interest.

With the vast pool of prawns sitting in the vault, neither J.P.Hurgan nor the island will benefit. Like his ancestor Crystal, J.P.Hurgan loans them out to businesses and entrepreneurs based on an interest rate – *loans' interest rate*. By pooling everyone's capital and loaning it out, J.P.Hurgan can fund much larger projects and infrastructures, which were once impossible to fund.

THE PRAWN BANK makes money by the difference between *depositors' saving interest rate* and *loans' interest rate*.

Interestingly, the interest rates of the PRAWN BANK are set not by J.P.Hurgan, but the free market.

When the prawn reserves in THE PRAWN BANK run low, there are higher risks of issuing loans, and the interest rate of loans will be high. High interest rates attracts depositors to put more prawns into THE PRAWN BANK.

If there is an abundance of prawns in THE PRAWN BANK's vault, the interest rate will be low to encourage businesses to borrow more.

THE PRAWN BANK plays no role in setting any interest rate.

***

TAKE AWAY

So, this is the primary reason our banking system exists.

Interest rate is the demand and supply of money. It should be set by the free market, not by the central banks.

In our present economy today, we have record low-interest rates around the world.

If you are puzzled by low-interest rates, don't worry. We will explore more on this subject throughout the book.

Using Debts to Grow the Economy

For generations, using debts has been merely a subject between individuals who wants to raise capital to start businesses. Because of the limited lending capacity of any individual, the scale of how wealth is created and destroyed is minimum.

With THE PRAWN BANK established, everything changed.

Since J.P.Hurgan can approve loans on a much larger scale, he has the power to fund larger scale projects, which were once impossible to loan between individuals.

Take the construction of a hydroelectric plant on the island as an example. This project will cost 200,000 prawns to fund, and the return of this investment is 600,000 prawns. This project will benefit everyone and will grow the economy.

Other projects like Space-Travel-For-Fun will cost 1000 prawns to fund. They are high risk and have zero economic return.

THE PRAWN BANK must be very careful about who to lend to, how much is being lent, and the purpose of the loan. A good loan creates wealth and a bad loan destroys wealth.

Since the construction of a hydroelectric plant supplies electricity for the entire island, new businesses are created and will produce better products. The overall standard of living in the *Isle of Prawn* will soar!

The Birth of Employment and Jobs

The economy of the Isle of Prawns achieved an unprecedented level of prosperity because of **innovation** (e.g., Prawn net), **production** (e.g., availability of electricity to increase production capacity) and **savings** (e.g., deposit of prawn). Proper use of debt grows the economy.

Back then, everyone was an entrepreneur. They competed to create better and more efficient products. But as society becomes more complex, many people exchange their labor for prawns, which is called wages.

People without nets can only catch one prawn per day. But by working for those with nets, they can earn two prawns per day as wages. So, they are one prawn wealthier than working for themselves.

Sam is a mega prawn net producer. His device allows anyone to catch ten prawns per day. But Sam wants to be rich. So by employing people for two prawns per day, his employee can help him to earn 8 prawns per day! All Sam must do to get rich is hire more people and make more tools.

Employment became popular on the *Isle of Prawn*.

Most jobs are created to improve the overall productivity on the Island.

These types of jobs grow the economy, because they increase the number of prawns in the economy.

After generations of catching prawns, more people became richer. So, Islanders had more time to pursue other interests and lifestyles. The concept of the service sector was born.

Then business transformation happened.

Businesses that were previously non-existent, like retail, hairdressing, fingernail polishing, makeup, and massage, emerged. More people shifted from prawn catching jobs to service sector jobs.

Despite the business transformation and the increased number of jobs, more service sector jobs do not benefit the economy of the island. And the reason is simple. The number of prawns in the Isle of prawns does not increase through service sector jobs! They merely change hands.

***

TAKE AWAY

Job creation and employment is a hot topic in the everyday news. An increase or decrease in the unemployment rate does not really tell us whether an economy is improving. As you can see in the example above, an increase in Service sector jobs does not increase wealth. It merely shifts the wealth from one person to another in the same economy.

You may always hear on the news that governments report how many jobs they have created. This is misleading too. Theoretically, governments do not create real jobs – jobs that can directly grow the economy and create wealth. Real job creation is not part of a government's role. Jobs like doctors, policeman, and firefighters are essential, but they do not grow the economy. People who produce and create wealth fund the wages earned by public servants through tax.

[**Note:** In some cases, governments can invest wisely (e.g., Internet infrastructure).]

When Prawns Becomes Paper

As the size of the economy continues to grow, so does the size of the government. More government departments, like the department of art, the department of employment, the department of environment, and the department of education, were formed.

Since government jobs are better paid, more people shifted to become public servants. Fewer people are now willing to catch prawns. So the amount of prawns in the economy falls.

Finally, the island reached a critical point in which there are insufficient prawns to fund the big government.

One of the senior members of the Senate, Janet Yellow, realized that, if the situation continued, there would be riots, and the government would be shut down for good reason.

But there are still too many infrastructure projects in the queue that the government had funded. The shutdown of the government would be a big loss to the island, as all the prawns invested into these projects would be lost. This chaos must not happen at all cost!

Since the government can only raise taxes to fund the project. Yellow knew it would be suicide if she told the public she would raise taxes. All the government revenues were derived from taxes. The Government really didn't catch a single prawn.

Throughout all the elections she had been through, she discovered people have one common psychology. Everyone *loves to have something from the government for nothing*. Politicians who promise the island more are to be elected. And those who tell the truth and offered nothing are doomed to fail the election.

Isn't that interesting?

Despite the emergency, Yellow saw an opportunity around the corner. She had a way to continue to grow and fund the government without raising taxes.

Here comes the **Prawn Reserve Note** - a piece of paper that allows people from the island to redeem prawns stored at the bank.

Yellow preached that the invention of **Prawn Reserve Notes** was one of the greatest inventions of the Treasury Department, since their ancestor Crystal invented the net. She proclaimed that, by introducing the **Prawn Reserve Note**, no one must ever carry prawns for trade; the note in their wallet will equate to the prawns backed by the government. And best of all, she promised everyone that she would make sure the government infrastructure projects would be completed on time. And the economy would continue to strive.

Yellow's plan was working perfectly. Everyone loved what Yellow had to say – except one man - J.P.Hurgan, who is in charge of THE PRAWN BANK. J.P.Hurgan knew the island was about to run out of prawns.

"Yellow, how can you make such a promise to the public? The island does not have enough prawns to support our big government. There are too many redundant departments. We should shrink the size of the government, and more people need to go out there and bring in more prawns! We must produce more!" J.P.Hurgan shouted.

"Don't worry, brother Hurgan; everything is under control. The Prawn Reserve Note will bring in a new era, and the economy of the island will continue to thrive. The people on the island need big government. We cannot afford to shrink in size," Yellow replied.

"But - "

J.P.Hurgan was puzzled about what Yellow was trying to achieve. His gut feeling told him that something was wrong. But no one supported him. All he could do was keep his fingers crossed and pray.

A few more months passed. Everyone adapted to the **Prawn Reserve Note**. Everyone seemed to like its portability.

The economy continued to grow, and the popularity of Yellow skyrocketed. She has now been promoted to Financial Minister of the Isle of Prawn.

One day, J.P.Hurgan went inside the vault of THE PRAWN BANK and did some auditing.

To his surprise, he discovered that, for every 10 **Prawn Reserve Notes** he received, there were only nine prawns in the deposit.

This was no good.

A wave of anger swept over J.P.Hurgan as he marched to the Financial Minister's office.

BANG!

He couldn't bother knocking, and he burst into Yellow's office.

"Wow, watch that; the door is quite expensive," Yellow was shocked.

"Yellow, you have got to be kidding me. I have run THE PRAWN BANK my whole life, and I have never seen such a ridiculous thing!"

"Slow down, slow down," Yellow tried to calm J.P.Hurgan and gave him a glass of water.

"Tell me what happened?" Yellow asked.

"This morning, I went and audited the vault. There were only nine prawns for every ten **Prawn Reserve Notes**. Do you know, if the savers discovered this, everyone would rush to THE PRAWN BANK and withdraw all the prawns they have immediately."

"So?" Yellow sounded cocky.

"So THE PRAWN BANK will have nothing to lend! My business will close down. The island lending activities will come to a halt, since the bank has nothing but an empty vault. Projects will not be funded. Everyone will hold onto their prawns at home and not put them in the bank. Since the vault is empty, the government will have no income. Our whole economy will collapse, riots will be on the streets, and we will return to square one. No saving. No lending. No security," J.P.Hurgan shouted angrily.

"Is that what you think?" Yellow laughed.

"What else do you think will happen? For the sake of the island, you must raise taxes immediately!" J.P.Hurgan narrowed his eyes, puzzled how Yellow had ever become the Minister of Finance.

Or could he be wrong about her?

Prawnflation

Two scientists in white lab coats came into Yellow's office with two plates. Each plate had two prawns on it.

"Thank you, just in time. Mr. Hurgan will probably change his mind about what he said after he tried this." Yellow smiled as she dismissed the two scientists.

"How much did you pay to employ these two freaks?" Mr. Hurgan whispered as the two scientists left.

"1000 prawns per month," Yellow replied.

Mr. Hurgan almost split. Reckless government spending.

"Just try it first," Yellow demanded. "You will love it."

"What is so special, anyway? Just look like typical prawns to me. And I don't need to have two prawns, by the way. One prawn is enough," J.P.Hurgan complained.

"Just try it first. You will need two; trust me." Yellow grinned.

Yellow was correct. It almost shocked J.P.Hurgan he still felt hungry after his first one.

"But how –"

"What do you think? Do you still feel hungry?" Yellow asked while flicking her pen, trying to look smart.

"Yes. But how -" J.P.Hurgan frowned. He never had more than one prawn per day for his life. Normally, one prawn was enough to last him for the whole day, just like everyone else and his ancestors.

He looked at the prawn again. They looked almost the same.

Strange.

"These are specially made prawns, unlike those you see in the ocean; the scientists have been collecting the dead prawns' exoskeleton, experimenting with putting fresh meat back inside, with some sweeteners. That's why they tasted better. They are processed," Yellow explained.

"So what are you planning to do?"

"If a prawn expert like you cannot distinguish the difference, no one can. With these and the Prawn Reserve Notes, the government can continue to grow, your bank can continue to lend more, and the public will continue to be happy."

***

TAKE AWAY

Although the story of Isle of Prawn is a narrative, throughout history, there have been many incidents in which the government grew too big, too out of control, and eventually devalued their currency supply. Whether it is by mixing real money, gold and silver, with copper to produce more coins with less weight, or simply print money, the result will be low inflation initially, and the public will be cheerful for the government's monetary policy, followed by high inflation. The economy will collapse in massive deflation or hyperinflation.

Almost everyone believes that, when there are rising prices, then there must be inflation. And when there is no rise in price, there must be no inflation.

This is incorrect.

Inflation, in general, means expansion. It is the same when you blow air into a balloon and cause it to expand. In economics, inflation is the expansion of money or currency supply. When newly created currency enters the economy and is spent, it will dilute the purchasing power of the existing currency supply, provided there is a constant or diminishing supply of goods. There will be more dollars chasing the same number of goods.

So, inflation is like the cause, and rising price is the effect. The more abundance of something, the less it is worth. And money is no different.

Question: Was there inflation before paper prawns?
Yes. Prior to issuing paper as a representation of prawns, prawns were money. Let's look at three scenarios.

- In the basic economy where every prawn caught is

consumed, there is no inflation. The money supply is always
zero.

- As the economy slowly develops, prawns becomes a medium
  to trade for other goods and service; prawns play the role as
  money. The prawn supply in this economy will expand and
  contract with the economy. But, eventually, the prawn supply
  will rise steadily. This is the inflation of the prawn supply.

- When paper prawns are introduced, more paper prawns issued
  relative to physical prawns' results in an artificial increase in the
  paper prawn supply in the economy. The inflation of the
  paper prawn supply is the type of inflation we are
  experiencing today.

*Question: I notice that when the government launched QE 3, prices did
not rise like they did when QE 1 and QE 2 were launched. Does that
mean inflation does not cause a rise in price?*

Generally, when currency or money is created, it needs to be spent in the
economy before any rise in price results.

Now here is the catch. QE 1 and QE 2 caused asset prices to rise. But
not all these QE currencies entered the economy.

Figure 2.1 refers to the adjusted monetary base, and Figure 2.2 refers
to the excess reserve of depository institutions (i.e., The reserves of the
banks).

[**Note**: The blue line is our base money, and the gray rectangular bars indicate the U.S.
recession period.]

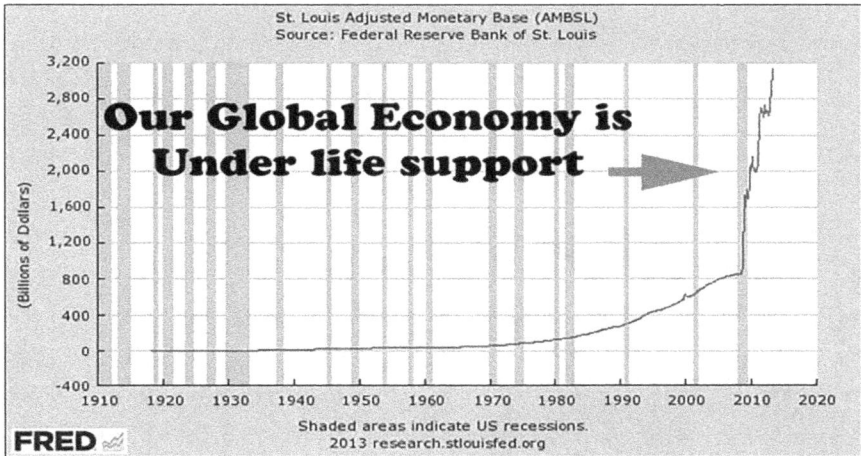

Figure 2.1: Adjusted Monetary Base

Source: Federal Reserve

If you pay close attention to Figure 2.2, you will realize that the excess reserves from 1960 to 2008 is tiny. The graph only surges at a 90° angle after 2008.

But what does that mean?

It means several things.

First, it means the commercial banks were keeping a low reserve prior to the financial crisis of 2008. Second, it means the commercial banks suddenly had very large reserves sitting in their vault after 2008.

Figure 2.2: Excessive depository Institutions

Source: Federal Reserve

[**Note**: The first book *Corruption of Real Money* explains how this works at length]

This is a good indicator that, despite the rise in asset price, not all the currencies from QE 1 and QE 2 entered the economy. These excess reserves are sitting tight in the vault of the banks. The reason the rising price due to QE 3 is not as dramatic as QE 1 and QE 2 was because the majority of the currency created by the Fed in QE 3 was sitting in the vault of the bank!

In other words, QE was a gift to the banks.

Now, do you know why some banks still make record profit, even after the financial crisis?

The banks are sitting on over trillions of dollars, and it can loan them out at a low interest rate, causing asset prices like houses to grow.

Please do not worry if you do not understand this part at the moment, we will come back to QE later. In the meantime, let's look at the economic landscape after the paper prawns were introduced.

***

A New Era

Yellow's plan worked like a charm. With introducing paper prawn, the Government could make any promises and spend at will.

The economy expanded tremendously like never before in history.

The excessive capital allowed the Government to modernize and improve infrastructure.

Instead of shrinking the size of government, more government jobs were created.

People and business were happy, because they suddenly received more prawns than they used to gain.

So every year, the government issued more paper prawns, and as the physical prawn supply reduced, the prawn scientists would use their magic.

The sudden abundance of paper prawns in the economy makes everyone feel like the island had entered a new economic era.

No one figured out why the island suddenly enjoyed a period of prosperity. Why bother? Almost everyone thinks Yellow and the Government have done a fantastic job at managing the economy.

More people began to diverge from traditional production jobs and shifted to government jobs, because they are more comfortable and better paid.

"So you see, J.P.Hurgan, the public only accepts what benefits them. It is human nature," Yellow explained. "The job of the government is to take care of the people. We cannot afford the economy to shrink. If it does, many people will lose their jobs; many businesses will fail. We must always use whatever it takes to grow it, and only then, will we stay in office."

"But what is the difference between someone who counterfeits and you, devaluing the prawns in this way? One day, they will find out when all is left on their plate is nothing but bones. This is unconstitutional!" J.P.Hurgan argued.

"There is a big difference. The government is doing this for the public, and theft is doing it for their own self-interest. Besides, it depends on how this generation reads the constitution," Yellow explained.

J.P.Hurgan sighed, still unconvinced.

"Maybe the island is entering a new era…"

Fractional Reserve Prawn Banking

"Because of the 'fractional' reserve system, banks, as a whole, can expand our money supply several times, by making loans and investments"

-Federal Reserve Bank, New York: The Story of Banks, p.5.

Several years later, the financial landscape of Isle of Prawn had become so different and complex. Several rival banks had opened to compete with THE PRAWN BANK by offering higher interest rate to depositors.

Slowly, J.P. Hurgan lost his edge to his competitors. His business was suffering from a downward spiral, as more people deposited their prawns into other banks.

In a dire situation, he sought Yellow's advice.

"When was the last time your depositors demanded all the deposits at the same time?" Yellow asked

"Umm…I don't think I recall any," J.P. Hurgan scratched his head.

"Then that means depositors will not withdraw all their deposits at the same time," Yellow replied.

"But how does this help me?" J.P. Hurgan scratched his head.

***

Say, for example, if Marco initially deposits 1000 prawns in THE PRAWN BANK, THE PRAWN BANK can then set aside 200 prawns as a reserve and lend out the other 800 prawns, to say, Carrie, in the checkbook.

Resident	Amount Deposited	Lent Out	Reserves
Marco	1000	800	200

Table 2.1: Check Book of The Prawn Bank

Prior to the invention of paper prawns, the above table was straightforward. The bank can loan out 800 prawns and set aside 200 prawns as reserve. The total physical prawns in circulation are 1000 prawns.

[**Note**: This example assumes Marco will not withdraw all the prawns he deposits. He only withdraws what has been reserved. So if Marco suddenly withdraws 300 prawns, then THE PRAWN BANK will be in trouble.]

After paper prawns were introduced, the situation became entirely different. The bank can still loan out 800 prawns and set aside 200 prawns as reserve. But the total paper prawns in circulation is 1800 prawns as opposed to 1000 prawns.

The catch is here.

Marco's 1000 prawns deposit allowed THE PRAWN BANK to create 800 *paper prawns* on the checkbook magically.

The total *paper prawn* supply is the sum of Marco's deposit (i.e., 1000 prawns) and the bank's newly created *paper prawns* (i.e., 800 prawns), which is 1800 prawns in total on paper, with 1000 *physical prawns* backing it.

But this is only the beginning.

Once Carrie received the loan of 800 *paper prawns* from THE PRAWN BANK and deposited into her account, the same process repeats. Her 800 *paper prawns* deposited allowed THE PRAWN BANK to create 640 *paper prawns* magically, while keeping 160 paper prawns as reserve.

The total paper prawn supply in this stage is 2440 *paper prawns,* with 1000 *physical prawns* backing it.

Resident	Amount Deposited	Lent Out	Reserves
Marco	1000	800	200
Carrie	800	640	160

Table 2.2: Check Book of The Prawn Bank

So, what will happen if this continues?

Resident	Amount Deposited	Total Amount of Paper Prawn Created
Marco	1000	1000
Carrie	800	1800
Jane	640	2440
Peter	512	2952
Zoe	409.6	3362
Emma	327.7	3689
Brad	262.1	3951
Angela	209.7	4161
Paul	167.8	4328
Jennifer	134.2	4463
Maram	107.4	4570
Michael	85.92	4656
Mark	68.73	4725
...	...	...
Mr X	0.2	5000
Total	**5000**	**5000**

Table 2.3: Fractional Reserve Prawn Banking

You will eventually find out that, after several processes, the original 1000 physical prawns deposited by Marco will eventually create 5000 paper prawns in circulation by the bank. This is called fractional reserve prawn banking.

By reducing the reserve requirement, more loans can be made.

So if the reserve requirement is down to 10%, the total amount of paper prawns created by the bank will be 10000.

But this is not the end of story.

Since every loan is a form of debt, there will be interest repayment to the bank by the borrower, so the paper prawn supply will be much larger.

***

"So, from now on, you will never need to worry about whether there are sufficient deposits in your vault to loan out. Your bank will always have enough paper prawns under fractional reserve prawn banking," Yellow concluded.

Yellow is right. J.P. Hurgan quickly regained power in the banking sector by being the pioneer of fractional reserve prawn banking. He made record profit he'd never imagined. Paper prawns really do more good than harm.

But beneath the surface, real problems evolved.

***

TAKE AWAY

So, fractional reserve banking and inflation are some of the core elements, which constitute the *legacy of debt.*

The term, fractional reserve banking, literally means lending out many times more money than you have on deposit and only keeping a fraction as reserve.

If you put this concept into perspective in the *Isle of Prawn*, it is like banks can magically spawn imaginary prawns into existence and charge interest (i.e., more prawns) from those imaginary prawns, which never existed in the first place.

What is our Total Prawn Supply?

Initially, where no debt exists, the total *physical prawn supply* is the total number of prawns caught on the island.

M (Prawn Supply) = Total Prawns Caught on the Island

If we step backward and re-read the beginning of this chapter, you will see the *physical prawn supply* represents true value in an economy.

With banks invented and paper prawns notes backing 100% reserves, the total prawn supply will be like this.

M (Prawn Supply) = Physical Prawns in Public
+ Paper Prawns in Public
+ Demand Deposit of Banks

The *paper prawn supply* represents the true value of an economy if it is backing the *physical prawn supply 100%*.

With *prawnflation* and *fractional reserve prawn banking*, the government and the banking sector expanded the *paper prawn supply* many folds.

M (Prawn Supply) = Physical Prawns in Public
+ Paper Prawns in Public
+1 / (Reserve)

[**Note**: Reserve is expressed in a percentage of total demand deposits.]

Without going too much in-depth, I hope that, by now, you have a basic understanding of how the prawn supply on the Island evolved from a simple economy to a paper prawn based economy.

Whenever there are loans, there will be debt.

But in a simple economy, prior to banks existing, wealthy individuals must be careful about who they loan to. The wealthy individuals decide if a loan should be made. A loan happens if both sides agree on the risks.

A good loan will expand the economy by increasing the physical prawn supply; whereas, a bad loan will destroy the number of physical prawns on the island.

THE PRAWN BANK exists because it can boost the economy's growth by collecting everyone's prawns as deposit and lending them out to fund projects, which are otherwise impossible to be funded by individuals.

Before prawnflation, the total amount of physical prawns represents 100% of the island's deposit. This banking method has a lot of constraints to prevent reckless spending. However, constraints do not mean bad loans are impossible.

Prawnflation allows the government to spend recklessly. If government projects are over budget, all they need to do is to inflate the prawn supply.

As long as people on the island are not taxed, they will gladly accept prawnflation as a normal phenomenon, even though the effect of inflation means a rise in the price of every good and service in the economy.

Prawnflation is an invisible tax in disguise.

Fractional reserve prawn banking allows banks to have multiple times the total prawn deposits to loan out. Under this arrangement, the paper prawn supply is always expanding faster than the goods and services produced in the island economy. These newly created paper prawns dilute the value of the existing physical prawns, causing the goods and services on the island to rise.

I hope I have explained the fundamental concept of debts well. Although this chapter might not truly reflect what is happening in our economy today, these are important economic concepts.

By understanding this chapter, you will see why the nature of our economy has changed.

Chapter 3

In Debt We Trust

"I want to give everybody the right to issue banknotes so that nobody should take banknotes any longer."

-Ludwig Vo Mises

For most of you reading this book, I guess you are most likely millennial or baby boomers born in the age of debts. And I hope you have enjoyed the story.

Like everyone, we grew up with our economy being mandated by the central banks' monetary policy. We grew up believing our government should take care of us, and social welfare is taken for granted. We grew up in the age of fiat currency accepting currency as money. We grew up with the perception our economy grows by consumption through debt. We grew up in an age of turbulence where debts become the new money.

In debt we trust.

In this chapter, I continue with the story of the *Isle of Prawn* to illustrate the financial ideas we live.

Where do these ideas come from? Why do we need central banks? How did bonds markets begin? How did our economy slowly manifest from a production economy to a pure debt-based economy? What is the difference between debt-based business cycle and free-market business cycle? How did social welfare even begin? What is wrong with our money supply? Since when did the world buy into the idea of Dollar Standard? And why?

Are you ready to continue with the journey of debt?

The Story So Far

In the last Chapter, the head of Treasury Department on the *Isle of Prawn*, Janet Yellow, helped the government to avoid the crisis with a financial idea called prawnflation.

Prawnflation artificially expands the prawn supply to fund the government's project without the need to raise taxes: now, the government can make any promises. Everyone was happy. Everyone welcomed this monetary policy initially, as they seemed to get richer.

At the same time, J.P. Hurgan, the founder of the first bank on the island – THE PRAWN BANK, was facing increasing competition from several rising rivals in the loan business. His bank was constantly facing insufficient deposits to meet the loan demand.

In a dire situation, he sought Yellow's advice.

Yellow suggested J.P. Hurgan to keep a minimum reserve, just to meet depositors' withdrawal. She introduced the concept of fractional reserve prawn banking to expand the bank's capacity to make loans.

The tactic work flawlessly.

No one knew what fractional reserve banking is. No one cares if the balances in their checkbook are correct. Within months, J.P. Hurgan's business was revived.

Since J.P. Hurgan was the pioneer to introduce this idea, once again, he regained his power and came back as the wealthiest banker on the *Isle of Prawn*.

The Birth of Central Banks

With fractional reserve banking in place, the once tight constraint of lending disappeared. A bank's lending capacity was no longer only governed by the total reserve in their vault but by the reserve requirement as well. By setting a lower reserve requirement, a bank can make more loans, thus, more profits.

But who decides the reserve requirement?

Is it set by the bank? Let's find out.

***

With more immigrants from other islands entering the island, so came an unexpected epidemic.

It was the first time in the history of the *Isle of Prawn* where an outbreak happens. Many villagers were infected. Those infected lost their ability to work. There were no vaccines available yet. Many businesses closed. The island's demand for loan was reduced significantly. So did banks' profits.

Some people feared the banks might closed just like other businesses; others simply want to withdraw most of their savings because it was too risky to travel multiple times to the banks due to the outbreak. So they withdrew most, if not all, of their deposits.

Unprecedented long queues were forming outside every bank on the island.

"What do you mean you haven't got them?"

"Where are our deposits?"

Waves and waves of angry customers stormed the banks as they discovered the banks did not have what they deposited!

Unlike depositors, who can borrow from the banks, banks themselves can borrow from no one but among themselves. But, no banks will lend, so that set the short-term interest rate for loans to historically high levels. Since most banks have only fractions as reserves, weaker banks are forced to foreclose and disappeared from the industry. Depositors in those banks lost all their life savings. As loans from these banks turned bad, businesses that borrowed from these banks are collapsing like a house of cards.

For the first time in history, an epidemic revealed the shaky foundation of the banks.

This incident is the first bank run in the *Isle of Prawn – The Great Panic*.

Yellow, the Head of the Treasury Department, and all other bankers formed an emergency meeting with all the bankers in the industry.

"It is a matter of confidence that we have to restore," some bankers suggested.

"Somehow, we have to come up with a huge sum of prawns to keep the system from collapsing," others bankers replied.

No one on the island except one man had such power – J.P. Hurgan.

Yellow quickly sealed a deal with J.P. Hurgan to form a rescue package of one million prawns designed to prop up failing banks. The government also injected more liquidity into the system to prevent it from collapsing. Banks could apply funds they saw fit to prevent further panic.

At last, the panic was settled.

J.P. Hurgan was recognized as the savior of the banking system and depositors of the island. He is the man, who single-handedly turned things around.

Yellow learnt a valuable lesson from this banking crisis.

For the existing banking system continued to avoid the loss of confidence again, they need a **lender of last resort**. They need a banker's bank.

They need a central bank.

One year after, THE PRAWN BANK officially became the CENTRAL BANK of the *Isle of Prawn*.

To understand how a central banking system looks like and how it will change the financial landscape, let's look at the diagram below.

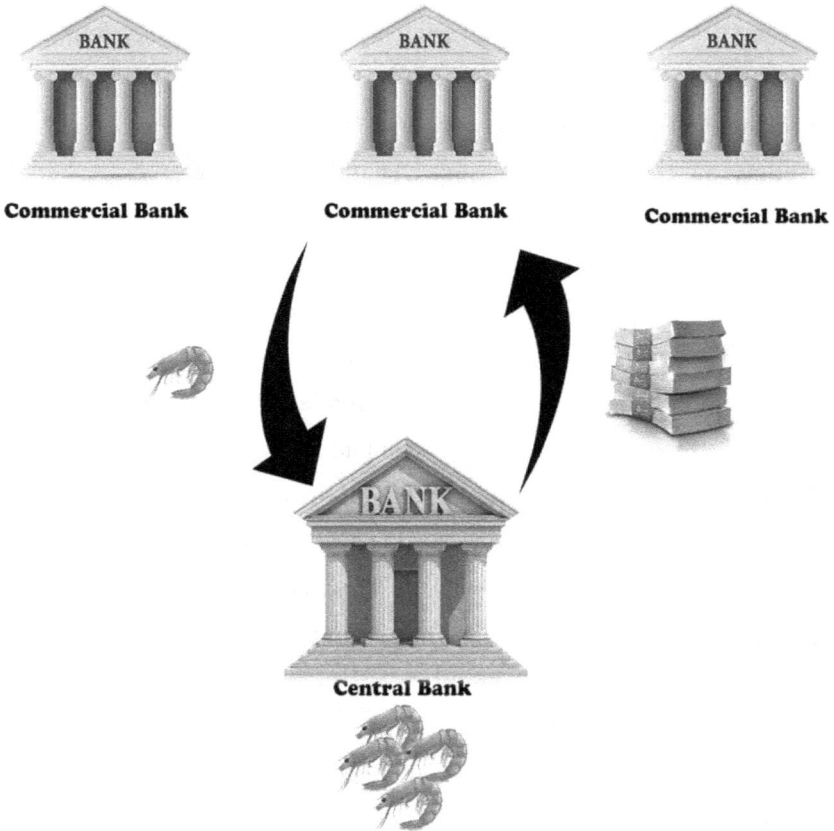

Figure 3.1: The Central Bank System

The central bank is like the bank of all commercial banks.

It is a government owned institution that controls and regulates the entire banking system of the island.

Every commercial bank has an account with the central bank, just as the public keeps checking accounts with the commercial banks.

Unlike previously where each bank can print its paper prawn, only the central bank will have this monopoly privilege.

When a customer wants to cash in from his commercial bank, that commercial bank must obtain the paper prawns from the central bank and reduce its checking account balance. Conversely, when a customer deposits prawns in a commercial bank, these prawns will be transferred to the vault of the central bank, and the central bank will update that commercial bank's checking account balance.

So, all the prawns in the vault of the central bank and the prawns in the hands of the public is the actual prawn supply – **the money supply**.

Theoretically, the money supply should be plain and straightforward.

Now, let's have a second look at the scenario below.

Let's say, the central bank of the Isle of Prawns has one million yummy prawns in the vault, and the ten commercials banks have a checking account showing 100,000 prawns each (i.e., paper prawns). If the central bank set the reserve requirement to 20%, through the magic of fractional reserve banking, all the commercial banks will have 500,000 paper prawns in their checking account.

Following this logic, there should be five million paper prawns in the vault, whereas the actual number of physical prawns in the vault is one million.

Do we call this five million phantom prawns our money supply too?

When Money Become Complex

"Any Intelligent fool can make things bigger and more complex... It takes a touch of genius – and a lot of courage to move in the opposite direction."

-Albert Einstein

So how much money is there in our economy? It is a simple question with no easy answer.

If you revisit the debt free economy like at the beginning of Chapter 2, where everything saved is consumed, the money supply in the island's economy is equal to all the prawns (i.e., money) that are saved.

As the economy becomes complex, the definition of money becomes complicated. Money is no longer merely what is circulated. Money can be deposited in the bank in a checking account - an account where a depositor can deposit and withdraw his money. Travelers from foreign countries can also use travelers' cheques as a medium of exchange. All this money together is commonly known as **M1 money supply**, which composed of the most liquid form of money in circulation. M1 focuses money as a medium of exchange.

M1 = Cash + Checking Account + Travelers Checks

[**Note**: In the Checking Account, the component included in M1 is the **reserves**]

So, are there more than one definition of the money supply? And are there other forms of money that are illiquid and cannot be used as a medium of exchange?

Before answering the question, let's look at other money supply definitions.

M2 is a conventional money supply definition closely related to M1.

M2 includes everything in M1 and near money - saving account and money market accounts and the certificate of deposits (CDs) less than $100,000.

A regular savings account allows you to earn interest on the money deposited into the account. Unlike CDs, the funds need not be held in the account for a specific period before you withdraw them. Depending on the bank you are with, you may receive a debit card for saving account. Unlike a checking account, a transaction limit for saving account, limits the frequency you can withdraw.

How about money market accounts?

Money market accounts are accounts that combine the benefit of a saving account and checking account. They offer account holders higher interest than a saving account but require them to have a higher balance. Money market accounts are available in other financial institutions besides banks.

CDs offer an higher interest rate higher than a saving account, but require you to set aside deposit for a fixed amount of time (i.e., maturity). Upon maturity, you can receive back your principal plus interest. Generally, the longer term your CDs are, the higher interest rate you will receive.

M2 = M1 + Saving Account + Money Market Account + Certificate of Deposits (CDs)

The crucial distinction to decide what constitutes part of the money supply is whether certain claims can be withdrawn instantly on demand.

That is a clause few people really pay attention to. And that is how we saw commercial banks engineer credit inflation in the 1920 s by changing deposits from demand to time deposit.

Imagine two people, Crystal and John, have a transaction of furniture. Crystal, being the seller, demands cash for the transaction to happen; John replied that all his savings are tied up in CDs earning interest and Crystal must wait 30 days before he can withdraw cash for the transaction to happen. If you were Crystal, would you wait 30 days or seek another buyer with cash already available? Besides, nobody is foolish enough to know the money that sits on the CDs is still with the bank as this deposit is already loaned out until maturity.

M3 is another commonly used measurement of the money supply.

The M3 figure is simply M2 plus various term loans, plus a larger denomination time deposit (> $100,000), and L figure, is M3 plus other liquid assets, such as bonds and treasury bills, etc.

M3 = M2 + Larger Term Deposit (>$100,000)

All loans should not be considered as money.

Money represents the final payment medium of exchange and purchase goods and services in our economy. Treasury securities and other financial instruments, such as CDs and stocks, are merely goods to be sold for money, no matter how liquid.

**Global Money Supply from Jan 1970 - Oct 2008
Measured in US$ Trillions**

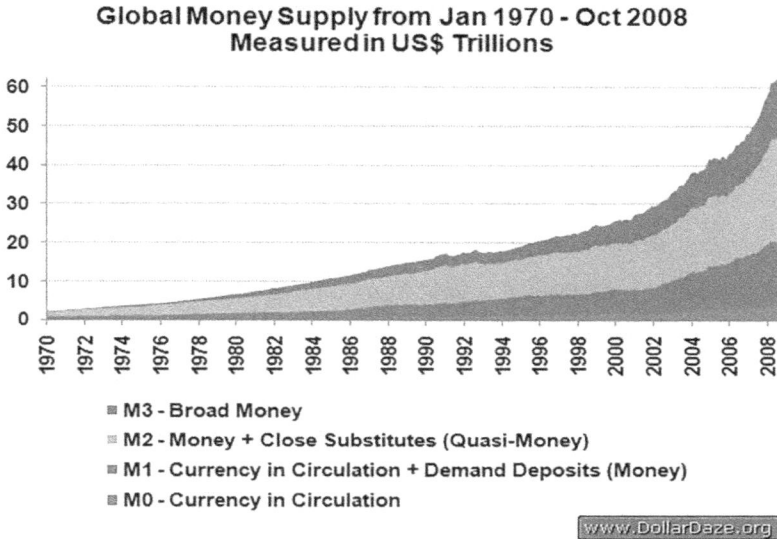

Figure 3.2: Global Money Supply

Source: www.DollarDaze.org

In the diagram above, you can see a graph titled global money supply from Jan 1970 to Oct 2008.

By now, you should understand the flaws of the term - money supply.

Instead of calling Figure 3.2 a global money supply, it is a graph showing the credit in the world. The exponential increases you saw from 1970 to 2008 is not money.

It is credit.

But isn't credit and money the same thing?

Isn't Credit and Money the Same Thing?

One of the primary reasons the world suffers severe financial crisis and an increasingly lower standard of living is because of the misconception of money.

Money and credit are different.

Money is a store of value. Credit does not store value.

Credit can be expanded by the government and the central bank at will. Money must be accumulated through hard work.

In case of the *Isle of Prawn*, physical prawns must be caught, whereas paper prawns can be printed. The more prawns the *Isle of Prawns* wants, the more economic energy is needed, whether it is through time or talents such as the invention of net. Paper prawns can be created with little economic energy. The cost of creating a five-dollars paper prawn bill is the same as a one-hundred-dollar paper prawn bill. And economy energy is how value is derived.

But why is the world using credit today? Where does the value derive from?

Ironically, the value of the credit is derived from money itself. Without money, credit is nonexistent. Just like at the beginning of Chapter 2, when there is no saving, there will be no loans, hence no debtors and creditors.

Another important concept to understand is, unlike money, credit and debt are both sides of the same coin. One person's credit is another person's debt. The $60 trillion-dollar worth of credit in the world simply means there is $60 trillion-dollar worth of debt.

Before understanding how this expansion of credit transformed the global economy, let's go back to our story and understand different ways credits are expanded.

The First Bond

Due to the limit of resources and the expanding population of surrounding islands, invasion becomes inevitable. Struggles for power had caused islands to invade one another, which results in one group of people seek to expand its power at the expense of others.

The government of the *Isle of Prawn* knew from the early days of wars it could not count on the advance from its commercial bank to fund the growing costs of the war. So, instead of solely counting on tax, they need to raise far more capital to fund wars. Then the idea of bonds were formed.

A bond simply is an IOU - I owe you. The government uses bonds to borrow from the public. Say, the *Isle of Prawn* is facing an invasion from another island called the *Isle of Crab*. To defend themselves from the invasion, the government of the *Isle of Prawn* will need to improve their military strength that needs one million prawns.

But where did the money come from?

Well, there are three ways to get funding: (1) raising taxes, (2) borrowing from the public, and (3) printing it.

If the government goes with the first option and massively raises taxes, it might be insufficient. The government cannot finance too much from taxes; this is counterproductive and frightens the wealthy ones for their support for war. Morale and patriotism are important in this challenging time.

The government gives little consideration to printing paper prawns directly because of the bank run just happened a few years ago.

So, they are left with the last option - to borrow it from the public.

But how do they do that?

The government could issue bonds to the public to raise capital.

For example, the government issues a Liberty Bond, with a face value of $1000, with a maturity of 10 years and a coupon rate of 5%. Each year, the government pays the investor $50. This interest payment continues throughout the life of the bond, which is 10 years. Once the bond reaches its maturity (i.e 10 years), the investor can redeem its bond, which is the $1000 principal.

Besides only counting on the public, the newly formed central bank of Isle of Prawn was granted the power to purchase *Liberty Bonds*.

When the central bank buys a bond from the government, paper prawns will magically spring into existence. These paper prawns are derived from nothing but the promise of IOU!

When a government spends more than it earns in tax, the result is deficit spending.

So when the government needs one million prawns, the government can issue one million worth of paper prawns. This is possible because the public has been using paper prawns as a medium of exchange; any newly created paper prawns by the government through deficit spending will dilute the value of the currencies held by the public.

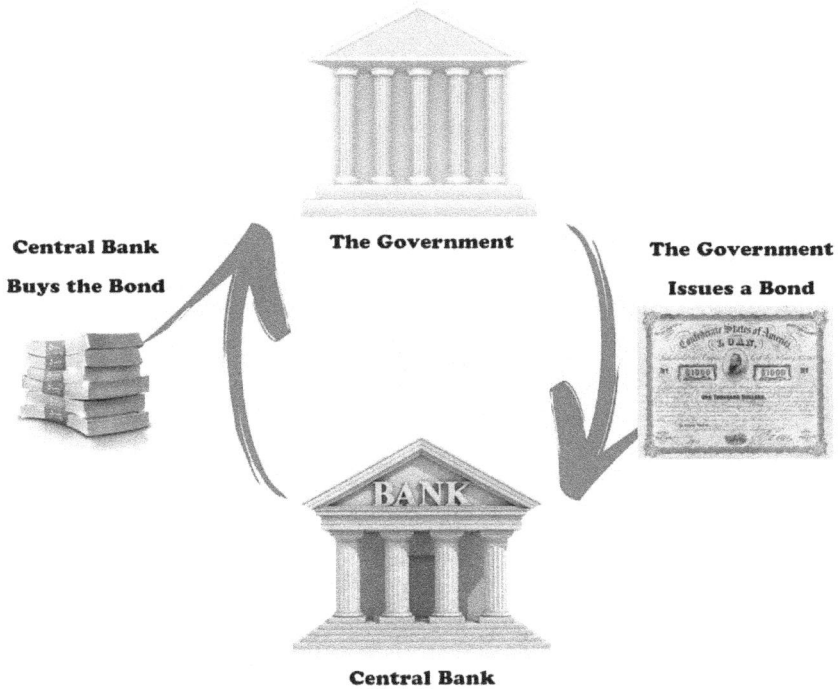

Figure 3.3: The Central Bank Buys Bond From the Government

When this paper prawns sit inside the vault of the government, nothing will happen to the economy. The effect of the increase in money supply happens only when the government spends it – whether it is to fund the military or to pay wages to the government employees.

Figure 3.4: Government Spending in Private Sector through Bond Purchase

When this newly created currencies enters the economy, it will be deposited back in the checking or saving account or held as cash. The result is an increase in the currency supply of the island.

Now, here comes a question.

Where does the value of these currencies for bond purchase come from?

Is the value comes from the 5% coupon rate? Or is it coming from the trust of the government?

The value comes from islanders' trust in the perception that paper prawns are fully backed by physical prawns.

With war and the birth of bonds, the government may spend more than it earns in taxes.

Bonds, the magic of fractional reserve banking and prawnflation had permanently altered the financial landscape of the *Isle of Prawns*.

In debt we trust.

[**Note**: A bond is simply a loan given by government to companies or investors. And a bond means a promise. The government constantly issues bonds to fund new projects or ongoing expenses. Investors use bonds to preserve the money they have or create an additional income.]

***

TAKE AWAY

A bond is simply a loan given by the government to companies or investors. The government constantly issues bonds to fund new projects or ongoing expenses. Investors use bonds to preserve the money they have or create an additional income.

The first ever bond issued by a national government was the Bank of England in 1694 to fund a war against France. This bond was issued by William III of England, who was inspired by the Dutch's approach of issuing bonds and raising government debt.

There are different government bonds, defined by their maturity date. **Treasury bills** (or **T-bills**) have a maturity period of one year or less. These bonds pays no interest before maturity and are zero-coupon. **Treasury notes** (or **T-Notes**) have a coupon payment every six months with a mature period from two to ten years; **Treasury Bonds** (**T-Bond**, or **long bond**) have the longest maturity, from twenty to thirty years, and a coupon payment every six months. All these bonds are collectively known as **Treasury securities** or Government Securities. These types of securities are very liquid and are sold in the **secondary market** – a financial market that buys and sells used financial products (i.e., assets not directly purchased from the sellers such as the government, which can be stock, futures, options, and bonds).

Today, the buying and selling of government securities are conducted by the **Federal Open Market Committee (FOMC)** of the Federal Reserve through a process called **open market operation (OMO)**.

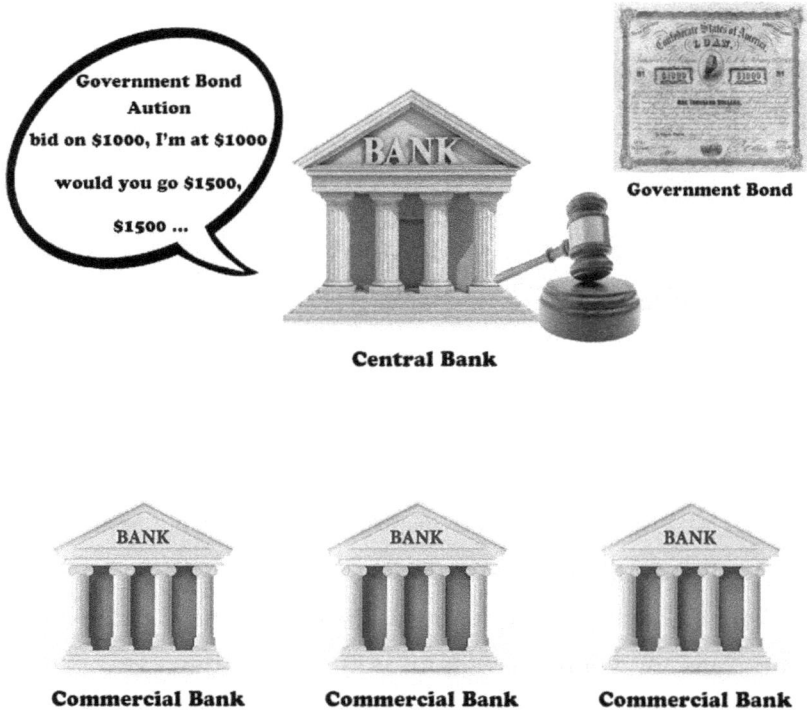

Figure 3.5: Open Market Operation

OMO is the activity of buying and selling government securities in the open market.

What Determines the Interest Rate?

So, open market operation is one way a central bank controls the currency supply. This is also called monetary policy.

Another common monetary policy where the central bank controls the currency supply is the interest rate. Interest rate is the demand and supply of credit (money). It is the cost of borrowing. An increase in demand for credit will raise the interest rate and a decrease in demand of credit will lower the interest rate. As more credit is available to an economy, the price of borrowing decreases and the interest rate decreases; conversely, when credit contracts, like you saw in the outbreak of epidemic scenario, the price of borrowing increases and the interest rate increases.

In reality, there are other things that influence the interest rate as well. One is non-repayment of loans. When people in an economy default on their loans, it reduces the credits available in an economy. Bank must then increase the interest rate.

Another one is the risk of the loan involved. A long-term bond (e.g., 20 to 30 years Treasury Bonds) usually has a higher risk involved, due to the uncertainties in the long-term; hence, it has a higher interest rate. A short term bond (e.g., T-bill with one year of maturity), is more readily convert back to cash; hence, it has a lower interest rate.

When a central bank purchases securities from banks (e.g., Home Mortgages) or the government (e.g., Treasury Bonds), this adds liquidity into the financial system, so that more currency is available in the market for lending. More currencies available lowers the cost of borrowing So, an expansion of currency supply lowers the interest rate.

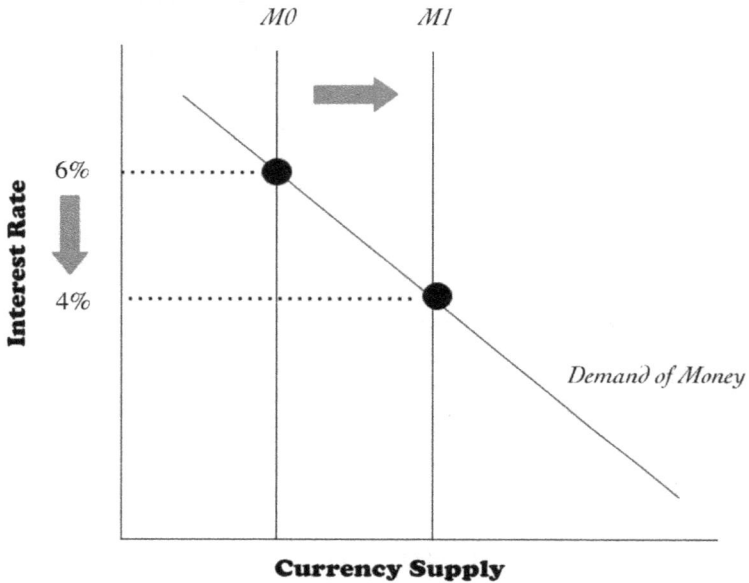

Figure 3.6: Cost of borrowing lowers when the currency Supply expands

Conversely, when a central bank sells securities to the commercial banks, this reduces the currency available in the market for lending. The tight credit supply means the borrowing cost will be high and a loan is more expensive to obtain. So, a contraction of currency supply increases the interest rate.

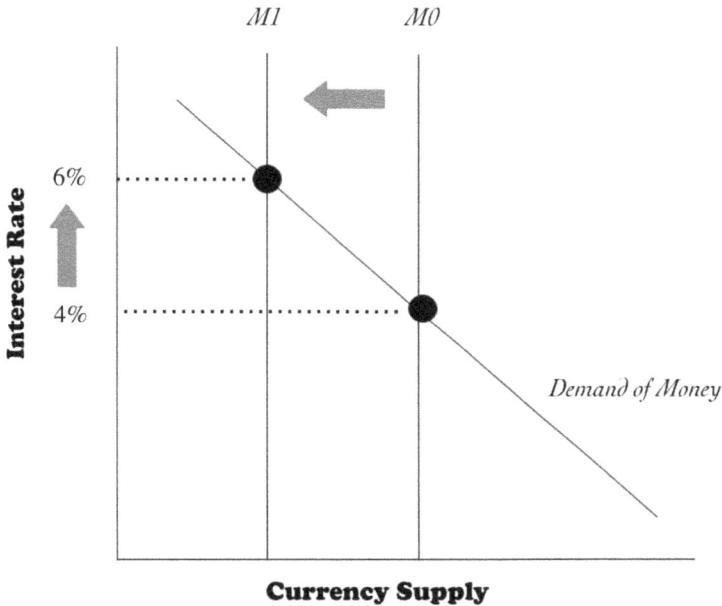

Figure 3.7: Cost of borrowing rise when the currency supply contracts

If you recalled in chapter 2, the same principle applies when everyone on the island pooled their physical prawns and stored them in THE PRAWN BANK.

The interest rate at that pre-paper economy is determined by the demand and supply of prawns.

For example, when winter is approaching, people on the island would rather stay home than go out to the ocean to catch more prawns. They will withdraw the physical prawns they saved for consumption. Here, the demand of physical prawns will increase as the total prawn supply decreases. The borrowing cost will be high, and the interest rate rises. This also encourages more people to deposit prawns back into the vault to enjoy a high interest rate.

On the other hand, if there is a new device that boosts the islanders' prawn catching efficiency, the additional prawns caught will increase the total prawn supply and lower the borrowing cost in the island. This lowers the bank's interest rate.

In the pre-paper era, an interest rate is mainly set by the demand and supply of physical prawns in the island by the free market.

This is the *interest rate of the money supply*.

However, this is no longer true, once paper-prawns are introduced. Instead of being set by the free market, the interest rate of paper-prawns is set by monetary policy of the central bank through expansion and contraction of credit.

This is the *interest rate of the currency supply*.

So, even though both interest rates refer to the cost of loans, their underlying meanings are different.

[**Note**:When talking about interest rate today, we are referring to the interest rate of our currency supply. Despite our money supply being irrelevant because our currencies are no longer backed by gold, it is important to know about the history.]

The Value of the Currency Supply

Although the story of the Isle of Prawn is simple, it can reduce a lot of complex economic concepts down to its essence.

What is the value of the currency supply?

Imagine that if everyone on the *Isle of Prawns* gets a government job, and no one is left to catch prawns; what do you think will happen? You might think this is unrealistic, as the whole island will run out of physical prawns one day. However, this is exactly what is happening in our economy today.

Originally, the reason the Isle of Prawn's economy grows is obviously not because of the expanding of paper prawns. If you recall the beginning of Chapter 2, it was Crystal who took the risk to create a net that transformed the economy of the Isle of Prawn. The net is a capital that can increase the productivity of the island. Islanders can slowly save more prawns than consuming everything they caught. It is innovation, production and savings that drive economic growth. The value of the money supply is the sum of all the prawns caught on the *Isle of Prawns*.

However, as the economy becomes more complicated, and banks are given the power to issue paper prawns to represent physical prawns, the financial power becomes more powerful. People's trust and confidence in using paper prawns comes from their experience that paper prawns bought them something yesterday.

Instead of having an economy that grows by saving, the economy grows by expansion of credit through monetary policies.

The expansion of credit gives a false signal to people that the economy has plenty of saving. And this drives the interest rate of the currency supply low.

As the money supply becomes a fraction of the total currency supply, it is the supply and demand of credit that decides the interest rate of the currency supply.

But who decides this demand and supply of credit?

It is no longer the business and individuals who decide the supply and demand of credit of the *Isle of Prawns*. The demand of credit from the government played a leading role.

But how did the government do that?

[**Note**: The interest rate of a country is also determined by trading partners. We will explore that later.]

Relationship Between Interest Rate and Bond

Today, the demand and supply of credit is largely determined by the purchase of Treasury securities. (e.g., Treasury Bonds).

Say, the Treasury Department issues a T-Bond for $1000 (i.e. Par value) with ten-year maturity and a coupon rate of 5%. So every year, an investor will receive $50. The par value and this coupon rate are fixed at the time of purchase. They do not change.

Suppose I bought this bond for $1000, and due to speculations in the economy, instead of paying 5%, the newly issued T-bill is now paying 8%.

Would you pay me $1000 for my bond?

Certainly not.

Why would you pay $1000 to receive my bond, which pays you 5% per year? In reality, you can buy a new bond for the same price, which pays you 8% per year, instead of 5%.

Now, how do I sell my bond? To do so, I must find out the present value of the bond.

Price of Bond = Interest / Yield = $50/ 8% = $625

I can sell my bond for $625 to match the market interest rate of 8%.

So, when the interest rate has gone up, the price of the bond comes down. Interest rate and bond price are inversely proportional to each other.

Myths of Business Cycles

Grandad's stories are engaging as they break down complex concepts to its essence. It is so amazing how much I learn in a few short hours listening to Grandad's stories, compared to sitting for hours in traditional school. Often, teachers must rush through the curriculum because of our so-called exams. Everything we learnt is within the boundary of the syllabus. There is little room of creativity. The result is that we become a product of doing exams for the sake of doing exams. Do you have similar experiences?

One of the unsolved mysteries that puzzled me for a long time is called the business cycle. The concept of economic boom and bust cycles is nothing new.

However, what is interesting to me is how different our global economy behaves today.

I was listening to the financial news one night, and it surprised me to hear these financial experts proclaim that the free market should be held responsible for the economic crisis. And what we need is more government regulations. Do you agree with them?

Let's join Grandad's conversation with Crystal and listen to what they have to say.

***

"Grandad, I listened to the financial news yesterday, and the expert says the financial crisis in 2008 happened because of the failure of the free market, and we need more government regulations. Is that true?" Crystal asked.

"I doubt it. We do not really have a free market economy. If we have a free market economy, a crisis of that magnitude simply would not have happened."

"What do you mean we do not have a free market economy? I just learned about it in my economy class," Crystal protested.

"In a free market economy, prices of goods are set by the demand and supply. The government does not manipulate the price of goods in a free market," Granddad explained.

"So free market actually does exist today! I bought some brand new shoes yesterday, and the demand and supply of shoes have not been manipulated by the government; I also bought a whole bunch of other things too, and the government did not get involved," Crystal disagreed.

"Those goods are not manipulated by the government. However, there is one good that the government manipulated the price. And that good is the most important good in the economy,"

"Which good is that? I didn't buy any other things," Crystal frowned.

"It is money, or precisely, currency," Grandad answered.

"Did you say money? So, money is a good too?" Crystal was puzzled. "And it has a price?"

"Yes, money is the single most important good in our economy. And *the price of money is the interest it charges to borrow*,"

"Oh, I see. So do you mean the price of the money should be set, based on the demand and supply of money in a free market society?"

"Exactly. And banks are the seller in this case. They charge interest to lend money, which is called interest rate. Ideally, the interest rate should be set based on the demand and supply of money. Come with me to my room; I will show you in detail."

"Suppose you are a banker in the *Isle of Prawn* in the pre-paper period. Let's pretend you have a tiny bit of deposit so your supply of prawn is low. What would you do to encourage more people to deposit more prawns in your vault?" Grandad asked.

"Hmm… I would raise the interest rate?"

"Correct. You would raise the interest rate to encourage more people to deposit more prawns. In other words, you encourage them to save more." Grandad gave her a thumb up. "Now, let's pretend a lot of people take advantage of the high-interest rate and deposit prawns into your bank. And you have a lot of other people's savings. To make more money, you need businesses to borrow money from you. What would you do to encourage businesses to borrow more prawns from you?"

"Like other businesses would do, I would lower the price of my product. In this case, I would lower the interest rate."

"Excellent! You are following. So, the interest rate serves as a very important signal to businesses. When the interest rate is low, people are saving a lot of prawns; when the interest rate is high, people are not saving enough prawns."

"But is that important?" Crystal asked.

"Yes, it is. It is because if you are running a business, you want to make sure consumers are saving enough to spend in the future. So, if consumers are not saving, that means they rather spend on the present but not the future. In this scenario, business should not be borrowing as consumers will not have enough prawns to consume their products."

"Okay. That makes sense. Businesses should borrow and invest when consumers are saving and avoid borrowing when consumers are spending everything now."

"That is correct. Businesses do not need to figure out whether consumers are spending or saving. They look at the interest rate. When the interest rate is low, people saved a lot of prawns. And this is the right time businesses should borrow. This is ideally how a free market works."

"Okay… but didn't you say there is no free market anymore?"

"Yes. The free market is no more because the government manipulates the interest rate."

"But how do they do that?"

"If you still recall the central bank in the story of the *Isle of Prawns*. It can lend prawns to the commercial banks at a very low rate through monetary policies."

"But isn't this good? Banks will always want to lend to make more profits?"

"This is the trick. You have a lot of prawns to lend not because of consumers saving, but the central bank gave it to you. Since you have a lot of prawns to lend, you will lower the interest rate of the commercial bank too. But remember the interest rate serves as a signal to businesses."

"Oh. I see the problem now. When the central bank influences commercial banks to artificially lower the interest rate, it sends a false signal to businesses to think it is a fantastic time to borrow and invest. Businesses are misled to think that consumers have a lot of savings."

"You are right. Having low savings and low-interest rate are very dangerous. Businesses will misinterpret the signal and invest in projects they shouldn't have invested in. They will hire more people."

"But isn't that good? The central bank indirectly helped to create jobs!"

"Yes, you are right. But these jobs are created, based on wrong economic signals. The artificial boom caused by low-interest rate will be followed by a bust. Imagine what happens when a business spends all the prawns and realizes that the projects that they are doing now are no longer profitable?"

"Oh. I get what you mean. Then businesses will begin to lay off employees because they cannot support them."

"This is call business cycle. Business expands at the wrong time."

"Now, I understand why you disagree with the so-called expert.

Government and the banks should be held accountable for the bust. They should be responsible for the loss of businesses as well as the loss of jobs."

"Yes. Businesses would have been better off not expanding until consumers start saving again," Grandad explained. "So you see, if the government and the central bank would allow the free market to decide the interest rate, the scale of the bubble would not be as devastating. The free market is built with a self-adjusting mechanism by signaling businesses when to borrow and invest. And it is this type of economic expansion that leads to prosperity."

In Debt We Trust

I hope I have done a good job to demystifying the role of the central bank, the money supply, the definition of credit and money, the concept of bonds, interest rate, and the business cycle in a way that is rather easy to understand. More importantly, I hope you enjoy this chapter as much as I did writing it.

Please congratulate yourself for finishing this long chapter as it serves as a foundation which grassroots the legacy of debt. However, don't worry if you do not fully understand it, as these concepts are not meant to be digested easily in the first go. Please reference them occasionally, as they will be building blocks in the chapters ahead to discuss the global economy.

One reason why I wrote *Legacy of Debt* is because I believe the lifespan of our debt-based monetary system is coming to a turning point. In my first book, *Corruption of Real Money*, I have briefly mentioned a chart called the Total Credit Market Debt (TCMD).

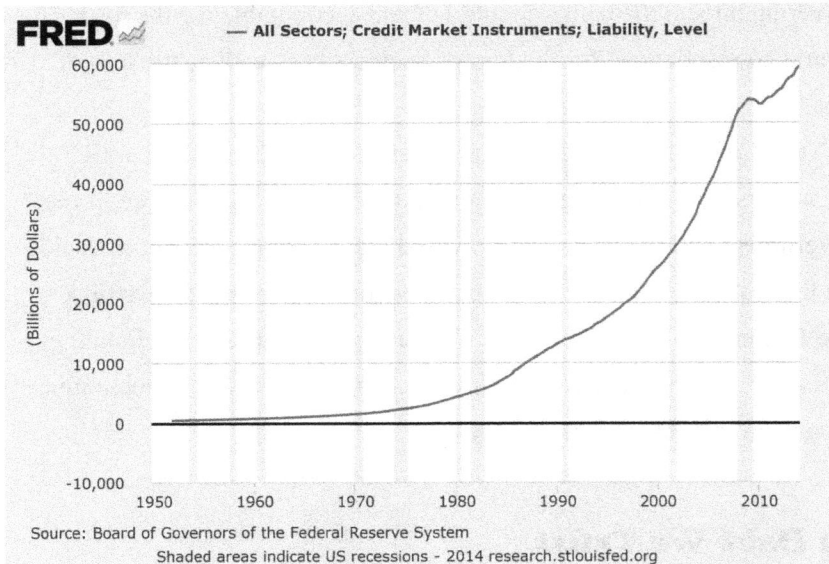

Figure 3.8: Federal Reserve - Total Credit Markte Debt (TCMD)

If I were asked to tell you in one diagram to explain where we are in the global economy, I would pick the above diagram. TCMD is the total debt in the U.S. If you remember, credit and debt are both sides of the same coin; you will come to realize this chart also affects the rest of the world, which is also holding the same amount of credit.

From 1971 – 2016, in just 45 years, the total debt in the U.S. had increased almost 60 fold!

In debt we trust.

This unprecedented amount of credit transformed the global economy.

So, if you are a baby boomer (1946 – 1964), you probably feel that everything was relatively cheap in the 50s and 60s. The price rise was relatively stable. This is not by accident as it coincides with the curve of TCMD. Back then, the dollar we were using was backed by gold. Everyone in that generation still had the perception that gold was money. Despite the slower economic growth, the world had a higher prosperity level, just as I demonstrated in the Introduction of this book.

If you belong to Generation X (1960 – 1980), you were born in a period when there is great economic up heaven. In 1971, the Bretton Wood system had collapsed. And on 15th August 1971, President Nixon took the U.S. dollar off the gold standard and made the U.S. dollar as the world reserve currency. From that point forward, all the world's money became fiat, simultaneously. This is where the phrase - *The U.S. dollar is as good as gold* came from. Since the constraint of gold was removed, the U.S. government can borrow and spend at will. That is why you see TCMD accelerates. The unconstrained credit supply led to an unprecedented level of prosperity

If you are like me, who belongs to Generation Y or a millennial, you were born in the age of debt, when money is no longer money. You were born in an age when the economy is grown by the expansion of credit and government's promises. This is the generation when conventional wisdom from baby boomers of go to school, get good grades, buy a big house, put your money in the stock market and save for your retirement becomes out of date. We grew up in an economy that has grown by the expansion of credit since we were born, we expect this state of affairs is normal, and it is how the world works. We are led to believe by the government and the media that the world economy will continue to grow, and our prosperity will continue just as it did in the past 45 years. Behind the curtain, the majority of Generation Y or Millennial sense their standard of living going backward. What is happening?

[**Note**: You can refer to Corruption of Real Money to understand the history of these monetary systems.]

Winston Churchill famously said, the farther you look into the past, the farther you can see into the future.

If you examine the chart carefully, TCMD has a lot more stories to tell. Since the breakdown of the Bretton Wood system, the world's prosperity relies on the expansion of credit. For the economy to grow, our debt level must continue to grow.

Year	Total Credit Market Debt (Billion of Dollars)
1950-1960	763.95
1960-1970	1580.18
1970-1980	4397.43
1980-1990	14014.36
1990-2000	27220.72
2000-2010	53870.47
2010-2016	62523.94
2016-2020	A
2020-2030	B
2030-2040	C

Table 3.1: Source: https://research.stlouisfed.org/fred2/series/TCMDO

By studying the wisdom of history, we have discovered an interesting trend here.

For the world to maintain the same level of prosperity as previous generations, the world must go into twice as much debt, or the economy will collapse as it did in 2008.

In the table above, I purposely left out three parameters for you to fill in – A, B, and C. They are your projected TCMD by the end of this and the next two decades. These three important parameters will determine your investment plan and how will you position yourself in the long run, financially.

So, can our government continue to grow its debt to maintain our prosperity? Can we have a debt level of quadrillion by the end of 2020, a quintillion by the end of 2030 or possibly a sextillion of debt by the end of 2040?

Let's find out together in the chapters ahead.

Chapter 4

The Emperor has No Clothes

"I want to give everybody the right to issue banknotes so that nobody should take banknotes any longer."

-Ludwig Vo Mises

Once upon a time, there lived an arrogant emperor who cared only about his clothes and to show them off. One day two tricky con men came to him and said they could make him the finest suit of clothes from the most beautiful cloth on earth. This cloth, they said, was very special. The cloth was invisible to the stupid and the low-class people.

The emperor was a bit nervous about whether he could see the cloth himself: he sent two of his trusted advisors to see this special cloth material. Of course, there was no cloth at all, but neither would admit what they could not see … so they praised it.

As word of this special cloth spread, the townspeople were now interested in learning how stupid their neighbors were.

One day, the emperor allowed himself to be dressed by the tricky con men in his special new suit – the one made of this special cloth for showing off. Although the emperor knew he was naked, he never admitted it. He was afraid the townspeople would think he was stupid.

Of course, all the town people wildly praised the magnificent clothes of the emperor: they also were afraid to admit they could not see the cloth until a small child said: "But he has nothing on!"

The child's parents gasped and attempted to silence the child, but the child would not be silenced. The child twisted and turned, pulling his parents' hands from his mouth, and continued to say, "The emperor is naked! The emperor is naked!" Soon, a few of his classmates were giggling and chimed in.

After a while adults joined their children and began to whisper, "The kids are right! The old guy has nothing on. He's a fool, and he expects us to be foolish with him."

The Law That Changed the Future

"I think the government solution to a problem is usually as bad as the problem and very often makes the problem worse."

-Milton Friedman

In early 2000, my granddad always emphasized that a change in law will change the future. He specifically talked about ERISA, which is The Employee Retirement Income Security Act of 1974. It is a federal legislation that sets a minimum standard for pension and health plans in the private industry to provide protection for individuals in these plans. I did not fully understand it nor was I interested in it since retirement is something from Mars for my age. Even so, at the age of 19, I was aware that some of the money I earned was set aside when I was working as a summer student librarian in the newly established Hong Kong Central Library. I remembered the head of the Human Resources department was speaking to a group of teenagers that Hong Kong was following U.S., and from now on, we have to contribute a proportion of our income for our retirement. Hong Kong Mandatory Provident Fund (MPF) was implemented in December 2000.

"Ching, pay attention to ERISA, a change in law will change your future. Watch out for the change in tax law just like a sailor constantly watching out for changing weather ahead."

Why is ERISA Important?

If you are a Millennial reading this book right now, you might be curious as to why I included the subject of retirement in this book. The reason is simple. As I am writing this book in 2016, I can foresee a potential crisis happening, which will directly affect the contribution you put into your retirement account. In other words, your retirement account could be wiped out in a stock market crash without your notice. Believe it or not, this is a global problem, and it has everything to do with the legacy of debt.

But could this be possible? Isn't the term ERISA supposed to protect employee so they can have sufficient funds to retire? How could it be related to the stock market?

To understand how this might happen, let's look at some facts and history and see how much we truly understand about this act.

[**Note**: The Employee Retirement Income Security Act or ERISA is a Federal law that sets standards of protection for individuals in most voluntarily established, private-sector retirement plans. The retirement plans under similar retirement protection in your countries comes with different names. For example, it is called 401(K) in U.S.; superannuation in Australia; and Mandatory Provident Fund in Hong Kong; Canada Pension Plan (CPP) and Old Age Security (OAS) in Canada, etc.]

Could Your Retirement be Wiped Out?

If you have attended a first year accounting class in university in early 2000, your lecturer would probably quote the story of the Enron scandal to teach the importance of accounting practice.

If you have read USA today, that was an issue with a large color photograph of an intelligent looking man in his late fifties with his arms crossed. Don't be mistaken he is not the CEO of Enron. Instead, he is a loyal employee of Enron – a company where a greedy CEO made millions at the expense of the bankruptcy of the company.

So why is this man on the front page?

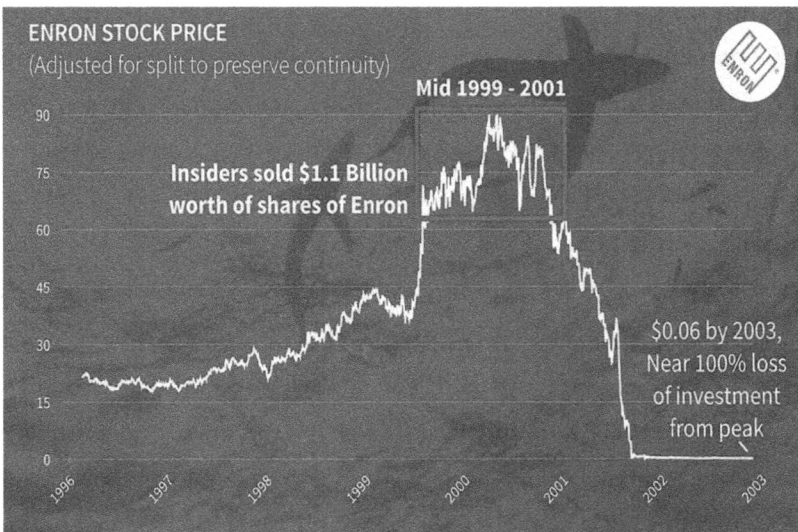

Figure 4.1: Enron Stock Price

Source: http://www.insidersense.com/blog/2015/9/22/swimming-with-sharks

This loyal employee lost most of his 401(k) in a stock market crash. At one point, he saw the share price of his company soar, and he decided to buy more shares. This employee felt so rich that he bought more and more shares and then put them into his 401(k). When the stock price collapsed, he lost almost everything – his job, his life savings, and his retirement package.

In fact, he is not the only one. Many Enron employees lost 70- 90% of their retirement assets after the company collapsed.

Is Enron just an extreme case? Could our retirement account be wiped out in a stock market crash? More importantly, who is in charge of your retirement account?

So What is Happening with my Retirement Account?

Take Australia as an example: when you have a job with salary package $60,000 including 9% super, you will contribute $5400 to your super account. The remaining $54,600 is the before tax income. On the other hand, if the employer quotes a base salary of $60,000 excluding 9% super, you will take home $60,000 before tax, and the employer would have to pay 9% into a super fund.

Either way, by law, the 9%, super guarantee (i.e., SG) is made compulsory to be paid to your super fund by the employer.

But do you think the employer will personally pay out of business profit to fund an employee's retirement? I doubt it as it makes no economic sense. Even though, by law, it is compulsory for your employer to make the 9% super guarantee, it comes from you. The company does so by reducing your salary. In other words, you are paying it yourself in the name of being contributed by the employer.

[**Note**: Super is the short form for superannuation in Australia. The 9% contribution is only for demonstration purpose. From July 1, 2014, the minimum rate for employer to contribute to super rate is 9.5%]

Please do not worry if you are not convinced. I will further explain it in this chapter, as there is history linked to it.

What is troubling the millennial is the fact below.

If you have ever opened up your retirement account and had a look, you will realize that it is not plain cash but a portfolio of "assets" you have not even heard of.

Portfolio overview

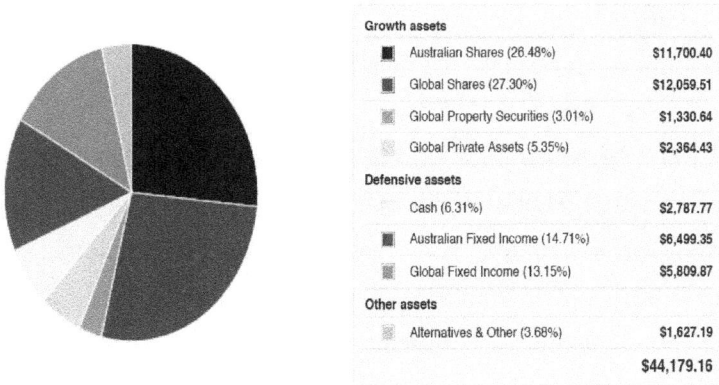

Growth assets	
Australian Shares (26.48%)	$11,700.40
Global Shares (27.30%)	$12,059.51
Global Property Securities (3.01%)	$1,330.64
Global Private Assets (5.35%)	$2,364.43
Defensive assets	
Cash (6.31%)	$2,787.77
Australian Fixed Income (14.71%)	$6,499.35
Global Fixed Income (13.15%)	$5,809.87
Other assets	
Alternatives & Other (3.68%)	$1,627.19
	$44,179.16

Figure 4.2: Super Portfolio Distribution

Source: Author

What is happening with your retirement account is that your retirement fund will be transferred into a **super fund** - a financial entity that helps you to manage your retirement account. Then this super fund will *help you* to invest in the stock market because they think it will grow over time. And in return for their help, you will be charged account fees, insurance, insurance premium, administration fees, total and permanent disability insurance premium, etc. for the rest of your life!

Do you smell anything fishy?

Do you want someone to manage your retirement in a stock market where "*they*" think it will go up forever?

I hope your answer is no.

You already know, from Enron's example, a company's stock price can crash all the way to zero. It can happen to Enron, Bear Sterns, and AIG, and it can happen to any company in the stock market.

[**Note**: In Australia, there are 250+ super funds. they are cooperate super fund, industry super fund, retail super fund and Self-Manage Super Fund (SMSF), etc.]

In addition, the government is encouraging you to put more of your savings into super because they are tax exempt.

But the Government gave me Tax incentive to put in my Super Fund

You may be aware that some of the governments in the world are encouraging people to put part of their income into retirement fund by setting it tax-incentives. In Australia, the money set aside in a retirement account is tax-free.

So who do you think benefits most from this tax law?

Will it be benefiting the young millennials, who are the backbone of society?

Obviously not. If you are in your early 20s, unless in extreme or special circumstances, normally your super will be withheld until you reached the legal retirement age (i.e., 65 or above) before you can claim it back. In other words, your net retirement fund will be locked up for the next 45 years before you can have your hands on it.

[**Note**: If you are in your early 60s and waiting for retirement, this is an excellent tax law to take advantage.]

Don't worry. The Market will always go back up

People may be thinking that despite the volatility of the market, the stock market will eventually go back up in the long run.

Imagine you are an employee waiting for retirement at age 65, and you have been religiously contributing for retirement for all your working life. By 1929, you saved up one million. As the market continued to go up, you waited and saw your portfolio grow since your super fund manager told you the market would go up forever. While he is happy to receive the administration fee and all other fees, you are happy to wait.

Unfortunately, time is not on your side, one year later, DJIA crashed, and 70% of your portfolio vanished. Instead of having one million to live off, you just have $300,000.

Figure 4.3: DJIA

Imagine you have a life span of 85: this means you have about $15,000 each year to live. Is it possible to live off with this amount? You know the answer too well.

Again your super fund manager will tell you the same thing – the market will always go back up.

It probably will, but the question is: Do you have time to wait for it to go back up?

Worse comes to worst, the Government will save us

If you think your retirement fund is insured by the government, you might be disappointed. Unlike your deposit in the bank, which is insured by the Federal Deposit Insurance Corporation (FDIC), most components of your retirement fund are composed of investment rather than a deposit. If you refer to the example of super Portfolio Distribution in Figure 4.2, you will realize 6.31% of the entire portfolio is cash. This amount is the only component covered by FDIC or similar entity in your country.

The Root Cause of the Problem

"Ching, do you know on Labor Day, 1974, President Gerald Ford signed a 200-page law called the Employee Retirement Income Security Act (ERISA)?"

"What is wrong with the current retirement plan?"

Grandad paused for a moment and wrote down four letters.

DB

DC

"What are these supposed to mean?" Crystal joined in.

"We are talking about retirement," I explained.

"I am glad you joined in as this is an important message to you in a few years' time." Grandad tilted his glasses and continued. "DB refers to *defined benefit*, which is a popular pension plan in the 40s and 50s. In a DB plan, a company takes care of you after you retire: you will receive a regular paycheck until the day you die."

"Wow, it sounds too good to be true!" Crystal exclaimed.

"Indeed. In fact, your parents are under DB pension plan working for the government."

"What about DC pension plan?" I asked.

"DC refers to defined contribution, which is the pension plan that exists today. In a DC plan, the employer, employee or both make a regular contribution to a super fund on a regular basis. The contribution in the super fund will be invested in the stock market. And the return is credited to the individual's account and assessable when he or she retired."

"What changes does it have on us now?" Crystal was puzzled.

"It will not have an immediate effect on you since you are still young, but it will affect your generation when you are about my age. The effect of DB pension plan to DC pension plan is so huge that it will just make retirement become a thing of the past."

"Are you serious?" Crystal sounded skeptical.

"DB pension plans means you will receive passive income for life after retirement. DC pension plan means you will fund your own retirement account out of your paycheck in the name of employer's contribution. The change from DB to DC pension plan means the government is shifting the responsibility of retirement back to individuals."

"Why did the government have to shift from DB pension plan to DC pension plan?"

"It is a long story. The narrative of DB pension plan begins in the second half of the 19th Century. American Express was growing railroad and freighter business at that time and was interested in developing a long-term relationship with the employees. The first DB pension was born in 1889. A worker was eligible upon completing 20 years of service and reached 60. Over the next few decades, the manufacturing, unions, and banking sector followed suits."

"How were the companies able to afford to sponsor DB pension plan back then?"

"Companies who sponsor DB pension plan can receive tax benefits. DB pension plan became increasingly popular in the mid-20th century. Following the Great Depression, WWII, and the Korean War, the corporate tax became very high. By 1941, the corporate tax had reached 31%, and by 1952, it reached 52%! This is the primary reason why companies prefer to fund employee's DB pension plan. It is a mean to avoid tax."

"Does that mean DB plan was popular throughout the 20th century?" Grandad had a cup of coffee and then continued.

"No, DB pension had its ups and downs during that period. During the Great Depression of the 1930s, not many companies could afford to start a new DB plan. In fact, 20% of the existing DB plans failed back then due to economic turmoil. Without government backing on pension, the employees under DB pension plan failed to get their pension."

"Do you mean people under DB pension plan lost their retirement in the Great Depression?" Crystal was amazed.

"Unfortunately yes. It was tragic and raised a lot of concerns. People who lost their retirement had nothing to rely on, apart from their saving."

"But the government must have done something to prevent this right?"

"They did. President Roosevelt signed the **Social Security Act of 1935**, which was enacted by the Congress. In this act, there was a retirement benefit to protect the elderly from poverty. Unlike today, the original idea of **Social Security Act** was intended to be a floor of protection only and is not a retirement income vehicle."

"If DB pension was so good, what triggered the shift away from DB pension plan to DC pension plan we have today?"

"Good question. It all started when a company called Studebaker terminated its employee DB pension plan, and more than 4000 auto workers at its automobile plant in South Bend, Indiana lost some or all of their promised pension plan. When a company goes out of business, employee's pension will be lost and has nowhere to call for help. This incident creates a ripple effect in the world about reforming the existing pension plan. And on Labor Day 1974, ERISA was formed."

"But if DC pension plan is much better, why is the world experiencing retirement crisis?" I sighed.

"The truth is, like society security, DC pension plan is a Ponzi scheme. They rely on younger workers like you to contribute to pay off workers that are retiring."

"Are you serious?"

"One of the reasons so many pension plans are in trouble today is because it is underfunded. In other words, if your generation does not contribute, or the stock market does not go up, the retirees who depend on the growing portfolio in their DC pension plan will be toast. That is one reason the government keeps extending the retirement age and encourages or enforces the younger generation to contribute more into their super fund. After all, saving is a merit."

"Yeah right. It almost reminded me the story of the Emperor's New Clothes."

Entitlement Wagon

"But the Emperor's New Clothes does not only end with the trouble of pension. In fact, Social Security, originally signed by President Roosevelt as the **Social Security Act of 1935**, is in deep trouble as well." Grandad added.

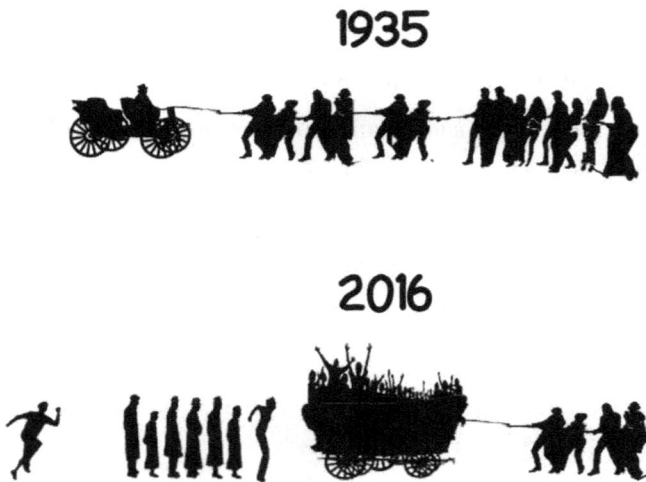

1935

2016

Figure 4.4: Entitlement Wagon

"But business and taxpayers are constantly contributing to social security through taxation; it helped a lot of people in the Great Depression to sail through the difficult times. And the Great Depression is long gone. How is it in trouble?"

"Although the Great Depression is over, people's dependency on social welfare is not. In fact, social welfare can be like a drug, apart from those who ready need it to alleviate temporary financial stress, it encourages the society to develop an entitlement mentality. Do you know when social welfare was first introduced, people were embarrassed to take it? Some people even paid money back, because they felt guilty as they got the money they didn't earn?"

"Really? I can hardly imagine… many times on the news I saw people abusing the social welfare system with fraud claims."

"It is true. Unfortunately, we do not have that type of ethic anymore."

"Grandad, but how is it another Ponzi scheme?"

"In 1935, there were sixteen workers per Social Security recipient. After several generations, baby boomers (1946 – 1964), who once contributed social security to their previous generations (1901 – 1945), aged. As of 2016, there were three workers per social security recipient."

"But how do you know it is a Ponzi Scheme and will not last?"

"Think about it for a second. In 1935, for each dollar you received as a Social Security recipient, it was backed by $16 provided by the workforce. The system only functions properly if this 1:16 ratio stays. A reduction in this ratio means every dollar received by recipients is backed by fewer workers. That is why you are seeing governments worldwide trying to reduce the number of benefits."

"I see what you mean. Hang on a second? Could our generation get nothing when we retire?"

"I doubt your generation will get absolutely nothing, but your generation is getting is significantly fewer benefits than previous generations."

"Grandad, did the baby boomer's generation contribute a lot more than us so that is why the system worked in the past but not the present?" Crystal asked.

"No. In fact when social security was first introduced, it was only 1% of an employee's income. Now it is 6.2% of an employee's income and another 6.2% tax on employees, which is 12.4% in total going towards social security."

"So it is 11.4% more in contribution and less benefit than the generation that contributes only 1% of their income?"

"Calm down," Grandad chuckled and continued.

"Do you know Social Security and Medicare are some of the largest government programs in U.S. history? **Social Security Act of 1935** was just the beginning. In 1964, President Lyndon Johnson launched his **Great Society program** to save the poor. After that, Medicare and Medicaid were born. All these programs were expanded after that."

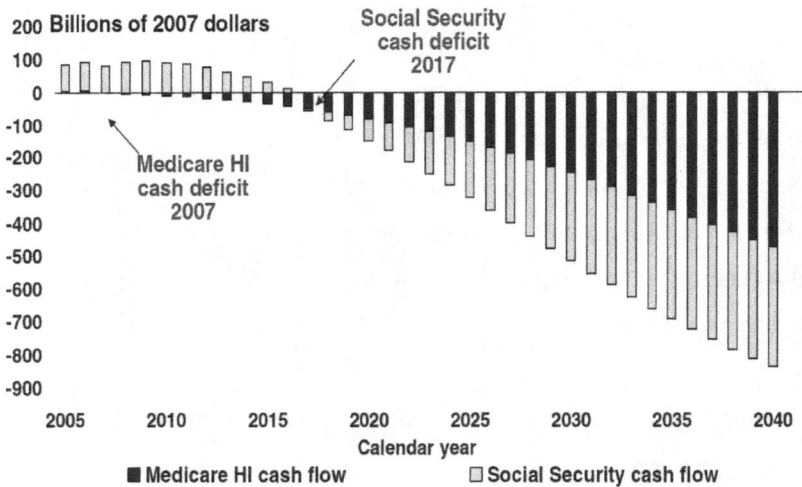

Source: GAO analysis of data from the Office of the Chief Actuary, Social Security Administration and Office of the Actuary, Centers for Medicare and Medicaid Services.

Note: Projections based on the intermediate assumptions of the 2007 Trustees' Reports. The CPI is used to adjust from current to constant dollars.

Figure 4.5: Social Security and Medicare Projections

"So what is the current situation with these social programs right now?"

"The picture is worrying. In fact, Medicare has been running deficits since 2007, and social security is projected to follow next year. If nothing is done, at the current rate Medicare will be exhausted by 2026, and social security in 2033."

Growth in constant dollars 2007-2032

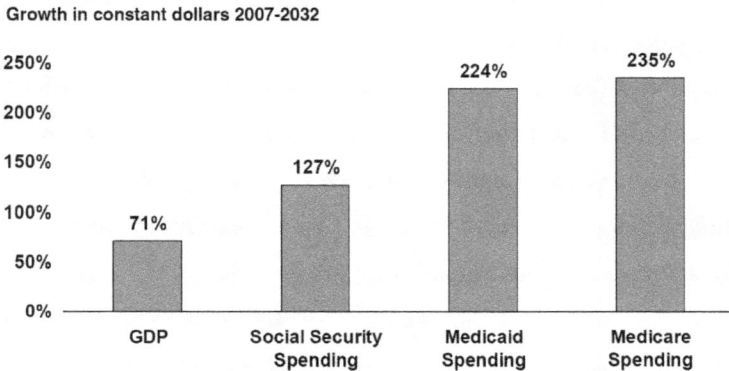

Source: GAO analysis based on data from the Office of the Chief Actuary, Social Security Administration; Office of the Actuary, Centers for Medicare and Medicaid Services; and the Congressional Budget Office.

Notes: Social Security and Medicare projections based on the intermediate assumptions of the 2007 Trustees' Reports. Medicaid projections based on CBO's August 2007 short-term Medicaid estimates and CBO's December 2005 long-term Medicaid projections under mid-range assumptions.

Figure 4.6: Social Welfare Spending

"So you mean the welfare state will be bankrupt by 2033?"

"If you recall the National Debt clock of the U.S., you will notice that U.S. has about $18 Trillion in national debt at present. Unfortunately, this is only a small part of the total debt. The U.S. government excluded a much larger sum – the unfunded liabilities."

"What are unfunded liabilities?"

"Let's say you want to buy me dinner tomorrow but you have no money. This is an unfunded liability. It is a liability because you promised to pay. It is unfunded because you have no money."

"But how did the government accumulate unfunded liabilities?"

"The government borrows it through bond purchase or by future taxation."

"So how much are the accumulated unfunded liabilities?"

"Credible research groups estimate unfunded liabilities can go up to $127 Trillion, which dwarf all other liabilities combined…."

"Are you serious? That is seven … seven times the monstrous national debt… How did that happen? Didn't we and employers pay social security tax, which is deposited into the Social Security Trust Fund? So, if it is in a Trust Fund, then…how?"

"One reason is that the U.S. government is promising more in Social Security and Medicare benefits covered by our contributions to the Trust Fund. Another reason is that the Congress is focusing the Trust Fund to invest in U.S. Treasury. In other words, Congress spent the money in the Trust Fund on other government programs."

"So, Grandad, you are telling me the contribution we put into the Social Security Trust Fund is spent by Congress on other programs?"

"Indeed. Even so, the root of this massive bill is because of entitlement mentality and the greed of politicians wanting to get elected. As a politician, if you want to be elected, the only way is to promise something. And, in order to deliver that promise, one way is to raise taxes, which is politically unpopular. So, the politician will choose an easier path, which is to offer it for FREE – that is to use debt."

"But $127 Trillion is a staggering figure. How does the U.S. government expect the future generations to repay that much?"

"They don't. So they expect younger generation like you and your sister to contribute new money to pay for the present beneficiaries. They just assume there will be more participants entering the scheme. When it reaches a point of defaulting, retirees and workers will realize that their contribution and pensions have been robbed."

It is a Global Pheonmenon

Although this staggering unfunded liability is U.S.'s problem, I challenge you that the problem of pension, social security, and Medicare is a global issue of different scale and urgency. All the world governments are facing the same challenge due to the aging population, pension, and healthcare cost. 2016 is just the beginning as baby boomers are beginning to turn 70 and starting to retire. That means the demand for Social Security and Medicare will continue to increase. Contribution by the younger generation and higher tax are unlikely to fill this gap.

One reason I am writing this doom and gloom is not to scare you but to let you know the facts in advance and to reveal the emperor has no clothes. Being informed is better than uninformed.

What is so fair about young people who are 18 or 25 years old today, having to pay 15% on social security tax for older people, who are much wealthier than they are and paying much lower social security tax, to go and play golf?

If the government today is going to keep the promises for people who are baby boomers, the social security tax for the next couple of generations is going to go up to 25% or 30% of payroll as shown in the graphs above. Do you think further generations will put up with that kind of taxation?

If the government cannot make the payment and they choose to print them, then the value they we are going to get from social security will be stolen.

If so, what are your solutions?

What is the solution that is going to be fair to all generations?

My Proposed Solution

It is interesting to see many politicians such as Republican or Democrats, holding one point of view. When the Liberal party says they want to cut Social Security and Medicare, others will bombard them as being inhumane; when Republicans vote for raising the payroll tax and Medicare levy, they will be labeled as unconstitutional.

Ironically, both solutions inherit flaws. The solution of cutting social security and Medicare will be unpopular for the older generation; raising the payroll tax and Medicare levy will also be unfair for the later generation. Buying Treasury Bonds to fund these unfunded liabilities are also nothing more than kicking the can down the road.

Despite the situation we face, the best solution is to minimize the damage to all generations as much as possible.

Because we cannot continue to do what politicians are doing now, my solution in this chapter is a transition.

Please note that my solution of transition is intended to ensure fairness for all generations and to reduce future generation's dependency on social welfare slowly. By no mean is it to resolve the fundamental problem. It is a cosmetic solution.

In order to resolve the fundamental problem, we must factor monetary policy, the value of our dollar, and the global economy into account. Only then will we have a structural reform.

Here is how the transition should begin:

Transition No 1: *Transition from dependent mindset to mindset that treats it as a Safety Net:*

In order to have a smooth transition, a good starting point will be the mindset. Instead of turning a blind eye to the fact that social security is going to deplete in the future, a good move will be to acknowledge and accept it. Instead of being dependent on it, the public should treat this as a safety net. This is a crucial step, as understanding that the Social Security fund might not exist will alert the present generation to be aware.

Then an immediate question comes up: "Why am I still paying for social security?"

Transition No 2: Provide Young people the option to opt Out of Social Security:

The second step I propose will be to make it an option to opt out of social security.

Instead of making it compulsory for the younger generation to fund the liability of the older generation to continue the Ponzi scheme, we should allow young people to have the option to opt out.

Under a society where people are responsible for themselves, people have to suffer the consequences of spending more than they earn. If they don't, they have to depend on charity, friends, and families. This way, the society will have fewer people depending on social security, where everybody is disillusioned that they are entitled, and the government is going to take care of everybody.

But this will accelerate the possible bankruptcy of the social security trust fund. So how do you deal with this?

Transition No 3: Massively Cut Government Spending

Governments in the world should shrink its size by massively cutting spending and subsidize. One common feature among all government infrastructure projects is that it tends to be over-budget and behind schedule.

Recently in Hong Kong, the construction cost of the high-speed rail link to Mainland China by Mass Transit Railway Corporation (MTR) ballooned from HK$65 billion to HK$85.3 billion, 31% more than the original estimated.

In Australia, according to Treasurer Joe Hockey, the government is spending over $100 million a day more than what they are collecting in revenue and $40 million a day on the interest on the debt.

General government deficit

% of GDP, 2012

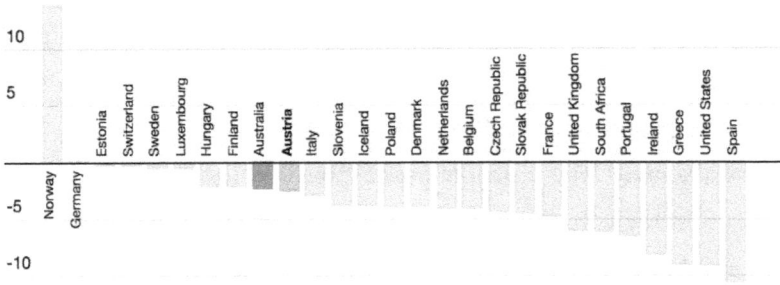

Figure 4.7: General Government Deficit

Source: OECD https://data.oecd.org/gga/general-government-deficit.htm

By reducing the amount of wasteful spending, we can extend the time period and pay the previous generations what they contributed, without putting pressure on the younger generation.

Transition No 4*: The Government should stop funding the Social Security by buying Treasury Bond*

One of the core reasons why all social programs are increasingly expensive is because the government makes up for the shortfall through debt. This is exactly the same as an individual swiping a credit card to fund what they cannot afford. In the short term, the politicians might feel it is politically feasible as they promise something for free. The problem is that these unfunded liabilities needed to be repaid the future generation through taxation or inflation. Most of the $127 trillion unfunded liability is accumulated through this process.

Transition No 5*: The Government is restricted to use the Social Security Trust Fund for the purpose of providing Social Security only*

The Social Security fund should only be used on social security alone and should not be invested nor used to buy Bonds. The reason is that the market goes up and down. Social Security could be a loss in a stock market crash. It shall not be invested in Bond either due to the reason in Step 4 above. It should stay as cash.

But doesn't cash devaluate due to inflation, if it isn't invested?

It does. But that is related to the problem of our money supply in which I will list how to resolve in Part II of the book.

The Emperor Has No Clothes

Ponzi Scheme or pyramid scheme can never work as they will eventually fall apart. Our social welfare in the world today is running on the exact same principle. Government calls it PAYG.

This is no conspiracy theory but public information.

The only difference that makes the government able to disguise as not a Ponzi scheme is that they say the social security they received is invested in government bonds. However, if you take a step back and analyze these financial jargons, you will immediately notice that a government cannot invest in its bond. A government bond in your account or my account is an asset whereas a government bond in a government's account is a liability.

So when a government says they invest the Social Security Trust Fund in a treasury bond, it means there is nothing in a trust fund!

But how?

The reason is simple. For the trust fund to get money, they have to sell the government bond.

But what if no one is buying these bonds?

Then the government must get into debt to fund these liabilities. This is why there is $127 trillion unfunded liability accumulated.

Social welfare is a good deal for people who got it early, those who put in just little bit of money and then entitled to collect a lot of benefits. People who are 80 or 90 and have been collecting Social Security tend to like Social Security. They pay pennies and can receive a lot. However, for people who are paying the social security taxes now, they hate it because they are going pay in a lot and eventually get back very little of it.

I hope you can all see through this, and that is why our emperor actually has no clothes – he is simply naked.

Chapter 5

The Marriage for Debt

On 10, October 2000, U.S. President Bill Clinton signed the U.S.-China Relation Acts of 2000, granting Beijing permanent normal trade relations with the U.S. and paving the way for China to join the World Trade Organization in 2001.

Between 1980 and 2015, U.S. - China total value of trade rose from $5 billion to $598 billion.

As of 2016, China's GDP is approximately 61% of U.S.'s GDP, and is the second largest economy in the world.

This chapter is about China's monetary history. In this chapter, I will take you through a helicopter ride to overview how the Chinese economy evolved to become the second largest economy in the world.

By the end of this chapter, you will understand the role of Chinese economy in the 21st century.

What Leads to the Marriage for Debt?

On the 15th August 1971, U.S. President Nixon, without the approval of Congress, took the U.S. dollar off the gold standard and made U.S. dollar as the reserve currency of the world.

Since all the currencies in the world were pegged to USD through gold at $35/oz, the unpeg of the dollar from gold caused all the world's currencies to become fiat simultaneously. No longer is our currency supply restrained by the global gold reserves. The rules of money have changed. Debt becomes the new money. This is when the world's marriage for debt truly began.

In my first book *Corruption of Real Money*, I detailed the history on what led to the global dollar standard at length. Please feel free to refer to it as refreshment.

So, how is a pure debt based monetary system different from a gold backed monetary system?

The Difference Between Gold and Debt Based Monetary System

Suppose U.S. and China are using gold as money. For the sake of simplicity, each country starts with 1000oz in their account.

When China trades with U.S., she exports the goods and services she produces and imports those she needs. When China exports more than she imports, China is in trade surplus. On the other hand, when U.S. imports more goods than she produces, she will have to pay gold to China. Such arrangement will cause less gold circulated in U.S.

The outflow of gold will cause the U.S. economy to contract, which will lead to a recession. Businesses will have to cut excessive employees and reduce the price of products through competitions.

The free market will readjust the price of goods until the U.S. economy is, once again competitive, then gold will flow back to the U.S.

As gold inflows into the Chinese economy due to trade surplus, China's economy will experience a boom. Too much gold chasing after too little goods will cause inflation. The price of goods in China will become more expensive locally. Eventually, Chinese goods will be less competitive. Export will decline, and China will rely on importing from U.S.

Gold will flow back from China to U.S. and this cycle repeats itself. This is how a gold based monetary system works. It is automated by the free market. No government needs to be involved in this case.

So how does a debt based monetary system work differently?

Under a debt based monetary system, trading works differently since the U.S. unpegged its dollar from gold and USD became the reserve currency of the world.

Suppose both U.S. and China start with $1 billion worth of USD in their current account. When China trades with U.S., she exports the goods and services she produces and imports those she needs. Imagine when U.S. imports more goods and services, she will have to pay USD to China.

However, unlike gold, where there is a constraint in money supply, U.S. can run a huge trade deficit by selling U.S. Treasury Bond to China. The currency supply in U.S. will not shrink because the U.S. government can print them. There is no automatic mechanism in place that encourages the U.S to cut local prices and wages to be competitive once again.

The U.S can continue to run a huge trade deficit as long as China accepts U.S. Treasury Bond as payment.

That is why China is able to run an ever-increasing trade surplus, and the price of goods in China will stay competitive indefinitely.

Who Holds the Most U.S. National Debts?

So far, we understand how U.S.'s dollar standard allows the U.S. to accumulate such a staggering amount of national debt, which destabilizes the global economy. We also realize that one country's debts are another country's credits.

Does that mean the astronomical credits from creditor nations from the rest of the world pose an equal risk?

Short answer: Yes.

But who is the biggest U.S. debt owner?

As discussed in the last chapter, the largest owner of U.S. debt is U.S. social security.

In fact, U.S. government owned 65.6% of the U.S. national debt, whereas foreign countries account for 34.4%, which is approximately one-third.

Allocation of U.S. Debt

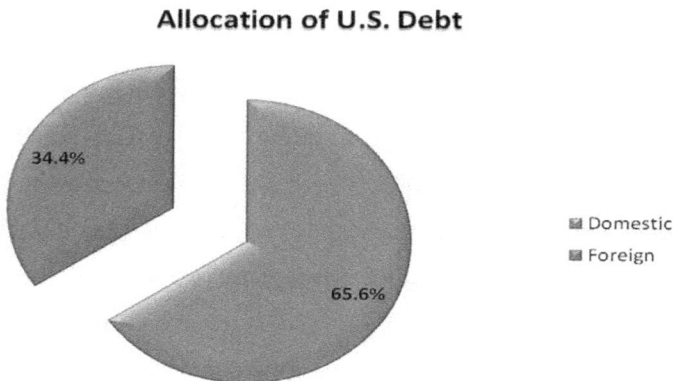

Figure 5.1: Allocation of U.S. Debt (August 2014)

So, who are the biggest foreign U.S. national debt holders?

According to the U.S. Treasury Department, the largest foreign holder of U.S. national debt was China (7.2% , ~ $3.23 trillion USD).

But Why Do Foreign Nations Hold U.S. Treasuries?

Smart readers like you might wonder why foreign nations must buy U.S treasuries?

It has everything to do with how the U.S. dollar becomes the world's reserve currency.

In the wake of WWII, U.S. had become the wealthiest country, the largest creditor nation with 60% of the world's gold holding. It was also the biggest lender; many countries were holding U.S. dollar-denominated securities.

During this period, countries around the world embarked on a lengthy period of reconstruction and economic development to recover from the devastation of war.

Because the gold exchange was incapable of coping with world trade, 44 Allied nations gathered together in Bretton Woods to agree on a new monetary system.

The conclusion was that all currencies were redeemable in U.S. dollar, which was pegged to gold at $35 per ounce.

The reserve status of the U.S. dollar means the demand for the dollar remains strong because:

1) Countries hold the dollar in reserve to buy oil.

2) The U.S. dollar is used to settle in international trade and to hold other nations' savings.

[Note: These dollar reserves do not necessary refer to USD. The dollar reserves can be dollar denominated assets like U.S. Treasury Bonds, which are debts.]

A Brief History of the Chinese Economy

"Our land is so wealthy and prosperous, that we possess all things. Therefore there is no need to exchange the produce of foreign barbarians for our own."

- Qianlong Emperor

When I was little, my Grandma used to tell me stories of a secret cycle happens roughly every 500 years, which is the wealth transfers from East to West and back. It is called the East-West cycle.

Do you believe it?

As a modern Chinese descendent, I was skeptical about older generation's saying. It is not until I did research that I realized the wisdom.

Below is a table extracted from *Maddison (2007), Countours of the World Economy*, you can see that from Year 1 AD to 1300 AD, China and Europe's per capita GDP were closely matched. Having a higher population, China had the largest economy in the world.

Year	1	960	1300	1700	1820	1952	1978	2003
China	450	450	600	600	600	538	978	4803
Europe	550	422	576	923	1090	4343	10972	16750

Table 5.1: Level of Chinese & European GDP Per Capita (1990 international dollars)

1 – 2003 AD

Source: See Maddison (2007), Countours of the World Economy (forthcoming)

In Chinese history, Ming dynasty (1368 – 1644) is believed to be when the sprouts of capitalism emerged in China. During the Ming dynasty, taxation was light. State tax of agriculture was only 2%, and commerce was on 1.5%. Under this liberalized economy where government was less intrusive, trade and commerce thrived.

Ming dynasty also had a thriving trade with Europe.

Sound money like silver was used as money.

During the Ming dynasty, there was an estimation of 300 million taels of silver, which is equivalent to 1900 billion dollars in today's money, flown into China.

However, despite the massive influx of real money, the Chinese economy stagnated from 1700 until the beginning of the 21st century.

So, what is causing such a great nation, with the largest economy in the world to stagnate behind the rest of the world?

It all began when Great Britain and other European nations desired China's silk and tea.

During Qing Dynasty 1644 - 1912, there was huge demand for China's silk and tea from the West.

China, however, had no demand for foreign products because she was self-sufficient.

China would sell, but buy nothing in return. If this could happen, Europe and Britain's gold and silver would go over to China to import goods, but would not return, because China was not importing.

This was unacceptable to the rest of the world, as it would cause an imbalance of trade.

So, Britian desperately needed a solution.

That was when using opium against China was born.

Opium is an additive substance. Opium addiction results in devastating consequences, such as job loss, financial problems, health problems, relationship problems, and possibly death.

Unfortunately, the Chinese did not realize this until it was too late.

In the late 17th century, over 1/3 of the Chinese reported smoking opium. China's massive import of opium resulted in trade deficit and the outflow of gold and silver.

To revert the situation, the Chinese government tried to ban the import opium. This plan did not work too well, because British merchants were smuggling opium into China. This illegal import of opium led to the Chinese government to take more aggressive actions.

In 1839, the Chinese government burnt over 20,000 bales of opium, which officially sparked *The First Opium War*.

However, due to the British advance in military, China was defeated during the war.

In 1841, China ceded the island of Hong Kong to Britian.

In 1842, China signed *the Treaty of Nanking* and formally ended *the First Opium War*.

In 1898, Britain was granted an additional 99 years of rule over Hong Kong under *the Second Convention of Peking*.

Unlike China, Britian was undergoing industrial revolution and had more advanced technological and military development.

Industrialization soon spread beyond Britain to continental Europe.

Years of oppression by foreigners had caused Chinese peasants to spark a movement to siege International Legations known as *Boxer Rebellion*. This attracted large European countries such as Germany, Russia, France, Britain and even Japan to invade China.

In the end, the Qing Imperials were defeated.

On 7th September 1901, the Qing Empire of China and the Eight-Nation Alliance signed *the Treaty of 1901*, a peace agreement between the Great Powers and China.

China was forced to pay 450 million taels of silver as indemnity over a course of 39 years to the Eight-Nation.

The Chinese peasants organized themselves to an anti-foreign power and protested against the Qing dynasty.

Eventually, Qing dynasty lost the loyalty of its people.

In this period of uncertainty, a Chinese revolutionary, Sun Yat-sen, formed the Republic of China on 1st January 1912, which is known as ROC (The Nationalists).

Sun Yat-sen was referred to as *"Father of the Nation"* in the Republic of China.

Over 2000 years of imperialism in China had ended.

China had no full sovereignty in the first half of the 20th century. The power was distributed among the foreign powers, the Nationalists and the Communists, remnant warlords, and later on, by the Empire of Japan (Second Sino-Japanese War 1937 – 45).

War, unfair treaties, indemnities, loss of sovereignty and huge foreign loans to pay off the creditors had saddled the economy of China with a lot a of unproductive expenses, which came from increased taxes on the Chinese citizens. Also, foreigners could carry out business within China, without paying Chinese taxes or obeying Chinese laws. And because of that, the local Chinese government had to collect these taxes from local Chinese business, which placed them in a position of comparative tax disadvantage.

From 1900 – 1949, the Chinese central government annually spent about 40% of its budget on loan and indemnity payment, and another 40% on military development, leaving merely 20% or less on other government expenses and economic development. All these cumulative effects of loss of tax revenues caused China's economy to stagnate and fall behind the rest of the world. That is why you see the per capita GDP of China went from parity to eight times below Europe by the first half of the 20th Century.

China During WWI

The beginning of the 20th century was a period of uncertainty and turmoil. Shortly after ROC was founded in 1912, WWI took place from 1914 to 1918.

Many people would have guessed WWI must have been detrimental to the Chinese economy. Interestingly, this period was a golden age of Chinese industrialization.

WWI caused a lot of foreign business to withdraw from China and reallocate back in their home country. This positively affected the Chinese business due to less competition.

However, Japan's influence in China had also spread for the same reason.

During WWI, export to China fell drastically, yet, the demand for Chinese goods such as raw materials, munitions and necessity increased. This helped to boost Chinese export and reduced the trade deficit inherited from the imperial predecessor.

Since the Chinese currency, Yuan, was pegged against silver. The strong demand of Chinese goods pushed the price of silver up, which led to double in value against both USD and the Pound. A stronger Chinese currency allowed China to pay off the foreign debt much more cheaply.

Overall, the effect of WWI had positive impacts on the Chinese people's economy. However, it is difficult to draw a generalized conclusion on how well the China's economy did, because it was split into several territories, including the nationalist party, the communist party, and foreign control.

Although WWI marked the end of China's economic independency of Western power, the withdrawal of Western business also paved the way to Japan's domination later on in history.

The Chinese Silver Standard

Prior to Chinese economic reforms and the trade liberalization in 1979, China's policies kept the country stagnant, centrally controlled, inefficient, poor, and isolated from the global economy.

It is a long story how China rose to become the world's second largest economy today. China's economy has grown at an average annual rate of 8-10 percent after 1978. That rate of growth (doubling of the economy every 7 years) is virtually unprecedented for a poor, third world country.

History suggests it was not until 1927, when Chiang Kai-shek, a leader of Republic of China, managed to re-unified China and brought political stability. China had a golden decade with relative stability from 1927 to 1937, which is known as the *Nanjing decade*.

Despite China suffering years of domination and colonization, Chinese benefited from access to advanced Western military and industrial technology, which were impossible to be adopted from stubborn Chinese leaders during the Qing dynasty. Chinese reformers also looked abroad for political and social models to help strengthen China. China's industry grew from 1927 to 1931.

The temporary prosperity level of China was quickly interrupted by The Great Depression of 1930. It is worth noting that back then China's currency was silver-based. Initially, the deflationary pressure from the Great Depression had caused a fall in silver price, which favored Chinese exchange rate and boosted exports. Shanghai, the financial center of China, benefited from large inflow of silver from other provinces.

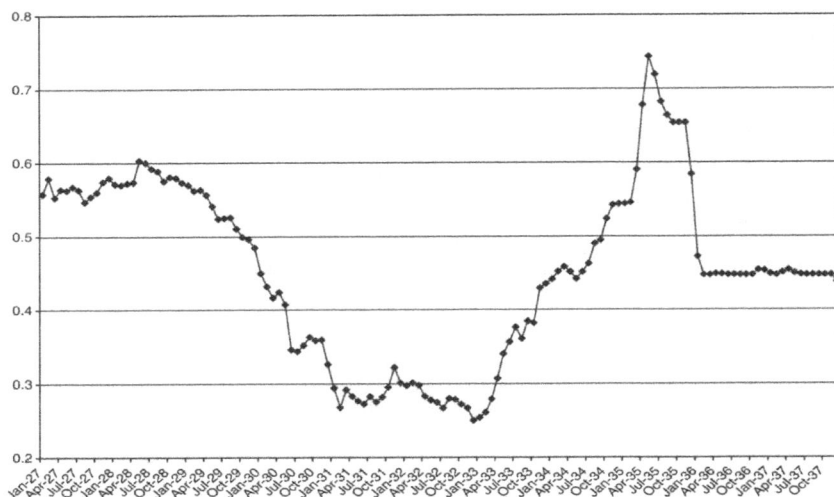

Figure 5.2: Silver Price in New York 1927 - 1939

However, the outflow of liquidity to Shanghai caused a large scale-banking crisis in rural areas of China. Shanghai was relatively stable only because the inflow of silver offset the outflow.

So, China, had not only weathered the international financial storm, but also experienced an export boom.

In September 1931, because British went off the gold standard, many countries had their currency depreciated. Chinese silver dollar was affected.

Like the British, under U.S. president Franklin Roosevelt's administration, the U.S. also unpegged from gold and remonetized silver. The U.S.'s *Silver Purchases Act* in 1934 meant massive purchase of silver. This action drove up the price of silver and caused a large outflow of silver from China to the U.S. The sharp rise in silver price led to a sharp appreciation of Chinese currency. The result is an immediate reverse of Shanghai's prosperity, causing a sudden crisis in Shanghai. The deflationary pressure due to a shrinkage in money supply became widespread in major Chinese cities during 1932 – 1934. Some cities experienced double-digit deflation rates.

In 1934, the Nationalist government needed to impose a foreign-exchange control on silver export.

By 1935, the Nationalist Chinese government had to abandon the silver standard entirely.

Afterwards, China was forced to be in fiat currency standard with the central government in direct and absolute control of the quantity of money.

Hyperinflation in China

China and Japan had a war that lasted 8 years, from July 1937 to September 1945. During the Japanese invasion, Japan controlled over one-third of China. The Chinese economy was devastated. Over ten million Chinese lost their lives in the fight. My grandparents were fortunate enough to escape to Hong Kong during those periods of turmoil and uncertainty.

The Nationalist government financed the war against Japan using a printing press covering 65 to 80 percent of the military expenditures.

The amount of Yuan created from 1937 to 1945 jumped from 3.6 billion to a staggering 1.507 trillion, which is 418 times!

The U.S. ended Japan's invasion in China through an air raid assault of Tokyo in 1945.

However, it was just the beginning of another civil war between the Nationalists government (lead by Chiang Kai-Shek) and the Communists (lead by Mao Zedong). The Civil war lasted 4 years. Another five million Chinese lost their lives during this Chinese Civil war.

In the end, the Communists triumphed and became the People's

Republic of China today.

The Nationalists lost the war and withdrew to Taiwan in later 1949.

Due to war, the money supply had reached an astonishing 399 trillion Yuan by July 1948.

In the end, China had a hyperinflation.

Wealth and saving for the Chinese middle class were undermined by the hyperinflation. To restore the public confidence in the fiat Yuan, the Chinese government created a new currency, which was backed by gold, to replace the old one. Queues with thousands of people lined up with bags of paper currency to trade their Yuan for gold. This eventually led to the government need to proclaim gold and silver ownership as illegal and enforced people to accept the new currency.

Guess what happened. It did not work.

The new currency introduced by the Chinese government depreciated as fast as the old one. Price doubled every 15.2 days.

By April 1949, the newly introduced fiat currency supply skyrocketed to 5.161 Quadrillion Yuan (i.e., 5,161,000,000,000,000 Yuan).

Figure 5.3: Chinese One million dollar bank note

If you refer to the foreign exchange market, just before China's war with Japan in 1937, the exchange rate of one USD was 3.7 Yuan, and by

April 1949, one USD increased to 5.161 Quadrillion Yuan.

The primary goal of the Communists Party was to restore the economy back to order. With the banking system nationalized under the People's Bank of China (founded in December 1948), the central government brought inflation under control by 1951 through unifying China's monetary system, tightening credit and central control of government budgets, and guaranteeing the value of the new currency in 1949 – *renminbi*.

The Origin of Chinese Communism

From this point forward, you might wonder how did China became the second largest economy in the world from the mid-20th century? What has the Communist Party done, such that China could achieve a stable average GDP growth of 10% ?

It might surprise you that China's economy did not really gain momentum until 1990. With most of China's unequal treaties abrogated during the Japanese invasion, China regained its sovereignty, once again.

Mao Zedong, who was a Chinese communist revolutionary, founded the People's Republic of China (PRC) on 1st October 1949.

To restore the order of China, he adopted Marxism-Leninism – a political philosophy that seeks to establish a socialist state.

Mao called it Maoism.

Unlike Capitalism, communism and socialism are political structures that promote equality and eliminate social classes. The two philosophies are interchangeable in some ways and different in others.

In a communism society, the working class owns everything and everyone works towards the same goal. There is neither wealthy nor poor. The community distributes what it produces based on needs.

Nothing is obtained by working more on what is required. Hence, communism often results in low production, mass poverty, and low advancement.

Socialism, promotes equality and allows workers to earn wages to spend as they choose. The government, but not the public, owns and operates the means of production, such as factories.

In a socialist society, workers receive what they need to produce and survive.

Like communism, socialism does not motivate people to achieve more. The primary reason Mao chose Marxism-Leninism is because he wanted to achieve a structural foundation and long-range goals to transform China into an industrialized nation with better living standards, reduced income polarity, and economic modernization. Hence, they nationalized and centralized the banks, and the industrial units and transformed enterprises into state-owned enterprises. Lands for agriculture were redistributed from landlords to farmers who previously owned little to no lands. Everything was gradually brought under government-centralized control and owned by the state. It was collectivism.

Failure of the Great Leap Forward

Mao's goal of restoring a viable economy in China was a success. From 1949 to 1952, China had progressively recovered from her economic scars due to decades of wars. The next steps were industrialization and socialization.

From 1953 to 1957, Mao promoted the *First-Five Year* plan to achieve his long-term goal for China. For this purpose, he sought help from the Soviet Union and adopted the Soviet economic model, which was based on state ownership and centralized economic planning to achieve a high rate of economic growth. The *First-Five Year* plan succeeded as China had built a strong foundation in heavy industry, including iron and steel manufacturing, mining and electricity generation etc. However, the Chinese government focused too much on industrialization, so that a growing imbalance between industrial and agricultural growth was being developed, yet, covered up by the government.

The *Great Leap Forward* (1958 to 1961) of the People's Republic of China was a very expensive disaster. During this period, farmers were told to stop farming and make steel. Mao forced people into schools, and universities, and villages to give up daily activities to forge steel.

In is worth noting that China was an agrarian country. By diverting millions of agricultural workers into industry and by pushing China to become an industrialized nation within 5 years, at the expense of agricultural, resulted in long-term failure. When this combined with three years of bad weather, the result was the famous *Great Chinese Famine* that caused the death of 30 - 40 million of people - the worst famine in human history.

China had a total economic collapse.

Socialism was not working as the Chinese government expected. Soviet's economic modal seemed unsuitable for China. China's goal to become the second largest economy in the world was filled with difficulties. A readjustment was needed.

For China to prosper, agriculture must come first. Hence, China's top priority was to restore agricultural output and expand it to a state that can meet the needs of the growing population. For that to happen, less centralization in agricultural decision was needed to restore the market efficiency. China relocated and mobilized the nation's resources into advancing agricultural technology. In addition, the Chinese government

also provided economic support for agriculture. They imposed policies
such as reduction of taxes on agriculture and increase in supply of
agricultural machinery concentrating on high yield areas.

During 1961 to 1965, the Chinese economic adjustment was a success.
The Soviet-style, industrial-orientated economic model was balanced
by agriculture first, decentralized ownership policy. Both agriculture
and industry output production level in China surpassed previous years,
growing at 9.6 percent and 10.6 percent annually, respectively. And with
a good foundation of agriculture, industries blossomed. Small-scale
industries, coal mines, and hydroelectric plants spread in China.

The Rise and Fall of the Cultural Revolution

Yet, the beginning of success in China's economic adjustment came
with a price. There was a secret war within the People's Republic of
China. Mao's failure in the *Great Leap Forward* reform resulted in many
political oppositions in the Communist party.

Mao, unwilling to admit his mistake, feared that other problematic
leaders (e.g., Deng Xiaoping) were a threat to the revolution. His power
was struggling. Hence, he plotted The Culture Revolution in order to
eradicate all the potential rivals.

Mao, with his fourth wife, Jiang Qing, who was a Chinese actress, used
propaganda to manipulate the minds of the young Chinese to be their
followers. Kids were taught to write *"Long Live Chairman Mao"* before
their own names.

In the Cultural Revolution, Mao's enemy included the old Communist
Party of China he built, but was no longer in charge of, rich farmers,
landlords, and the West. Old ideas, names and even news that was
sensitive were regarded as standing against Mao's revolution. The

purpose of the revolution was to identify who were his allies and enemies.

During the *Cultural Revolution*, Mao spread the idea that a second power is rising up to stand against him and to suppress his followers. Several militant universities and high schools formed a military unit as part of the revolution to fight for Mao. They were known as the *Red Guards*. Soon, this spread nationwide. Mao led the young people to rebel. They burned down schools and books, closed factories, encouraged young people to attack teachers, parents, government officers, and the education system.

Lin Biao, the head of Mao's army, made a "*Little Red Book*" for Mao's teaching, which almost became a bible to the *Red Guards*.

"War can only be abolished through war, and in order to get rid of gun it is necessary to take up the gun."

- Mao Zedong (Founder of the People's Republic of China)

You can imagine that the *Cultural Revolution* only stagnated the Chinese economy. The patrol of Red Guards disrupted the transportation system. Hospitals were non-functional. People with professional titles, such as teachers, engineers, and scientists, were jailed. The Chinese society was grinded to a halt. More citizens became peasants and worked in the farms to afford food and make a living for their families. Many people were left in poverty with the loss of education opportunities.

Yet, this economy halt could not last forever. The cultural revolution eventually ended by the Red Guards fighting among themselves. About of half a million people lost their lives during the *Cultural Revolution*.

Road to the 2nd Largest Economy in the World

The death of Mao in September 1976 was a major turning point for the People's Republic of China.

Deng Xiaoping, a Chinese Communist leader, won the power struggle in the People's Republic of China.

Deng witnessed that individual self-interest might be to key to strength China, which was unpopular under Mao's socialism framework.

Deng advocated a Chinese economic reform that introduced market principles into the existing Chinese socialism model.

Deng Xiaoping's *"Four Modernizations"* programs aimed to strengthen China's agriculture, industry, national defense, science, and technology to make China the most powerful nation by the early 21st century.

In the reform, economic self-reliance was the key.

Deng Xiaoping Theory summed up the positive and negative experience, since the founding of the People's Republic of China. It was a version of socialism with Chinese characteristics.

"It doesn't matter whether a cat is white or black, as long as it catches mice" was his famous quote, which means it is not important whether or not a person is a revolutionary, as long as he or she is efficient and capable to do a great job in the socialist economy; *"kai fang!"* which means open up, paved way to China's export-led growth economic model.

- **First Stage:** Opening up China to foreign-investments and permitting entrepreneurs to start business.
- **Second Stage:** Privatize state-owned industry; lifting price control and protection policies.

During the reform, the agricultural output increased at a rate of 8.2 percent annually. Food prices declined and profits for farmers rose. Agricultural technology improved the farming productivity, allowing workers to free themselves from farming and work in industries and other sectors.

To carry out the reform further, Deng needed to improve the relationship of China with the globe. He took an opportunity when U.S. President Jimmy Carter invited him to the U.S. in 1979. His visit inspired him. Unlike his ancestor, he was inspired and open-minded about foreign technology and invention, and he realized these are not a matter of socialism and capitalism, but ideologically neutral.

"Planning and market forces are not the essential difference between socialism and capitalism. A planned economy is not the definition of socialism, because there is planning under capitalism; the market economy happens under socialism, too. Planning and market forces are both ways of controlling economic activity."

- Deng Xiaoping (Chinese Leader)

These reforms gradually incorporated capitalism approach in a socialist market economy.

Since the beginning of the reform, the result had been remarkable. China's economy was growing at a rapid rate averaging 10% annually from 1979 to 2013. China's GDP per capita had risen tenfold.

China GDP per capita

1961 - 2013

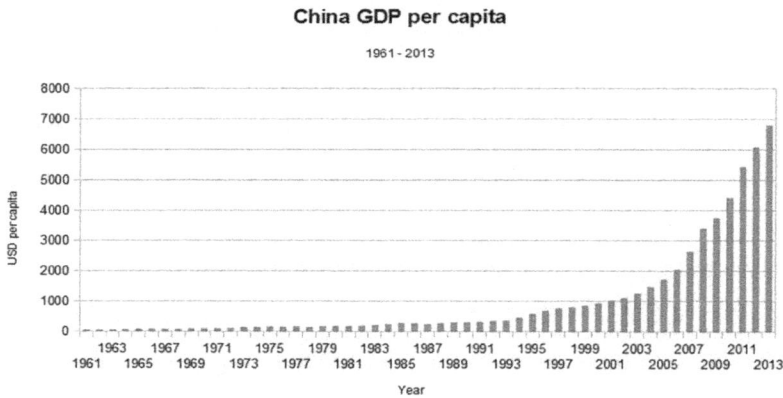

Figure 5.4: China GDP per capita (1961 – 2013)

Source: http://itbulk.org/country-codes/china/

From 1980 to 2000, Chinese steel production quadrupled and eventually accounted for one-third of the global market production level. China's openness to the globe quickly increased wealth for herself.

When China joined WTO in 2000, trade increased from under 10% of the GDP to 64% of the GDP.

Deng also exempted taxes and regulation for Special Economic Zones to attract foreign capital. His export-led, investment driven growth model allowed China to attain capital to accelerate economic growth, hence, his *"Four Modernizations"* programs.

The three decades of rapid economic growth in China had increased the income of average people and driven people out of poverty.

This is how China became the 2nd largest economy in the world at the beginning of the 21st century.

[**Note**: Deng Xiaoping famously advocated "One Country, two systems" that allows Hong Kong and Macau to retain their own capitalist economic and political system, while the rest of China runs the socialist system.]

How Fast is the Chinese Economy actually Growing?

To see how fast China's economy is growing, it is best to compare it as a percentage of GDP to other large nations in the world.

	1952	1978	1990	2000	2015
U.S.	9.5	13.6	27.9	51.7	61
Japan	78.5	38.5	70.5	165.9	266
Germany	N/A	50.8	113.3	244.8	327
India	63.9	78.0	122.2	190.6	525

Table 5.2: China's GDP as a percent of other nations' GDP (1978 – 2004)

Source: Heston, Summers, and Aten (2006) and IMF World Economic Outlook Database

A Closer Look at China's GDP Distribution

From 1980 to 2015, Chinese GDP increased 35.86 times: it went from $330 billion to $11 trillion.

In 2016, China is the largest exporting country in the world with export value estimated to be $2 trillion USD.

Prior to the economic reform in 1978, 81% of the population worked in the agricultural sector, which accounted for 40% of GDP.

Today, with the advancement in agricultural technology and increase in agriculture productivity, more people have shifted to other industries.

The agricultural sector accounts for 10% of China's GDP since 2009, consisting of approximately 34% of the total employed population.

China GDP Distribution

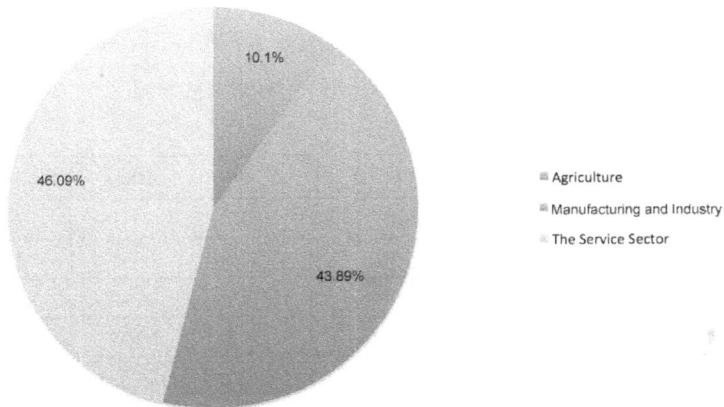

Figure 5.5: China GDP Distribution (2013)

Source: www.quandl.com

Manufacturing and Industry have always been the backbone of China's economy since the reform, accounting for 40% to 50% of the Chinese economy.

The service sector, which was fractional compared to the other two sectors prior to the reform, grew rapidly from 13% in 1970 to 46.09% by 2013.

The Great Chinese Trade Surplus

You probably remembered that for Deng's "*Four Modernizations*" plan to work, China must be self-reliant. China is already producing far more than she can consume.

But why is China the second largest importer in the world?

Unlike the U.S., where the main reason for U.S. to import is to consume, China's import is a function of export. The primary reason China imports from the rest of the world is for her to export, so that she can continue the export-led growth economic modal to achieve their target economic growth.

From 1980 to 2008, China's export of goods and services as a percent of GDP had been rising sharply, increasing from roughly 5% to 35%.

China Export of Goods and Services as a % of GDP

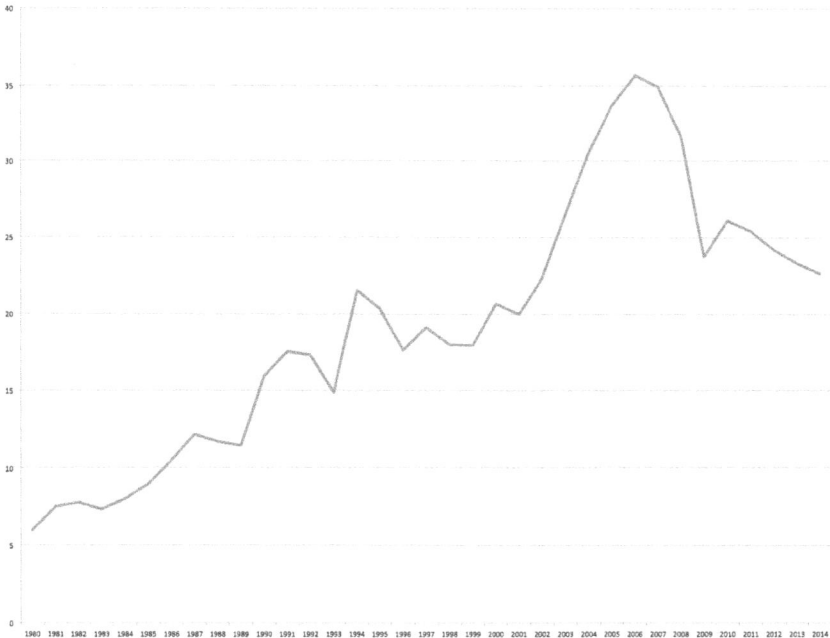

Figure 5.6: China Export of Goods and Services as a % of GDP

Source: World Bank Cross Country Data

Despite China's export as a percent of GDP declining since the financial crisis of 2008, China's trade surplus with the U.S. increased. From 1985 until 2015, China's trade surplus increased from $6 billion USD to $367 billion USD. This great Chinese trade surplus transformed the Chinese economy.

China's Trade Surplus with U.S (1985 to 2015)

in Billlion

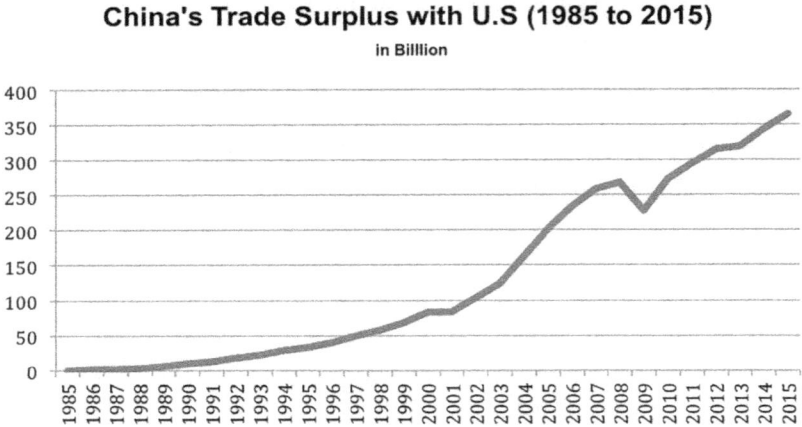

Figure 5.7: China's Trade Surplus with U.S.

Source: www.census.gov

In 2015, China trade surplus with U.S. was $367 billion USD, which accounts for 30% of China's GDP ($10,982 billion)!

This large trade surplus from U.S. demand indirectly triggered a lot of other factors driving China's local GDP.

If you recalled the definition of GDP,

$$GDP = C + I + G + X - I$$

Where

C = consumption

I = Investment

G = government Spending

X = export

I = import

This large trade surplus in China indicates that tens of millions of Chinese are moving into industrial and manufacturing sectors to produce goods and services for the consumption in U.S.

Their wages boost China's local consumption (**C**), which constitute part of China's GDP. The large U.S. demand also drives both local China and foreign investment (**I**) to enter China to construct factories.

So, China's export led growth and U.S.'s debt based economic models are like a marriage.

They depend on one another.

If one fails, the other will follow, and this is exactly what is about to happen.

Foreign Exchange Reserve Talk

At the beginning of this chapter, we briefly looked at the difference on how trade works between gold and debt based monetary systems. Prior to 1971, all currencies were pegged directly or indirectly to gold through the USD. When a country has trade deficit, gold outflows and the economy contracts.

International Monetary Fund (IMF) requires each country to maintain a fixed exchange rate (i.e., ± 1 percent) by tying its currency to gold.

Nothing will be gained by creating more fiat currency.

When the Bretton Wood system collapsed and the fixed exchange rate system ended, countries gradually discovered that by having their central banks create fiat currencies and using them to buy currencies of its trading partners, they can artificially push up the currencies of their trading partners and devaluate their own currencies, becoming more competitive in export.

To understand how it works, let's take a look at an example.

When Chinese businessmen export goods and services to the U.S., they are paid in USD. Since they cannot use USD in China, they have to convert it back to Renminbi (RMB). Imagine if this is done in a free market, where the price of RMB is based on demand; the conversion back to RMB will cause the value of RMB to appreciate sharply and reduce China's competitiveness in export. The Chinese government does not want this to happen, because this will hinder China's economic growth. So the Chinese government prevents this by instructing the People's Bank of China (PBOC) to print an equivalent amount of currency from thin air and buy up all incoming dollars at a fixed exchange rate. The Chinese businessmen will then accept this newly created currency and deposit it back to their local commercial banks. PBOC holds these USD dollars as foreign reserve asset. And this is how central banks accumulate foreign exchange reserve.

By creating RMB and using it to purchase foreign currencies from other countries, PBOC can prevent a deluge of foreign currency entering China and successfully hold down the value of RMB to favor its export led growth model.

According to IMF, the world's total foreign exchange reserve in Q4 2015 was $10.924 trillion USD. This staggering amount created over the last three decades is held by central banks around the world.

If you step back and look at the composition of foreign exchange reserve, you will understand that it is debt and fiat currency created by central banks around the world through bond purchase and fractional reserve banking.

Since the U.S. denominated assets account for 40% of the world's total foreign exchange reserve, it is easy to image how this mindboggling amount of debt created by the Federal Reserve transformed the world's economy.

[Note: Foreign exchange reserve includes only foreign banknotes, foreign bank deposit, foreign treasury bills, and short and long-term foreign government securities.]

How China Causes Global Inflation?

China is the largest holder of foreign exchange reserve. In May 2016, China's foreign exchange reserve was 3.19 trillion (~ 29% of the world's total foreign exchange reserve). To earn income on these foreign currencies, China must buy assets denominated in that foreign currency. This is how Chinese central banks add an enormous amount of liquidity to the rest of the world and caused global inflation worldwide.

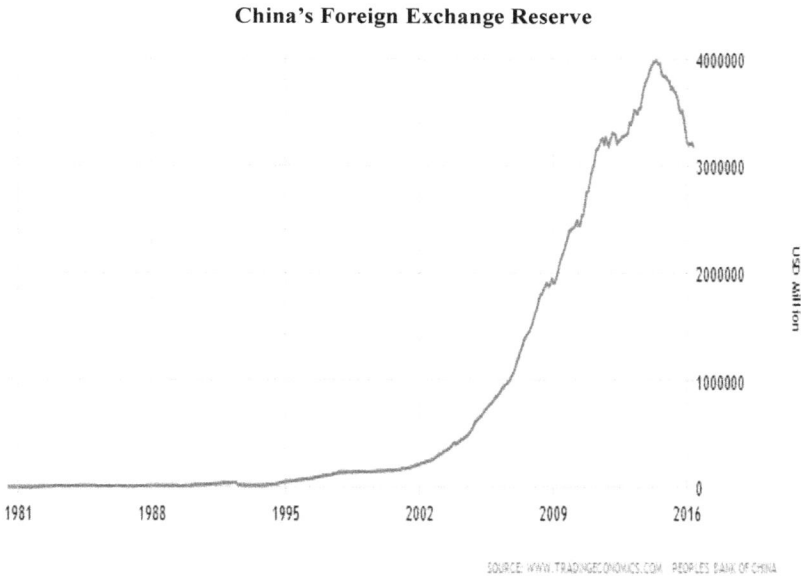

Figure 5.8: China's Foreign Exchange Reserve

Source: www.tradingeconomics.com/china/foreign-exchange-reserves

It is interesting to compare U.S. to China in terms of fiat currency creation.

When the Federal Reserve creates the dollar and injects it into the economy, it aims to add liquidity into the economy; when the PBOC creates fiat currency, it aims to prevent RMB from appreciating, resulting in adding liquidity to the rest of the world.

Who is the Currency Manipulator?

An interesting topic about currency manipulators has been circulating in the world of finance in recent years. The consequences of the huge gap between U.S.'s trade deficit and China's trade surplus has drawn a lot of attention.

Some countries accuse China of manipulating their local currency and robbing billions of dollars of capital and millions of jobs.

So, why is China labeled with such an accusation, and how does this currency manipulation mechanism work?

Imagine when China has trade surplus with the U.S.; the USD earned by Chinese businessmen will be purchased by PBOC, while an equivalent amount of RMB will be printed and given back to the Chinese businessmen at a fixed exchange rate.

These RMB will be circulated in the local economy, and the dollar held by PBOC will act as the foreign reserve.

While holding USD will earn China nothing, China must invest it.

Since China is the biggest holder of the dollar as foreign reserve, if China uses these dollars to buy the Swiss franc, it will cause the Swiss franc to appreciate sharply. The result is that Switzerland's export will be hurt, which damages Switzerland's economy.

To avoid this, the Swiss central bank must also buy other foreign currencies to devaluate the Swiss franc. This is exactly what happened.

The Swiss central bank had bought $480 billion worth of foreign currency to devalue the Swiss franc in 2014; this is equivalent to 70% of Switzerland's GDP!

This race to debase where countries seek to gain trade advantage over each other is known as currency war.

It may surprise you that China is not the only country manipulating the foreign exchange market by holding down the value of its currency.

Central banks around the world have been doing this since the collapse of the Bretton Wood system, which ensured the balance of international trade.

If China is to be labeled as a currency manipulator, U.S.'s debt financed demand is the origin of trade imbalance that destabilizes the global economy.

I hope my explanation of currency manipulation gives you an insight of the whole picture of what is going on in the currency war.

Next time, when listening to the news on currency manipulation, maybe you too might have something to say.

Climbing China's Great Wall of Worries

Right now, as I am writing in 2016, the Chinese economy is in serious trouble.

Despite China not officially admitting the slowdown, the economic data suggests its future economic outlook is not optimistic. China's export-led growth and investment driven economic model is coming to an end.

In 1979, China leader's "Four Modernizations" plan had adopted an export-led growth model for China's economic growth.

From 1990 – 2013, China's export grew an average of 18.4% annually. The U.S. has been China's largest export market.

In 2015, China trade surplus with U.S. was $367 billion USD, which accounts for 30% of China's GDP. It is this extraordinary trade surplus that transformed China from a very poor third world country to the second largest economy in the world.

As China's export grew, it has more money, allowing her to import.

Hence, this allows China to be the second largest global economic growth engine.

In order for China's economy to grow by export, China must invest in building factories and manufacturing equipment. This amount of investment can be shown in China's Gross Fixed Capital Formation (GFCF). From 1960 until today, China's GFCF has reached $4.5 trillion USD. Since 2003, over 40% of China's GDP depends on GFCF.

All these data suggest that China's economy depends on investments into factories to continue its export led growth economic model.

China's Gross Fixed Capital Formation (1960 – 2016)

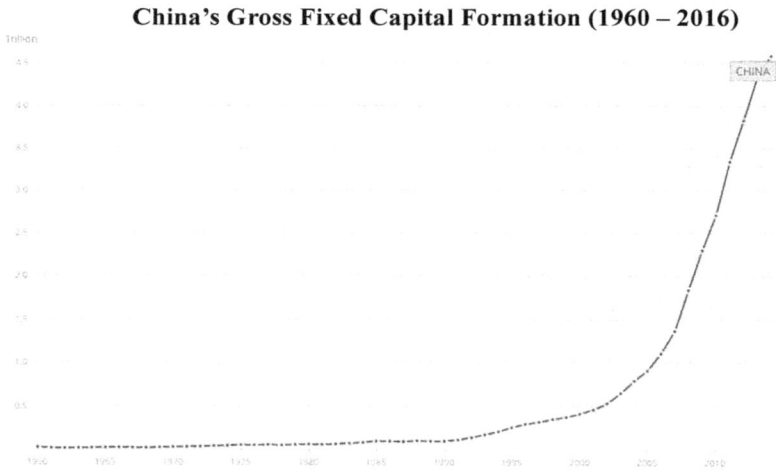

Figure 5.9: China's Gross Fixed Capital Formation (Source: World Bank)

China's Gross Fixed Capital Formation as a % of China's GDP

(1960 – 2016)

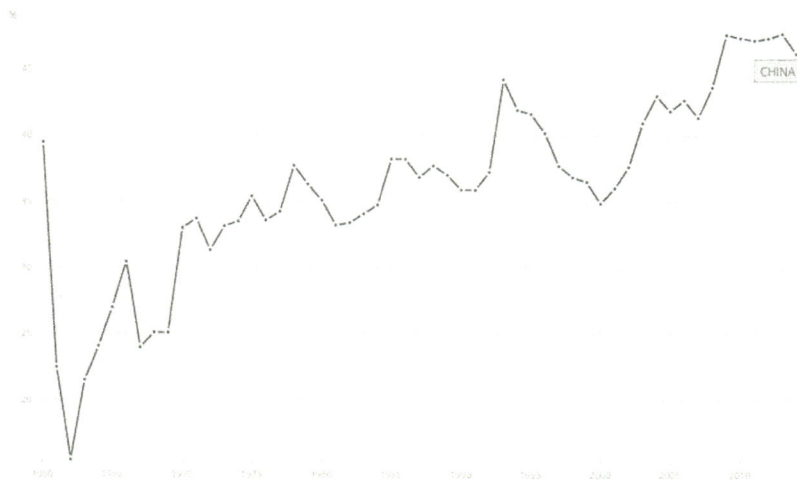

Figure 5.10: China's Gross Fixed Capital Formation as a % of China GDP

Source: World Bank

Eight years after the financial crisis of 2008, the world is showing no signs of recovery. The U.S., Europe, and Japan all have their own economic problems, and China is left with few big trading partners to export to. With a reduction in demand of global import from China, China is left with excessive production capacity. This means that further investment into building factories and manufacturing will be a loss. The gross fixed capital formation, which accounts for 40% of China's GDP will decline. Factories will close down due to becoming unprofitable. Unemployment in China will rise. And the Chinese economy will contract. This is the situation China is confronting now.

Can China's domestic demand absorb the excessive production?

Unfortunately, even with 1.36 billion people in China, it cannot absorb this excessive production capacity.

Despite China's per capita GDP rising dramatically and the poverty rate in China declining, it is astonishing to see that the average annual salary of a worker in China's private sector is only 28,752 RMB or $4323 USD, which is approximately $12 a day!

Not surprisingly, Chinese factory workers do not earn enough money to buy the products they produce.

If you have read my first book, *Corruption of Real Money,* you probably recall how too many goods relative to the money (credit) supply causes deflation. This happened during *the Long Depression* - the first global recession during *the Industrial Revolution.*

In order to sustain China's economic growth, China is left with few options but to expand its credit rapidly.

The Chinese economy today is in a very similar situation to that in Japan in the 90s. The Japanese economy depended on export-led growth, which allows it to accumulate a gigantic amount of foreign reserves. In the post-bubble period, deflation happened. To avoid a 1930 style depression, the Japanese authority stimulated its economy by massive government spending, expansion of credit through quantitative easing. Japan's government debt had risen above 200% of GDP. All this fiat currency creation is merely to offset the deflationary force and put the Japanese economy in a coma state for over 23 years, even today.

***

The reason this chapter is titled *Marriage for Debt* is because the Chinese economy and the U.S. economy are closely synchronized. Chinese export led growth and investment driven economic model would not be possible without the U.S. being able to run a huge deficit through debt-financed demand. I hope you have a deeper understanding on Chinese economy and its role in the 21st century economy. Next, we will look at how U.S.-China economic relationship affects the rest of the world.

Chapter 6

Decoding Credit Bubbles

"Men, it has been well said, think in herds; it will be seen that they go mad in herds, while they only recover their senses slowly, and one by one."

-CHARLES MACKAY, *EXTRAORDINARY POPULAR DELUSIONS AND THE MADNESS OF CROWDS*, 1841

If you listen closely enough, you can almost hear the hissing sound of bubbles deflating all around the world. The problem with bubbles is that they are so difficult to see, especially for the ones who lived within them for a long time. They adapt bubbles as their reality. Even when the air seeps out, they rarely sense it, until it is too late.

Does Real Estates Always Goes up?

Until 2008, very few people believed real estate could go down.

The truth is it went down.

Perhaps, the U.S. housing bubble caused by the subprime mortgage crisis is a special event.

Well, if you pick up your phone and call anyone in Tokyo and asked them about the real estate in Japan, they will tell you that real estate in Japan went down 65% since the last crash in the early 90s.

26 years later, today, it is still down 65%.

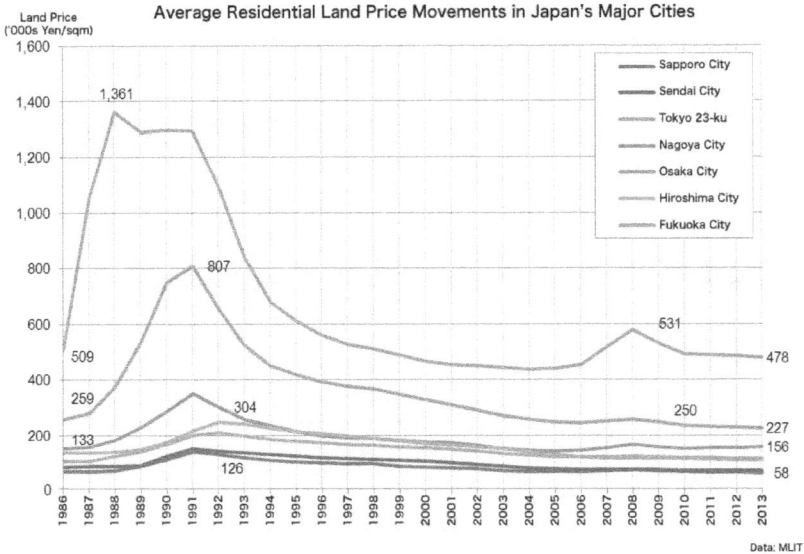

Figure 6.1: Average Residential Land Price Movement in Japan's Major Cities

Source : MLIT

But could your country be different?

After all, different countries have different economic backgrounds, different credit ratings, different amounts of land available, different population growth rates, and different demands from foreign investors, different legislation and monetary policies by governments.

Some countries, like Australia, even have negative gearing where a property investor can claim tax deductions from their taxable income when the interests they pay for their mortgage is more than the rental income they collect.

So, comparing countries to determine whether a property bubble exists is like comparing apples to oranges, or is it?

This chapter is about decoding credit bubbles. We will explore some of the mysterious credit bubbles around the world. By the end of this chapter, you will gain insight in the world's credit market few people can comprehend.

The 60 Trillion Story

At the end of Chapter 3, we left off with how the U.S. Total Credit Market Debt (TCMD) increased to $60 trillion USD in 45 years. We also understand that credit and debt are both sides of the same coin. This means this $60 trillion worth of TCMD also affects the rest of the world, which is holding this amount of credit.

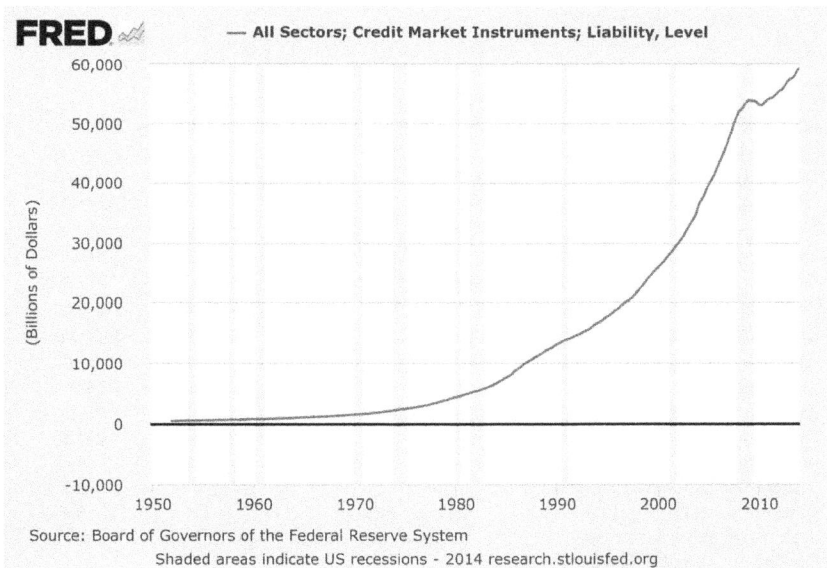

Source: Board of Governors of the Federal Reserve System
Shaded areas indicate US recessions - 2014 research.stlouisfed.org

Figure 6.2: Federal Reserve - Total Credit Markte Debt (TCMD)

So, who is responsible for this staggering $60 trillion worth of debts, which destabilized the global economy?

To understand it, let's investigate the $60 trillion story.

The *Flow of Fund* breaks down all the debts and credits in the U.S.'s economy and can be downloaded from the Federal Reserve website. Table 6.1 is a table extracted from the *Flow of Fund* comparing TCMD owed by debtors between 1945 and 2015. Similarly, Table 6.3 compares TCMD held by creditors over the same period. Since the total amount of debts is equal to the total amount of credits, the total TCMD in the two tables are the same.

U.S. Federal Reserve's *Flow of Fund* decomposes TCMD into three main sectors:

1. Domestic nonfinancial sectors,

2. Financial business

3. Rest of the world (ROTW)

	1945	2015
All sectors; TCMD (in billions)	**354.9**	**59045.7**
Domestic Nonfinancial Sectors;	**348.1**	**41735.8**
Households and nonprofit organizations;	27.4	13508.6
Nonfinancial corporate business;	45.1	7717.7
Nonfinancial noncorporate business;	4.8	4460.2
Federal government;	251.5	13086.7
State and local governments, excluding employee retirement funds;	12.6	2962.6
Others	6.7	-
Financial business;	**1.9**	**14104.6**
U.S.-chartered depository institutions;	0.1	669.9
Credit unions;	0	34.9
Life insurance companies,	0	75.4
Government-sponsored enterprises;	0.9	6234.6
Agency-and GSE-backed mortgage pools; total mortgages;	0.1	1642.5
Issuers of asset-backed securities;	0	1359.7
Finance companies;	0.4	1249.4
Real estate investment trusts;	0	674.4
Security brokers and dealers;	0	107.4
Holding companies;	0	1380.5
Funding corporations;	0	675.8
Others	0.4	-
Rest of the World;	**5**	**3205.3**

Table 6.1: U.S. Total Credit Market Debt Owed by Debtors (1945 and 2015)

Source: Federal Reserve – Total Credit Market Debt (TCMD) : Flow of Fund

To understand how much these debts are affecting the economy, it is best to analyze it as a percentage of GDP.

1945		2015	
Real GDP	Nominal GDP	Real GDP	Nominal GDP
$2.218	$0.218	$16,349	$17,947

Table 6.2: US real and nominal GDP in 1945 and 2015 measured in trillions

But which GDP will we use? The government statistics usually publish two GDP figures - the Real GDP and the nominal GDP.

Real GDP is the GDP adjusted for inflation and nominal GDP is the GDP measured in the year, where the data is being taken. Since we are only interested in knowing the size of debt corresponding to the nominal size of an economy of a year, we will use the nominal GDP.

	1945	2015
All sectors; TCMD (in billions)	354.9	59045.7
Domestic Nonfinancial Sectors;	125.9	6388
Households and nonprofit organizations;	91	3271.4
Nonfinancial corporate business;	21.6	170.2
Nonfinancial noncorporate business;	0.6	102.1
Federal government;	5.2	1196.1
State and local governments, excluding employee retirement funds;	7.5	1648.2
Others	-	-
Financial business;	226	42292.7
U.S.-chartered depository institutions;	24.3	10885.2
Credit unions;	0.2	964.8
Life insurance companies,	41.2	3582.6
Government-sponsored enterprises;	2	5975.3
Agency-and GSE-backed mortgage pools; total mortgages;	0.1	1642.5
Issuers of asset-backed securities;	0	1328.4
Finance companies;	3.6	1312.8
Real estate investment trusts;	0	544.7
Security brokers and dealers;	0	397.5
Holding companies;	0	132.8
Funding corporations;	0	190.7
Others	154.6	15335.4
Rest of the World;	3.1	10365.1

Table 6.3: U.S. Total Credit Market Debt Held by Creditors (1945 and 2015)

Source: Federal Reserve – Total Credit Market Debt (TCMD) : Flow of Fund

[Note: Others under the Financial Business category are mostly commercial banks.]

To understand the $60 trillion debt story in the U.S. economy, it is best to look at how much debts are owed. So, we will use Table 6.1 for analysis.

Let's start by looking at the domestic nonfinancial sector.

Domestic nonfinancial sectors

In 1945, among the three sectors, domestic nonfinancial sectors owed $348.1 billion, which is 98% of the TCMD, or 160% of GDP!

So, why did the domestic nonfinancial sectors in the U.S. need to borrow that much? Which of its sub-sectors are behind this debt?

When you examine the sub-sectors of domestic nonfinancial sectors, the debt owed by the Federal Government was outstanding (i.e., 71 % of TCMD)!

The reason behind this massive amount of debts owed is simple – WWII. The buildup and involvement of the U.S. in WWII resulted in President Franklin D. Roosevelt massively increasing the level of public debt to pay for the fund needed before and during the war.

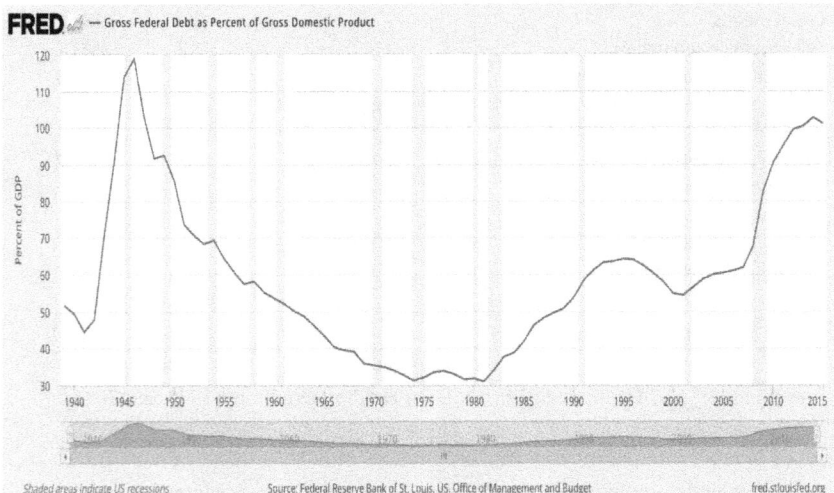

Figure 6.3: Gross Federal Debt as Percent of Gross GDP

Source: Federal Reserve

This gross Federal Government Debt, as a percentage of GDP, did not stay high and had been declining steadily after the war.

Between 1970 and 1982, the Federal Government Debt owed was only 30% to 35% of GDP.

If you examine the graphs carefully, one thing that might catch your attention is the grey shaded areas overlapping the graph. These are recession periods in the U.S., and the spike in Federal Government debt between 2008 and 2010 was quantitative easing, which caused the Federal Government debt to hike from 67% to 102% of GDP.

The second important subsector worth mentioning is the debt owed by the household sector. This subsector comprises home mortgages, home equity loans, student loans, and auto loans, and credit card debt.

In 1945, the debt owed by the households and nonprofit organization sector was merely 7.7% of TCMD, 12.5% of GDP. The reason is that most of these household debts that exist today did not exist in the past.

U.S. Government –backed student loans were first offered in 1950 and were not easily accessible; American Express had not introduced the first plastic credit card in the world until 1959. U.S.'s consumption was not the economic driver but production. WWII caused a lot of local U.S. citizens to go to war and caused a low demand in housing and home mortgages.

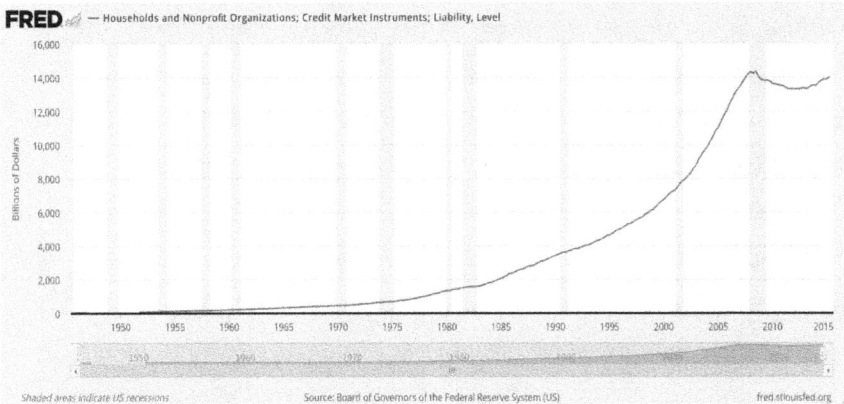

Figure 6.4: Households and Nonprofit Organizations; Credit Market Instruments

Source: Federal Reserve

All this changed when the Bretton Wood system collapsed because of U.S. President Lyndon Johnson's Great Society programs and a rise in military spending caused by the Vietnam War. High inflation caused the U.S. dollar's fixed exchange rate to gold struggles. The staggering debts accumulated during the post-war period caused high asset price inflation in the 60s. Eventually, in August 1971, President Nixon needed to close the gold window.

Household debts rose exponentially because of the U.S. dollar being the world's reserve currency, allowing the U.S. to run massive deficits with countries such as China and Japan.

Slowly, the U.S. became the world driver of economic growth through the expansion of credit by household sectors' consumption.

Record low interest rate for long periods also allowed the U.S. to go deeper into debt to consume. That is why U.S.'s credit card debt and student loan debt both hit $1 trillion in 2016. In 2015, total debts owed by households and nonprofit organization sector was 22.8% of the TCMD, 75% of GDP.

U.S.'s Household Debt Composition

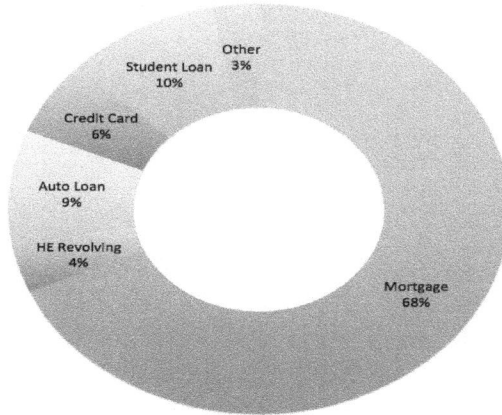

Figure 6.5: Breakdown of U.S. household debt

Source: Federal Reserve

Financial business

Beside the domestic nonfinancial sector, financial business is a major sector to focus on.

In 1945, the debt owed by financial businesses in the U.S. was fractional. Debts owed by many sub-sectors in financial business, such as credit unions, issuers of asset-backed securities, and real estate investment trusts (REIT), were small or virtually non-existent.

Commercial banks' deposits were mostly what were in the financial sectors.

It was not until the beginning of the 70s that debt owed by Financial Business took off. As the financial sector expanded, debt owed by Financial Business caught up with other sectors and officially overtook that of the Federal Government in 1995.

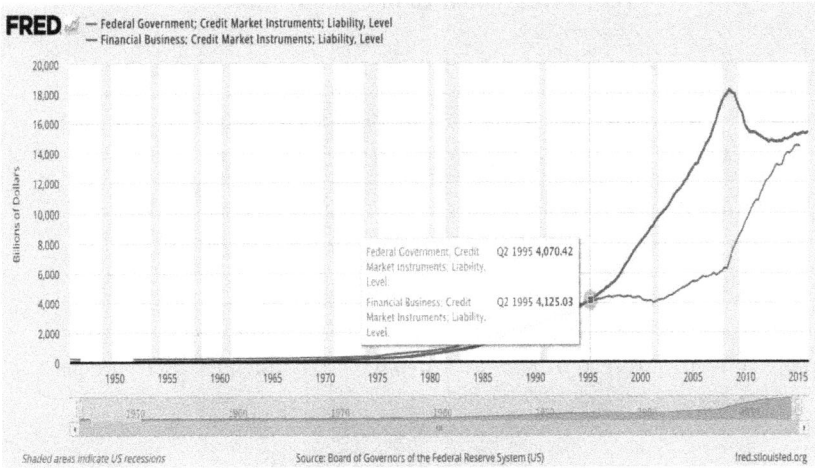

Figure 6.6: Debt owed by Financial Business overtook Debt owed by Federal Government

Source: Federal Reserve

By 1998, debt owed by the financial business sector overtook debt owed by the household sector for the first time in history and became the leading debt owed.

So, what are the forces that caused the financial business sector to borrow such an enormous amount of debt?

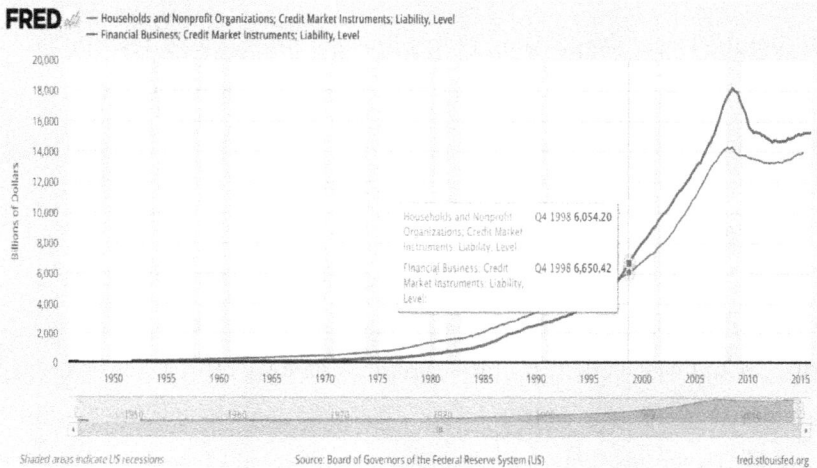

Figure 6.7: Debt owed by Financial Business overtook Debt owed by Households and Nonprofit Organizations

Source: Federal Reserve

If you examine Figure 6.1 closely, one sub-sector under financial business had outstanding debt among other sub-sectors. It is government-sponsored enterprises (GSE).

But what are GESs?

Generally, GSEs are created by the U.S. Congress. Their role is to allow more efficient and transparent credit flow into targeted sectors of the U.S. economy.

Housing GSEs are the greatest drivers of the U.S. housing bubble, besides the Federal Reserve. The *Federal National Mortgage Association (Fannie Mae)* and the *Federal Home Loan Mortgage Corporation (Freddie Mac)* are two GSEs that were supposed to make housing more affordable, but created a housing bubble.

But why were these two GSEs created?

When you look back at history, these GSEs were created for good reasons.

During the Great Depression, U.S.'s housing market was devastated. By 1933, there was an estimation of a quarter of U.S.'s outstanding mortgages defaulted.

As part of President Franklin Roosevelt's New Deal program to save the housing market, Fannie Mae was created in 1938. The original idea of Fannie Mae was to make housing more affordable for low-medium income earners. Unlike commercial banks, Fannie Mae does not issue mortgages to borrowers. It purchases and guarantees mortgages through the secondary mortgage market – a market where mortgages are bought and sold between mortgage originators, securities, and investors. By purchasing mortgages, Fannie Mae adds liquidity in the banking sectors and credit unions and allows them to create even more mortgages. These mortgages Fannie Mae purchased from the secondary mortgage market are then pooled and packaged to form mortgage-backed securities (MBS) – a process called securitization. If you refer to the sub-sector – Agency- and GSE-backed mortgage pools, they are one of the largest buyers of MBS issued by Fannie Mae and Freddie Mac. This sector is a special purpose vehicle (SPV) that acts as a subsidiary entity to allow GSE to hide debt. The word "pools" refers to the combination of financial instruments for resale in a secondary market.

Traditionally, when a commercial bank issues a mortgage to a borrower, it needs to keep the loan for the duration of the mortgage, usually 30 years, and bears the risk for non-repayment of the borrower.

GSEs help commercial banks, the mortgage originator, to free up capital by buying these mortgages.

Securitization through MBS allows the banks to shift the risks away to enjoy most of the benefits. Accredited credit rating agencies, such as Moody, will rate these pools of securities into AAA, AA, A and BBB grade etc., depending on the associated risk. Since GSE is a government-sponsored entity, its securities are believed to be performance guaranteed. These MSBs are sold to overseas investors, agencies, institutions, or even back to the mortgage originator.

GSE and agency-and GSE-backed mortgage pools account for a staggering $7.78 trillion USD, which is 43.8% of GDP!

Another sector that draws our attention is Issuers of asset-backed securities (ABS). Like MSB, ABS includes credit cards loans, auto loans, student loans etc., other than MBS. Issuers of ABS adopt the practice of GSE of securitization, which allows them to bundle all these loans, based on classes and the credit rating of the debtors, and then sell them to investors.

Although ABS are not backed by the government, the debts owed by Issuers of ABS reached $1.359 trillion USD by 2015, 7.57% of GDP.

Securitization of mortgages and loans has been driving the financial business sector growth.

Rest of the world

Apart from domestic credit creation from the two sectors mentioned above, the rest of the world also accounts for credit creation in U.S. from abroad.

To analyze this, we will have to use Table 6.3, since it shows the U.S. Total Credit Market Debt held by creditors. These are credits supplied from foreign central banks, such as European Central Bank (ECB), The Bank of England (BOE), People's Bank of China (PBOC) etc.

In 1945, TCMD held by the rest of the world was not even 1% or $3.1 billion; by 2015, this figure jumped to 17.6% of TCMD, which is $10.3 trillion USD! This $10.3 trillion USD worth of fiat currency creation is unprecedented and dwarfed the paper currency the Federal Reserve has been creating so far in the three rounds of quantitative easing!

***

Every economic bubble requires credits as fuel, just as fire requires oxygen, heat, and fuel to burn.

This $10.3 trillion USD credit, held by central banks around the world as foreign exchange reserve, caused asset bubbles around the world. Monitoring foreign exchange reserve is a very good way to understand the state of the global economic bubble.

So what causes these reserves held by the rest of the world to continue to expand?

Role of Trade Imbalance

One crucial indicator to understand the formation of the credit bubble is the Balance of Payment. (BOP).

BOP measures all the economic transactions of the dollar and goods. Every international transaction is an exchange of money (i.e., currency) with value (i.e., goods and services). For example, if the U.S. imports pencils from China, first it must supply the USD to exchange for the RMB to import the pencils. So pencils represent the goods flowing into the U.S., and the U.S. dollar represents the currency flowing out of the country. This happens when a country imports goods and services into a country. Values come in and currencies go out. The U.S. dollar is sold in the foreign exchange market to buy RMB.

How about export?

Say, for example, when U.S. exports soybeans to China, the Chinese buyer must convert RMB in the foreign exchange market into USD to pay for the soybeans. So, currencies (i.e., USD) are flowing into the U.S., and values (i.e., soybeans) are flowing out of U.S. If you add up all these transactions, the dollars flowing in and out have to balance somehow. This is what the BOP is all about, which is summarized by the formula below:

Current Account = Capital and Financial Account + Reserve Asset.

The *Current Account* is an effective method to measure the balance of trade. It measures the trade of goods and services between countries. Let's say, if China and the U.S. trade with each other, and if China exports more than she imports, China is said to be in *trade surplus*; conversely, since the U.S. imports more than she exports, the U.S. is said to be in *trade deficit*.

The *Capital and Financial Account* tracks how many one country owns of another country's financial assets. The Capital Account includes assets like patents, copyrights, royalties, migrants' transfer of fixed assets etc.; The *Financial Account* records the movement of ownership of financial assets (e.g., bank deposits).

If China purchases foreign assets, like properties in Australia, then capital outflows from the Chinese economy into Australia economy. This is a debit item (-) in China's financial account. A negative Financial Account means a country's ownership of foreign assets is increasing.

Under the Bretton Wood system and the Gold Standard, an automatic adjustment mechanism ensures the trades between countries remain balanced. When the Bretton Wood system broke down in 1971, that automatic adjustment mechanism ceased to function. Afterwards, U.S. was allowed to run enormous trade deficit with the rest of the world; that trade deficit destabilized the global economy and created the biggest global credit bubble in history.

Understanding how this automatic adjustment mechanism works is the key to decode the credit bubble.

If we travelled back in time in 1800s, when England had a trade deficit with Germany, England's gold would literally be put on a ship and sent over to France. Since gold was money, England's money supply would have contracted. England would be in a recession and unemployment would rise. The result would be deflation. Germany would experience an influx of gold and an expansion in money supply. Credit in Germany would have expanded accordingly. The Germany economy would have boomed. The result would be inflation. After a while, the wealthy Germans would have the purchasing power to buy cheap English goods. And the poor English would not have the purchasing power to buy as many expensive German goods. Eventually, the trade would be balanced, until England had a trade surplus with Germany and the cycle repeated. This is how the automatic adjustment mechanism works. Surplus countries will experience inflation and deficit countries will experience deflation.

Today, however, the balance of trade does not work this way anymore.

Before the Bretton Wood system broke down, the U.S. had a balance of trade. However, when the U.S. dollar became the world's reserve currency in 1971, the U.S. discovered that she no longer needed to pay in gold, but the U.S. dollar or U.S. dollar denominated credit instrument (e.g., Treasury Bond).

When you look at the U.S.'s current account, you will see the U.S. quickly ran a larger and larger trade deficit. Ironically, the first country to fall victim to this trade deficit was not the U.S., but Japan, which was the second largest economy in the 60s.

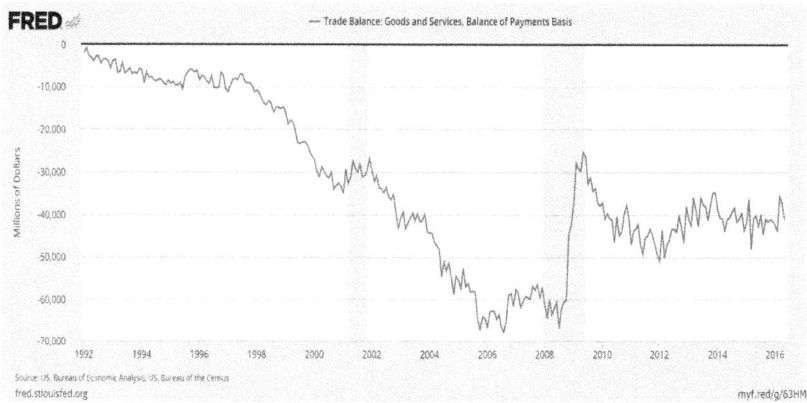

Figure 6.8: U.S. Current Account Balance
Source: Federal Reserve

If you replaced Germany with Japan in the previous example, Japan would have a trade surplus and U.S. would have a trade deficit. Theoretically, such an arrangement would cause the U.S. to enter deflation, whereas Japan's economy would inflate.

In reality, U.S.'s economy did not deflate, because she was not paying in gold, which is limited in supply. Instead, she was paying in the U.S. dollar and U.S. dollar denominated credit instruments, which were unlimited in supply.

Hence, U.S.'s trade deficit continues to grow larger and Japan's economy continues to boom.

Figure 6.9: Japan's Stock Market Nikkei 225

Source: wikimedia commons

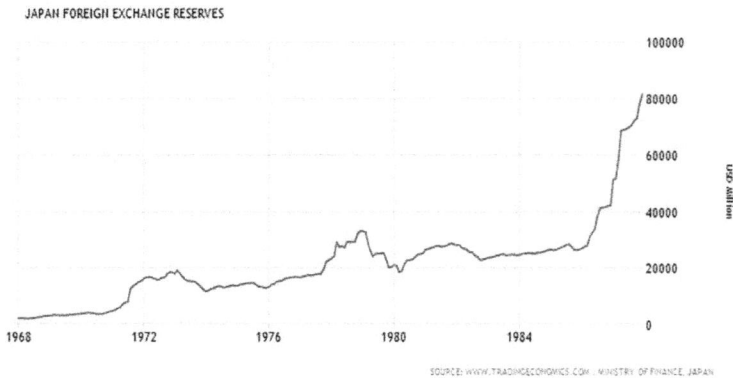

Figure 6.10: Japan's Foreign Exchange Reserve

Source: Ministry of Finance, Japan

The result was that the growth of the Japanese economy became very dependent on the U.S. to continue running a larger and larger trade deficit. The astronomical trade surplus allows Japan to hold a lot of foreign exchange reserve.

From 1968 to 1988, Japan's foreign exchange reserve went from $3 billion to more than $80 billion. Too much credit entering the Japanese economy as bank deposits caused bank loans to grow. Through fractional reserve banking, the currency supply expanded and caused asset prices to rise. Loan growth causes economic growth. This large influx of credit ballooned Japan into an economic bubble. That is why Nikkei 225 jumped from less than 5000 in 1970 to 38,957 by 1989. That also explains the sharp rise in Japan's property price in the beginning of this chapter. At the peak of the bubble, the imperial palace of Japan was said to be more valuable than California!

Do you see any similarity to the world economy today? What do you think happens next?

At the end of the 80s, despite all the signals alarming of a major economic bubble, everyone in Japan felt very optimistic about the Japanese economy. Japan's export led growth modal had created a new economic era. If you revisit Figure 6.1 (Average Residential Land Price Movement in Japan's Major Cities) and Figure 6.5 (Japan's Stock Market Nikkei 225), you will find out that the real estate price and stock market had never been down. People in Japan believed land and real estate price always go up as shown in the graph – before 1990. Demographic analysts will have theories saying the rise in population will make the demand of real estate outpace the supply.

Again, do you feel any similarity today?

Winston Churchill once said that the further you look into the past, the further you can see into the future. Despite not having a crystal ball, events are predictable. The only factor that is unpredictable, but important, is time. How could one who bought properties in Japan in the early 90s have guessed his home could go down by 65%, and 26 years later, it is still down 65%?

Japan's example is a classic episode of how credit growth drives economic growth until a point it doesn't.

The Myth of Foreign Exchange Reserve

In the last Chapter, we used the example of China to illustrate how foreign exchange reserve is accumulated. We understand that, when China businessmen sold goods to the U.S., the dollars coming into China were bought back by PBOC to exchange back to RMB before entering the local Chinese economy. We also know that PBOC printed these RMB to buy back the dollar at a fixed exchange rate to favor her export-led growth economic model by holding down the value of RMB.

Foreign exchange reserve is one of the least understood aspects of the global economy. Yet, it is important to understand the entire picture of the global credit bubble.

Foreign exchange reserves are currencies of other countries held by central banks in the foreign exchange market. These currencies can be U.S. dollars, Yen, Euro etc. The foreign exchange reserve is one way to measure the global currency supply.

Historically, central banks around the world hold gold as their reserve. Like the example between Germany and Britain, gold will outflow from a country when she has trade deficit. Since gold is money and the supply of gold cannot be magically created to finance the trade deficit, a country has no reasons nor advantages to accumulate other currencies.

However, everything changed when the Bretton Wood System broke down.

Under the dollar standard, the system works differently. When PBOC prints RMB in exchange for the U.S. dollar from Chinese businessmen, these U.S. dollars can be used to purchase currencies of other countries to drive up their price and indirectly depress the value of RMB. Since a weak currency will favor more exports, which in turn, helps employment and economic growth, countries around the world are having a currency war to enhance their own country's export competitiveness.

China is not the only country that has been using this method to benefit her own economy. Countries around the world with huge trade surplus are using the exact same tactic to fuel their export-led growth economy. During this process, their central banks have been printing local currencies in an unprecedented rate.

Total World Total Reserve Exl Gold and SDR

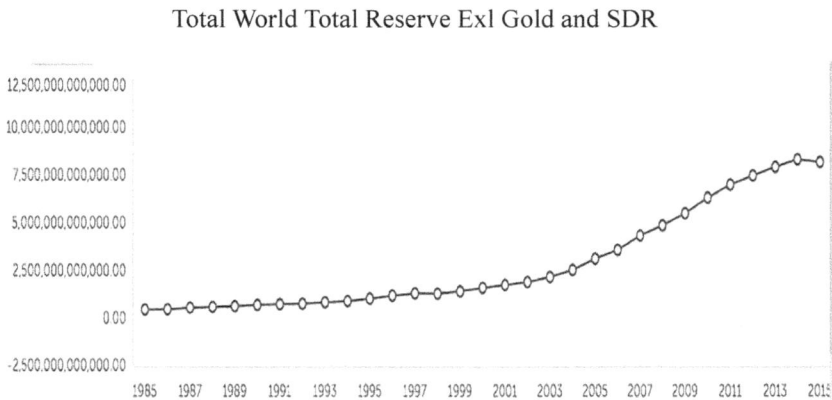

Figure 6.11: World Total Reserve Exl Gold and SDR

Source: IMF

This is how the foreign central banks around the world created $10.924 trillion USD! But please remember this amount of fiat money creation would be impossible without the U.S. running a huge trade deficit with the rest of the world. The growth of credit around the world depends on the U.S. to continue to run a huge trade deficit. A decline of trade deficit would severely stagnate the global economy, as shown in recent years.

So, to summarize, we have:

1. Foreign central banks creating local fiat currency to buy back the U.S. dollar entering a country.

2. Then, we have foreign central banks now holding these U.S. Dollars.

Next, we will look at how this astronomical amount of fiat money creation by foreign central banks is affecting the entire world. And then, we will look at how these U.S. dollars accumulated by foreign central banks affect the U.S. and the global economy.

Where does China's Wealth Come From?

China has been an important driver of the global economy in the past two decades. The $4 trillion surplus in China, fueled by the U.S. running a huge trade deficit in the past three decades, transformed China's economy. Through fractional reserve banking, the $4 trillion worth of credit is multiplied in unprecedented scale to $21.3 Trillion by 2015.

This astronomical amount of credit growth in China benefited everyone domestically. First, a Chinese billionaire class emerged. Second, the Chinese middle class grew to the size of hundreds of millions. The world demand for cheap Chinese products caused huge demand from factories. A massive amount of credit is used to invest in infrastructure and constructions. That is why people from rural parts of China have opportunities to work in factories and moved on from farming. Above all, the Communist government officials in China suddenly became very wealthy.

By 2015, the total credit in China was $21.3 trillion USD.

It is worth emphasizing that, similar to Quantitative Easing by the Fed, these credits are not savings by local Chinese citizens. These are fiat currency printed by PBOC to artificially suppress the value of RMB.

If you investigate the total credit between China and the U.S. carefully, you can see that, from 1985 to 2010, China took 25 years to grow its credits from what was considered insignificant to $10 trillion USD. Yet, it only took China just another 5 years to double this amount to $21.3 by 2015.

The U.S. traditionally had its total credit doubled every 10 years, and she is growing its debt at a less aggressive pace after the financial crisis of 2008.

Total Credit : U.S. vs China

US$ billion, 1985 to 2015

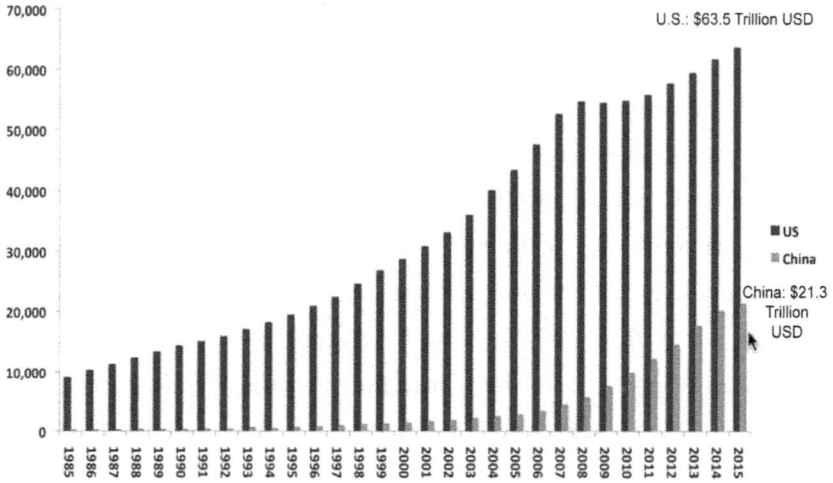

Figure 6.12: Total Credit : U.S. vs China (Billion USD), 1985 to 2015

Source: Federal Reserve, CEIC

[**Note**: In reality, the data for total Credit in China is more than $21.3 as of 2015, due to different financial calculation methods being used.]

With this credit expansion in China, does that mean China's economy is set to expand?

Before answering this question, let's look at how China's expansion of credit affected the other parts of the world?

We will choose Australia.

What is Wrong with the Kangaroo Economy?

Australia had an unbroken growth record of 25 years, uninterrupted by recessions. Despite the global financial crisis in 2008, Australia was one of the luckiest countries, least affected by it. Immigrants and the Reserve Bank of Australia's monetary policy of continuously cutting interest attracted a lot of foreign capital influx into Australia. Homeowners are seeing their home price surge. Many people believe Australia is a lucky country.

I am living in Sydney, Australia. From my observation, Australia followed a course of economic development very different from other countries.

Despite being a country rich in natural resources, Australia has been consistently experiencing trade deficit or current account deficit every year.

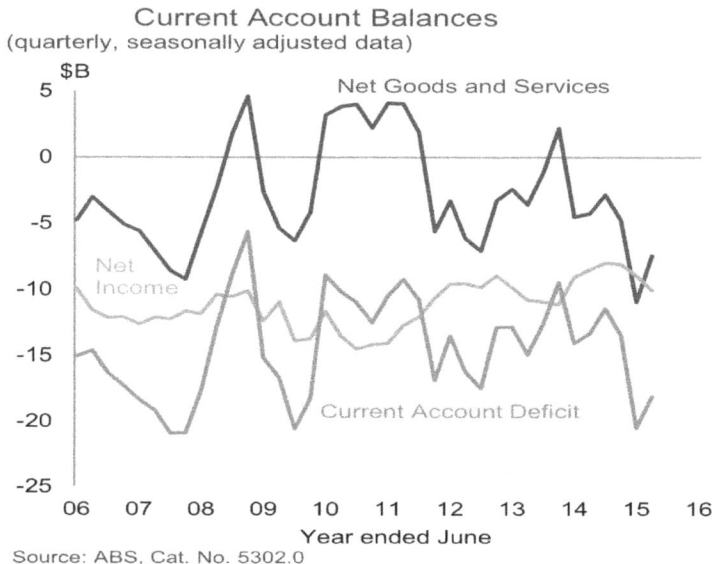

Figure 6.13: Australia's Current Account Balance

Source: ABS

In 2015, Australia's current account deficit was $20.5 Billion AUD.

When a country is in current account deficit, it is a debt-financed economy. This is not necessarily a bad thing if the government used the debt for future growth, not consumption.

If Australia must temporarily incur debt by importing to create a final good for export, then it is a good deficit. However, if the Australian government is spending the borrowed money non-productively, such as giving it to refugees or Medicare, then it is a bad deficit.

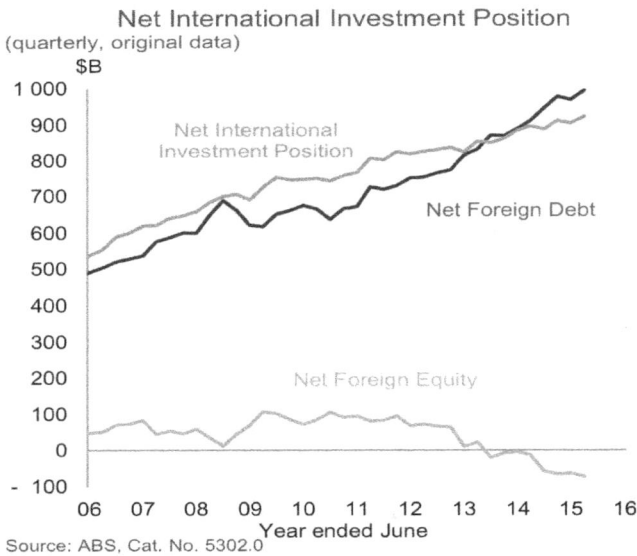

Figure 6.14: Australia's Net International Investment Position

Source: ABS

Beside BOP, Net International Investment Position (NIIP) is an indicator that tracks how many one country owns of another country's financial assets. In Figure 6.14, the *net foreign debt* in Australia means how much the rest of the world owns assets in Australia. And *net-foreign equity* refers to how much Australia-owned assets are abroad. If a country's net foreign debt is higher than her net foreign equity, this means the country is indebted to the rest of the world.

NIIP to GDP is a gauge to see whether a country is creditworthy.

[Note: NIIP is the sum of past current account deficit or surplus adjusted for valuation changes]

If you revisit Figure 6.14, you can see that Australia's net foreign debts have been increasing at an enormous pace. This means that countries that had incurred a trade surplus with Australia are reinvesting the AUD credits to buy AUD denominated assets aggressively.

Australia's net foreign debts in 2016 had just broken the $1 trillion AUD mark. It is this massive influx of capital inflow from the rest of the world that has been sustaining the Australian economy.

So, what is wrong with the kangaroo economy?

For the Australian economy to continue to grow, it must go deeper and deeper into debt. To avoid paying high interest on net foreign debts, the Reserve bank of Australia (RBA) must continue to keep its interest rate low.

Now, we have a basic understanding of the current status of the Australian economy; let's look at one of the widely disputed topics happening in Australia - The Australia Real Estate Bubble Talk.

Is there a Real Estate Bubble in Australia?

There is a widespread disagreement about whether Australia is in a real estate bubble. Since 2006, economists in Australia advocated dire warnings about the massive real estate bubble Australia is facing; real estate agents described the Australian real estate bubble as a fantasy like the existence of Loch Ness monster.

Below are just a few of the many commentaries about the real estate bubbles in recent years.

"But make no mistake, the notion that in a country the size of Australia, with a population of 23 million people, that in some way high house prices are a consequence of investors from China, frankly it's laughable."

-Australia's Trade Minister Steve Ciobo, 2016

"There is no evidence that international investment is swamping the residential housing market or influencing prices".

-Property Council of Australia, 2014

"Australia is a unique housing market and sometimes offshore investors don't realise the key differences,"

-Sydney director at JPMorgan, Sujit Dey, 2016

"In a nutshell, I got the cause of the Aussie House Price Bubble right, but the direction of the cause wrong. The fundamental determinant of house prices is mortgage debt. I thought that -- as had happened in Japan after its bubble economy burst -- the Australian economy would start to de-lever after the GFC, and that this process would take house prices down with it. This is what happened in the USA and most of the First World."

-Prof Steve Keen, Head Of School Of Economics, History & Politics, 2016

All of these are interesting ideas, and they are logical in their own way. All of them are worth considering. There is one important element among them that was not talked about – credits.

An economic boom cannot happen without credit, just like fire will not occur in the absence of air, heat, and fuel. As opposed to most of the above commentaries, I think how the Australian housing market will play out depends on whether the credit in Australia expands or contracts. This is not only true when the credit expanded in the Roaring 20s, which eventually led to the Great Depression in 1929; it is also true for the post Bretton Wood bubble, such as the Japan Economic Crisis in 1990, the Asia Financial Crisis of 1997, the Russia financial crisis in 1998, and the most recent subprime mortgage crisis in U.S. in 2008.

"In fact, every nonmonetary trade –cycle doctrine tacitly assumes – or ought to assume – that credit expansion is an attendant phenomenon of the boom. It cannot help admitting that in the absence of such a credit expansion no boom could emerge and that the increase in the supply of money (in the broader sense) is a necessary condition of the general upward movement in price"

- Ludwig von Mises

Sydney Median House Price

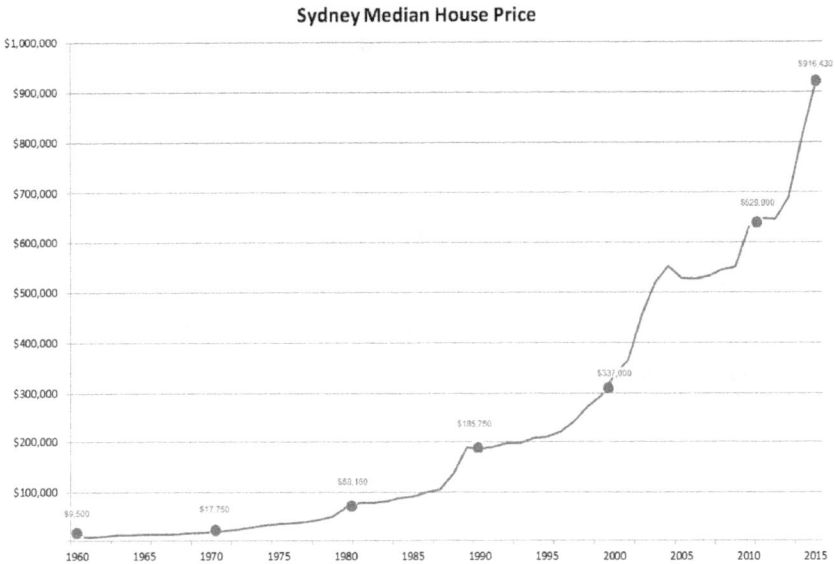

Figure 6.15: Sydney Medium House Price

Source: Jonathan Tepper, founder of research house Variant Perception

If you looked at the housing prices in Sydney, it's no wonder why local Australians agree that Sydney's housing market is unique, compared with the rest of the world. Sydney housing prices experienced no decline as shown in the graph. As I am writing now, the average medium house price in Sydney is above $1 million AUD. So if you own a house in Sydney now, congratulations; you are a millionaire.

Despite being a lucky country, young Australians are not that lucky. With the rapidly surging home prices in recent years, most young Australians are priced out of the property market. The average property price-to-median household income ratio is 12.2 times. Those who are lucky enough to save up for a deposit must take out huge mortgages not to miss the property train. If you are a young Australian reading this book now, I guess you should have the same synergy.

Australian Debt Clock

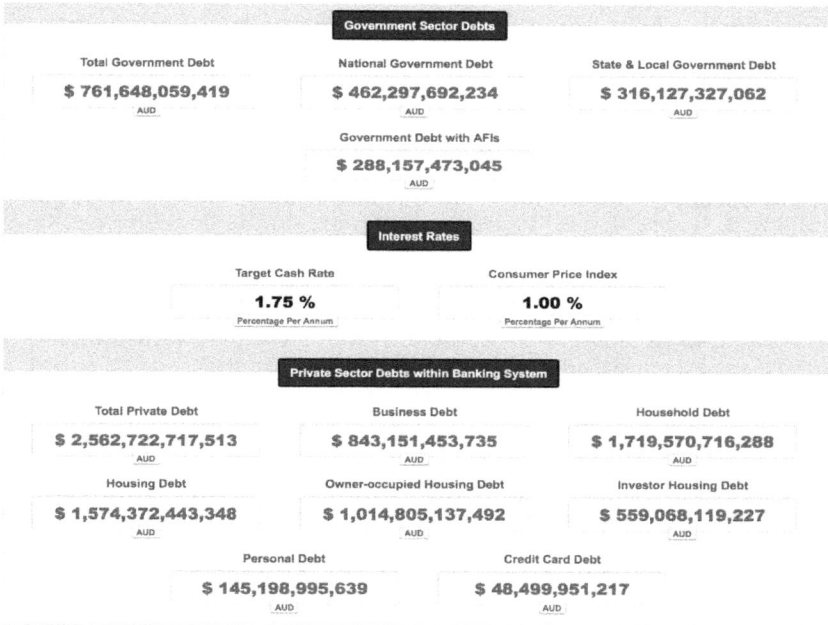

Government Sector Debts		
Total Government Debt	National Government Debt	State & Local Government Debt
$ 761,648,059,419 AUD	$ 462,297,692,234 AUD	$ 316,127,327,062 AUD
	Government Debt with AFIs	
	$ 288,157,473,045 AUD	

Interest Rates	
Target Cash Rate	Consumer Price Index
1.75 % Percentage Per Annum	1.00 % Percentage Per Annum

Private Sector Debts within Banking System		
Total Private Debt	Business Debt	Household Debt
$ 2,562,722,717,513 AUD	$ 843,151,453,735 AUD	$ 1,719,570,716,288 AUD
Housing Debt	Owner-occupied Housing Debt	Investor Housing Debt
$ 1,574,372,443,348 AUD	$ 1,014,805,137,492 AUD	$ 559,068,119,227 AUD
Personal Debt	Credit Card Debt	
$ 145,198,995,639 AUD	$ 48,499,951,217 AUD	

Figure 6.16: Australia Debt Clock, 2016

Source: www.australiandebtclock.com.au

To understand the economy of Australia and the housing market, it is necessary to look at different sectors and their size in the economy. The owner of australiandebtclock.com.au did a great job displaying this information in real time.

If you look at the Australian Debt Clock, there are two large components:

1)   Total Government Debt   ($ 761,648,059,419 AUD)

2)   Total Private Debt   ($ 2,562,722,717,513 AUD)

Interestingly, despite severe Federal budget deficits in recent years, the total government debt in Australia is only 30% of the total private debt. For simplicity, if you use 2016's GDP as a reference point, the total government debt accounts for 47% of GDP, whereas the total private debt is 177% of GDP!

[**Note**: Australia GDP was $1.62 trillion AUD by 2015]

But which sector is the biggest sector in the private sector contributing the most debt?

It is the housing debt under household debt.

Household debt to GDP in Australia today ranks No 1 in the world!

According to RP data, in 2016, the total market value of Australian residential property is $5.8 trillion AUD, which is approximately 3.4 times larger than the total market value of the stock market!

If RP data and the Australia debt clock are precise, and you subtract the total housing debt in the private sector (i.e., $1.57 trillion AUD) with the $5.8 trillion AUD, you will get a figure of $4.23 trillion AUD. This figure is telling us that 73% of Australian residential property market value is actually not based on debt!

So, despite the Australian household debt being ranked 1st in the world in 2016, it appears that there are forces in the Australian housing market still having a lot of capacity to buy homes – without mortgages. This force is unlikely to be young Australian middleclass.

"Chinese investors and immigrants purchased more than $8 billion in Australian residential property in the space of 12 months (2013 – 2014), with growing demand forecast to pump another $60 billion into the market over the next six years....There were 1.2 million Chinese with more than $US 1 million in China, the report said, who "can easily afford to buy an apartment in either Sydney or

Melbourne".

- **Credit Suisse, 2015**

To find out the force behind it, it is worthwhile to revisit Figure 6.14. The $1 trillion AUD worth of net foreign debt indicates the rest of the world owns $1 trillion AUD worth of Australian assets; it also means $1 trillion AUD capital inflows from the rest of the world into Australia.

Which country in the world today owns most of these net foreign debts in Australia? The answer is obvious if you pay a visit to some of the most renowned universities in Australia. You can hardly see anyone who is not Asian. And take a guess which country has the largest population in Asia?

I remember, when I migrated to Australia in 1995, I was one of the few students in primary school with black hair and spoke Chinese; today, when I go back to the same primary school as a visitor, I rarely see anyone who is blonde or not speaking Chinese in the playground. It is interesting to see every building stays the same like they are stuck in time, except for the change in demographics and some wrinkles on my face.

So, by now, I hope I have enough evidence to convince you that the fuels behind the Australia housing market, especially Sydney, are:

1   Capital inflow due to net foreign debts
2   Australia domestic household debt

It becomes apparent to us that the Australia housing price becomes a function of continuous capital inflow and continuous increase in

Australia's domestic household debt.

Whichever direction the price of Australia's real estate will go depends on whether there will be **continuous** liquidity injected into the housing market by these two forces.

So our next important question becomes: Will credit growth in Australia expand or contract?

[**Note**: Like any countries that experienced a housing bubble, absent credit expansion, no boom could emerge. The housing market in Australia is no different, compared to the rest of the world. Whether the Australia housing market will continue to boom depends on whether credits in Australia will continue to expand or contract in the years ahead.]

Is Credit Growth in Australia going to Expand or Contract?

In a pre-Bretton Wood era, when money was backed by gold and supply of money was fixed, the huge federal budget deficit run by the Australian government would push the interest rate higher.

Since the supply of the money was fixed, when the government expenditure exceeded the tax revenue, the demand for money from the government drove the interest rate higher. Under this scenario, if the government continued to run a huge budget deficit, the rising interest rate discouraged private investment and consumption and crowded out the private sector.

Crowding out is true, at least in traditional textbooks, but no longer applies to the modern economy.

Today, in the post-Bretton Wood era, the Reserve Bank of Australia (RBA) can continue to cut the interest rates after 2008, despite the years of budget deficit.

Australia Federal Budget , 2000 - 2014 , AUD $millions

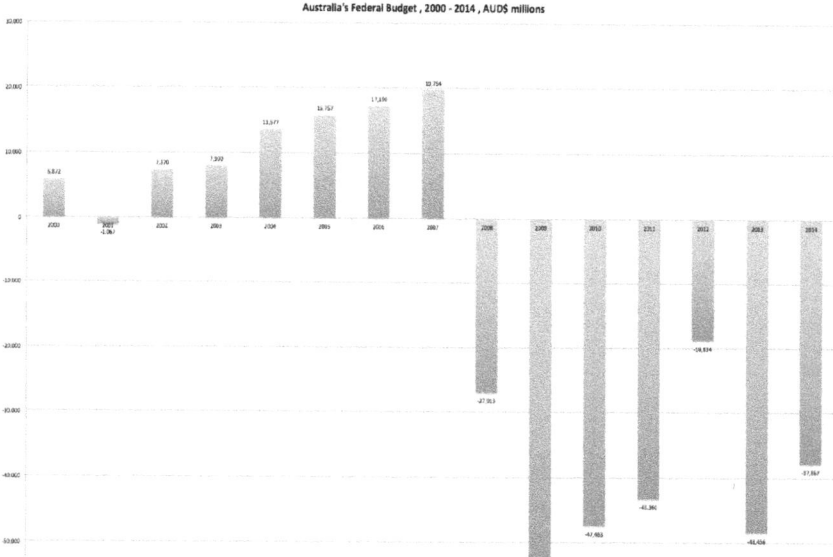

Figure 6.17: Australia Federal Budget, 2000 -2014

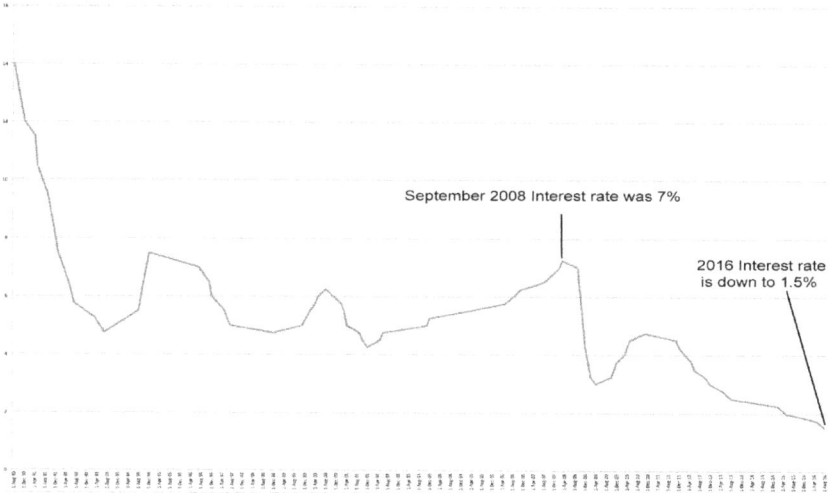

Figure 6.18: Australia Cash Rate

Source: RBA

This low interest rate encouraged the private sector to take on more household debts, and that is why you see the excessive liquidity enter the Australian housing market and cause a boom.

How can the Australian government run a large budget deficit and cut the interest rate for the past 8 years (2008 to 2016)?

This is the dilemma that is puzzling many economists, calling for the Australian real estate bubble. Low interest rates set by the RBA with a weak AUD encourages more foreign buyers from abroad to continue pumping liquidity into the Australia housing market, fueling credit growth. This makes the Australian housing market seem to defy the law of gravity.

However, the laws of economical physics have not changed. Interest rate is still governed by the demand and supply of money (credit). The only thing that has changed is that the supply of money (credit) is no longer fixed. The reason the Australian government is capable of performing deficit spending is because foreigners keep loaning Australians their savings through foreign capital inflow. The result is that the supply of the Australian dollar outstripped the demand. The federal budget deficit is not large enough to absorb the capital inflow.

More credit growth encourages more Australian homeowners to borrow and spend to stimulate the Australian economy, resulting in the higher the Australia house price. And this kept on perpetuating itself.

Beside monetary policies, government policies also dictate the direction of credit flow. In Australia, we have a policy called "negative gearing policy encourages" that is distorting the fundamentals of the Australian real estate.

"A bubble is a surge in asset price unwarranted by the fundamental of the asset and driven by exuberant market behavior. When no more investors are willing to pay for the elevated price, massive selloff happens, causing a contraction"

What is the fundamental of an asset?

In stock, you look at the dividend yield. If you get no good dividend yield, you are overpaying for the stock. High price to earning ratio in the stock market indicates there is a stock market bubble; in real estate, you look at the cash flow. Under normal conditions, and without government policy or external factors influencing the market, if an average investment property cannot generate 8% to 9% in the real estate market, an investor or homeowner is overpaying when they enter the market.

The negative gearing policy allows loss on property investment to be deducted from taxable income. This gives false economic signals to investors and encourages them to speculate and buy Australian real estate, even at a loss! These losses are paid by the taxpayers, which further worsen the severe federal budget deficit.

One common argument among mainstream commentaries is that the increase in population and lack of supply of housing in Sydney is a key driver of the price increases; therefore, the Sydney, Australia housing market is not in a bubble. And foreign investment is vital to increase this supply.

What do you think?

Before exploring this hypothesis, I want to tell you a story.

I was born in Hong Kong - a place where the population density is highest in the world; real estate is priced in feet, and the average property price-to-median household income ratio is 19 times; China is our next door neighbor.

Hong Kong Property Price Index

Figure 6.19: Hong Kong Property Price Index
Source: Rating and Valuation Department

Even in a housing market with a huge supply and demand imbalance, Hong Kong suffered a 60% decline in property price in 1997. This decline lasted for 6 years until 2003.

Although the burst of the Hong Kong real estate bubble was triggered by the talk of the 85,000-unit policy by the Hong Kong government that intended to increase the supply of housing, the fuels of the Hong Kong real estate bubble already existed prior to the trigger. The collapse of the Hong Kong housing market would not be so severe, without excessive foreign inflow due to being one of the four Asian tiger economies earlier in the decade.

By now, I hope I have convinced you that Australia has a housing bubble mandated by the government through monetary policies and fueled by excessive housing debt and foreign capital inflow.

It is impossible to predict the exact trigger that will collapse the Australia housing bubble or how long the boom will perpetuate. The $5.8 trillion AUD Australia housing market might be insufficient to absorb the huge demand from China (Total credit: $20.1 trillion USD) with 1.2 million citizen owning more than $ 1 million USD. As long as Australia's net foreign debt continues to grow, and Australians continue to go deeper and deeper into debt in the foreseeable future, the bubble will persist. If credits cease to grow, for any reason, I predict Australia housing will crash in a magnitude no Australian has seen in their lifetime. This will be financially devastating for many people.

Australia is not the only country experiencing an ongoing housing bubble. Many countries or regions in the East, like Shanghai, Hong Kong, Singapore, are experiencing the same bubble, and some are on a much greater scale.

As I am writing about this now, in 2016, a lot of has been happening in the Chinese economy earlier this year. Since a lot of countries' economy depends on China, whichever way the Chinese economy goes will dictate the credit flow to and from the rest of the world.

A Second Look at the Chinese Economy

Just as the world's spotlight was on the debt problems in the West, the credit bubble in China was formed.

In late June 2015, the Shanghai index plunged from a high of 5,100 to 3,700. More than $3 trillion was wiped out.

China was in shock.

In response to the crisis, the Chinese government immediately banned investors and executives holding over 5% of a company from selling any shares and began to pump hundreds of billions of dollars back into the market desperately to stop the free-fall.

Due to several months of continuous bad manufacturing data in China, the Chinese stock market plummeted on the first trading day of 2016,

The CSI300 index that listed the largest companies in Shanghai and Shenzhen plunged by 7% and triggered "circuit-breaker" to suspend trade nationwide for the first time.

When trading resumed on 7th January 2016, trading was again suspended for a second time in a week as the CSI 300 fell 7% when the market-reopened for less than 30 minutes.

Trading was halted, once again, to prevent further loss.

Since the beginning of 2016, in less than one week, the Chinese stock market plunged by 12%.

The Chinese government had no choice but to inject billions of dollars again in the equity market to instill public confidence.

So, what is going on with the Chinese economy?

Why would a country that is now the second largest economy in the world, with a high saving rate, experience such a sudden drastic decline?

What does it mean to the rest of the world?

China has been an important driver of the global economic growth after the U.S. Since the financial crisis of 2008, she becomes THE driver of global economic growth.

As shown earlier in this chapter, China's economic growth resulted from an export-led investment driven economic model. Decades of current account surplus allowed China to accumulate $4 trillion USD worth of foreign exchange reserve. As these foreign currency enters the Chinese economy,

1.   PBOC prints an equivalent amount off RMB to buy back the $4 trillion USD entering a country at an exchange rate that favors Chinese's export;

2.   Then, PBOC holding these U.S. Dollars invest abroad.

When these freshly printed RMB entered the domestic economy, through the magic of fractional reserve banking, the loan growth in China exploded. Figure 6.12 evidenced that the $21.3 USD worth of credit growth in China caused the Chinese economy to expand. That is how there is 1.2 million Chinese with more than $1 million USD in China.

PBOC invests the $4 trillion USD foreign exchange reserve in foreign assets, such as U.S. Treasury bonds and foreign currencies (e.g., USD, CAD and AUD etc.). These multi-trillion dollar investments by the PBOC are playing a leading role to cause economic bubbles in the globe.

[**Note**: When a Chinese buyer is buying properties in Australia, he/she will have to convert their RMB into AUD. During the process, the PBOC will buy the Chinese investor's RMB with USD, and then convert the USD back to AUD. The fuel of the global real estate bubble directly results from the trade imbalance between China and U.S.]

Apart from China's massive trade surplus due to export led-growth, its investment – driven model is another aspect that causes global imbalance.

Below is a figure showing China's Financial Account as the second component of the BOP. The meaning behind this diagram is greatly important – it is related to jobs and unemployment rate in the other parts of the world.

But how?

China's Financial Account US $million, 1983 to 2013

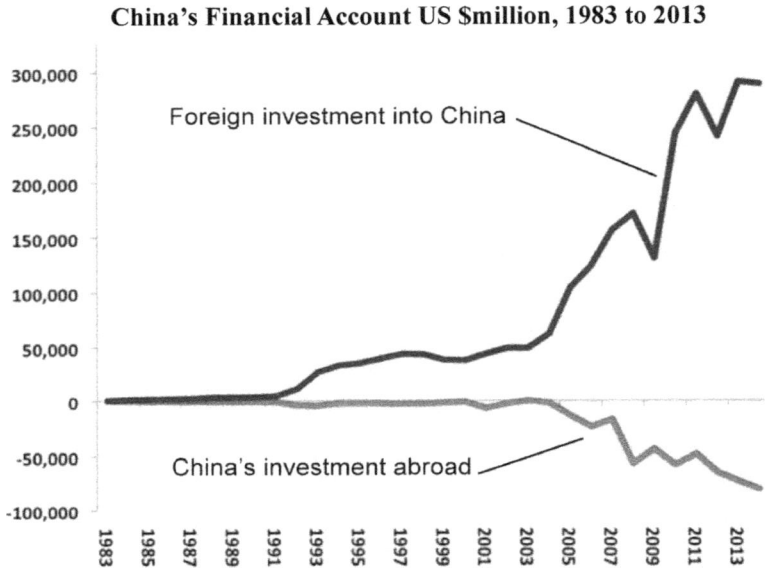

Figure 6.20: China's Financial Account US$ million, 1983 to 2013

Source: CEIC

The financial account in China shows how much foreign investments went into China and how much China invests abroad. Since 2009, China has been investing more than $50 billion USD abroad. (e.g., Real Estates, Treasury Bond, etc.). Part of this extraordinary amount of Chinese investment had already affected the real estate market of many developed countries as discussed previously. What is more interesting is how much foreign investment enters China. By 2013, foreign investment in China was approximately three times more than China's investment abroad. This means that multinational corporations, such as Apple, moved their manufacturing base to China; cheap labor in China means companies can earn a high profit at the expense of the jobs in other parts of the world.

By 2016, despite being the second largest economy in the world,

China's monthly minimum wage was only slightly above $200 USD, 20% of Japan's or 13% of U.S.'s.

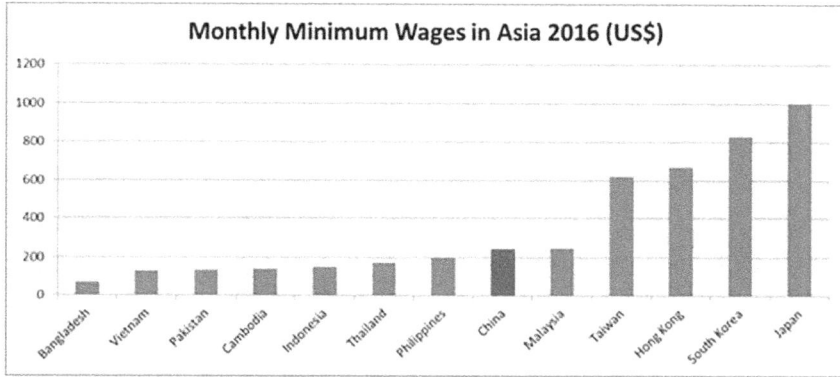

Figure 6.21: Monthly Minimum Wages in Asia in 2016
(The equivalent monthly rates are calculated on the basis of a 160 hour working month.)
Source: www.clb.org.hk

I hope you can see that, despite the growth in China, a lot of Chinese workers will work for $10 USD or less per day. A lot of these workers cannot purchase the goods they produce.

According to Global Wealth Report by Credit Suisse in 2015, about 71% of the world's population has less than $10,000. This means there is an abundance of population willing to compete for the $10 USD per day job in China.

The result is that workers in the developing world cannot compete with such low wages. Manufacturing bases of developed countries either must move offshore or close down. Jobs are shipped to the East. Products made in China swamped the globe.

The cheap labor in China allows the U.S. and the rest of the world to import goods cheaply from China. And the process keeps recursively reinforcing itself as we see in the trade imbalance.

This is globalization – a strong deflationary force as a result of the massive supply of cheap labor that fuels global imbalance.

Global Adult Population and Share of Total Wealth by Wealth Group, 2015

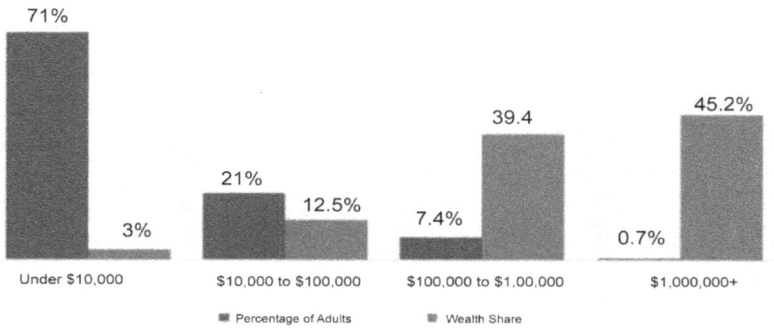

Figure 6.22: Global Adult Population and share of Total Wealth

Source: Credit Suisse Research Institute, Global Wealth Report 2015, October 2015

A Chinese Ghost Story

If you have ever been to China, you might accidentally stumble into some cities where hardly anyone is on the streets. The city is virtually empty.

Please make no mistake; these cities are not old and remote, but modernized with Bavarian-style structures and a magnificent medieval theme. And it is not only buildings, but new roads, railways, bigger airports, and even artificial lakes.

It seems to defy the law of gravity that Chinese developers continue to build empty cities after empty cities with no one moving in. If you boil down to the essence, you may wonder if the supply of real estate is driven by demand. If so, what is driving hundreds of empty megacities and towns to spring up in China in recent years?

Are they built for ghosts to live?

Figure 6.23: Complex in Huizhou in Guangdong province in the southeast of China

Source: dailymail.co.uk

The government is planning to move 100 million people from the countryside to the city by 2030. These ghost towns are produced by a Local Government financing vehicle (LGFV), which collected local farmland, moved farmers off the land, and rezoned them for urban uses. This land is then bundled into a bond and sold to China's most powerful bank – China Development Bank (CDB) – owned by the Chinese Communist party.

When the Chinese government buys the bond, they are financing the LGFV to develop these ghost towns.

This is a classic example of how government mandates the real estate market.

Urbanization is part of China's investment driven economic model to stimulate the economy by creating jobs and lending.

Despite many mainstream media warnings, this is a sign of a massive real estate bubble. It is too early to draw a conclusion based on the history and the dynamic of the Chinese real estate market. Wanda Group, one of China's biggest commercial real estate companies, built ten empty malls in China's second-tier and third-tier cities a decade ago. Back then, people did not see why these malls were empty. However, these malls are now fully occupied. So don't be surprised; the ghost town we are seeing today might be a different story in a decade or two.

Do you mean government mandated real estate of this magnitude could continue forever?

At first, it might appear obvious for economists to conclude that this massive supply in real estate disconnects the demand and supply fundamental. It is unsustainable and will crash the Chinese real estate market.

However, the Chinese real estate continues to escalate.

Government intervention can overwhelm the market force. And the more economic growth a country needs, the more urbanization.

Do you think so?

The Greatest Credit Bubble in the History of the world

Credit growth drives economic growth. Like other countries in the world, China's economy is not driven by savings, but by rapid expanding of credit. As long as credit continues to grow, so will the Chinese economy and the rest of the world.

By understanding this, decoding and understanding the dynamic of the credit bubbles becomes fairly easy – assets price becomes dependent on the expanding and contraction of credit.

This is exactly what is happening in China.

The two sharp declines in the Chinese Stock market in mid-2015 and early 2016 were no accidents. They were merely early signals, indicating that China's economic growth, the greatest credit bubble in the history of the world, is coming to an end.

If you look at China's annual change in import and export in the next page, you will see what is happening.

China is the second largest importer of the world. If you compare Figure 6.24 and Figure 6.25, you can see China's import is a mirror of her export. Precisely speaking, China's import is a function of her export. Since 2000, when China joined WTO, Chinese's annual increase in export has been increasing astronomically. China's GDP averaged 10% from 2000 to 2008.

Now, if you flip back a couple of pages to Figure 6.8 (U.S. Current Account Balance), coincidentally, you will see U.S.'s current is running a huge trade deficit. This is the source of credit that fueled the Chinese economy.

When you look closely at the U.S. current account deficit, you will see the financial crisis in 2008 resulted in reduced U.S. current account deficit tremendously from more than $70 billion USD in 2008 annually down to $40 billion USD in 2016.

Because U.S. is the largest importer in the world, a reduction in consumption means less trade with China.

China's Annual Change in Import 1991 to 2015

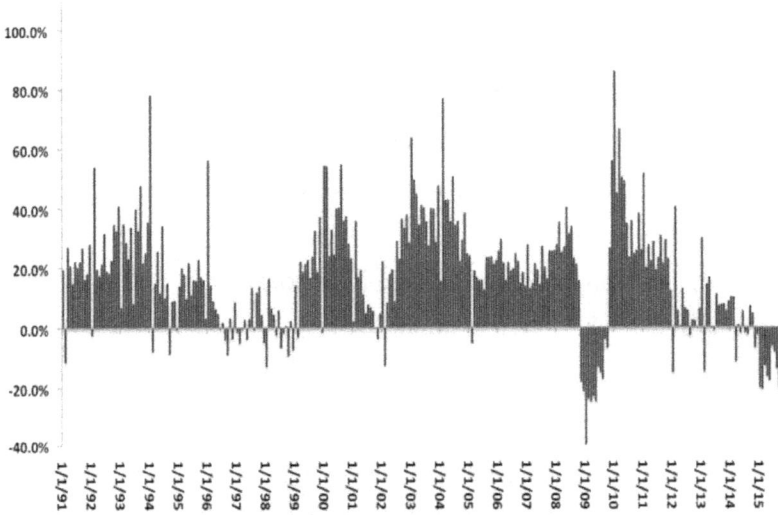

Figure 6.24: China's Annual Change in Import 1991 to 2015
Source: Bloomberg

China's Annual Change in Export 1991 to 2015

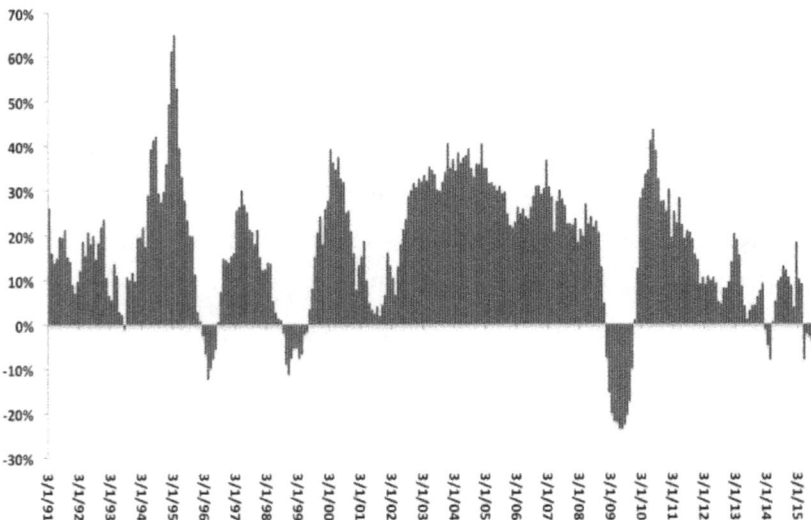

Figure 6.25: China's Annual Change in Export 1991 to 2015
Source: Bloomberg

If you look at Figure 6.24 and Figure 6.25, you can see that Chinese export declined from a peak of 40% in mid-2010 to -5% ~ - 7% in 2015; Chinese import declined from a peak of 80% to -20% over the same period.

That is telling us there is an emergency going on in China.

"In February 2016, the Chinese government announced plans to lay off 1.8 million workers in the coal mining and iron and steel industry as part of efforts to reduce industrial overcapacity. Later reports suggested China would actually lay off around six million workers from its ailing state-owned industries."

-Chinese Labor Bulletin

Instead of having an average economic growth of 10% annually historically, China's GDP slowed down to 6.9%.

China's GDP

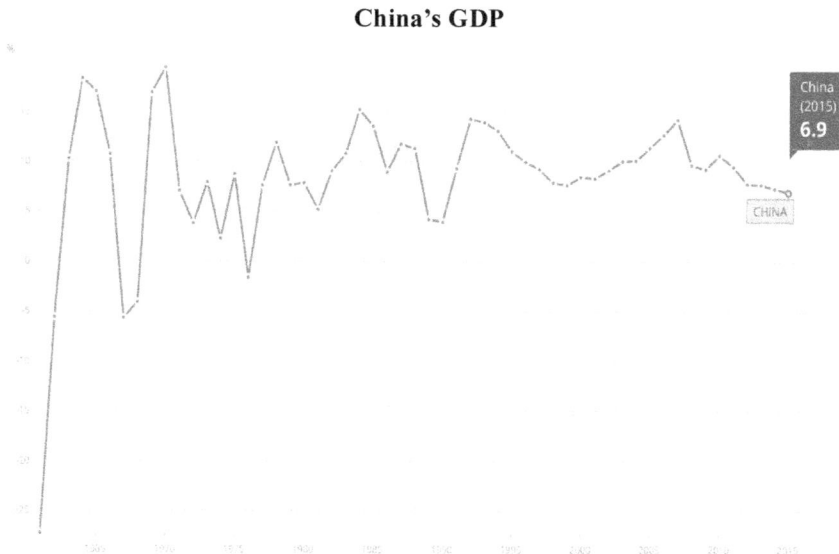

China
(2015)
6.9

CHINA

Figure 6.26: China's GDP 1965 to 2015
Source: World Bank

Beside U.S., couldn't the demand from the rest of the world continue to absorb the Chinese supply?

Apparently not. With U.S., Europe, and Japan's economies all in economic crisis, countries in the rest of the world simply do not have enough demand to absorb the excessive Chinese products.

Composition of Nominal Gross World Product

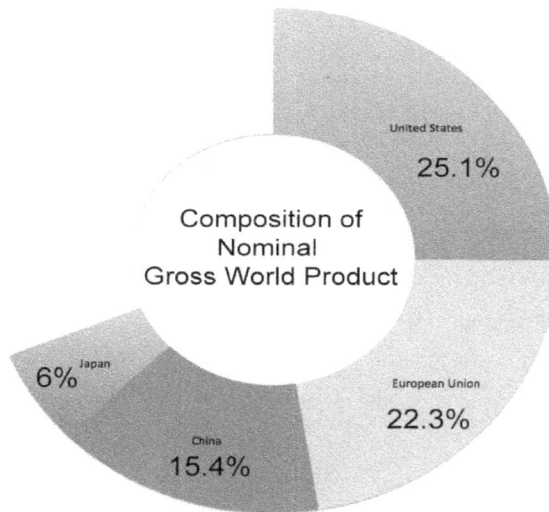

Figure 6.27: Composition of Nominal Gross World Product (2016)
Source: IMF

China is facing a different economic challenge, unlike other debtor nations, which is overproduction.

Overproduction is detrimental to China's export-led investment driven economic model that has been fueling China's economic growth in the past three decades. With less demand for Chinese products from the rest of the world, China's export reduced sharply, and this caused a sharp reduction in import from the rest of the world.

Commodities producing countries, like Australia and Brazil, which depend on exporting commodity to China, suffered badly. Brazil is experiencing its worst economic depression in a century. This can be seen in their preparation for the 2016 Olympics.

Overproduction in China forced industries that preceded during the boom to cut production and dismantle their industrial capacity. China, being the supplier of half of the world's steel production, is facing a serious challenge, as this will create massive unemployment. Earlier this year, China's plan to slash crude steel production capacity could eliminate 400,000 jobs!

Although investment is one way to economic growth, investment is good only if it is profitable. And to be profitable, the good sold must exceed the cost of manufacturing. If there is too much investment relative to demand, prices fall, and investments lose money. And in this credit-fueled economy, where investment is financed with credits from banks, loss in investment destroys our deposits. Overproduction in China simply means China's investment in buildings, manufacturing, and infrastructure outpaced the demand, both nationally and internationally.

Instead of generating profits, investment results in losses.

But doesn't credit growth drive economic growth? If China continues to expand its credit, doesn't that mean the economy will continue to grow?

Can Credit Growth Drive Economic Growth Forever?

Although credit growth drives economic growth, it is interesting how much an economy grows can be faster or smaller with an increasing quantity of credit.

If a unit of credit drives a unit of economic growth, that unit of credit is said to be effective in driving economic growth. As the economy becomes more dependent on credits, it might take two or more credits to drive the same unit of economic growth. If an economy becomes too dependent on credits, unless an extraordinary amount of credit is injected, asset prices will have diminishing returns.

After the financial crisis of 2008, China required an increasing amount of credit to generate economic growth.

Increase in Credit vs Increase in Nominal GDP in China (Yuan Trillions)

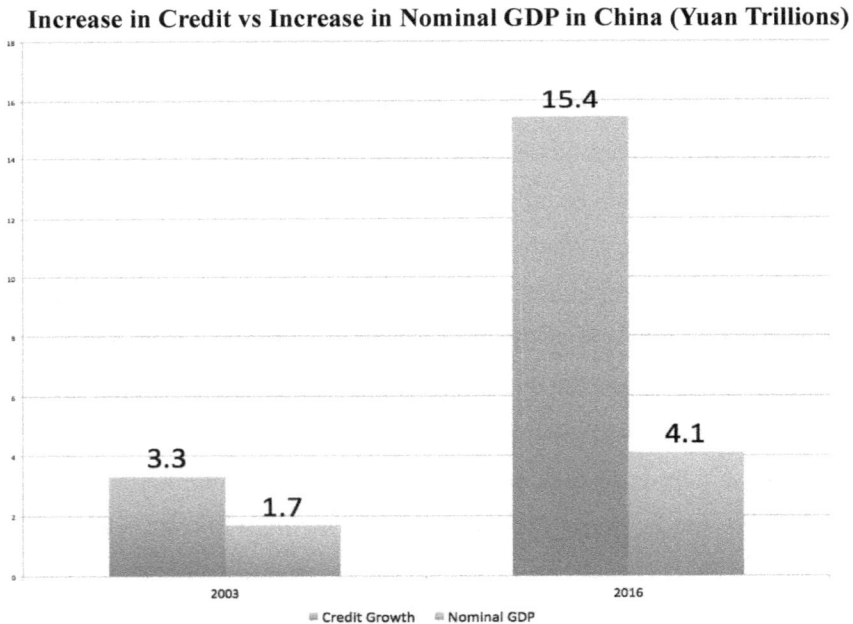

Figure 6.28: Increase in Credit vs Increase in Nominal GDP in China (Yuan Trillions)
Source: CEIC

The ghost cities in the previous example are possible because of the expansion of credit in China through bank loans.

Bank loans constantly receiving interest payment or principal repayment are good loans; the reserve, however, is called non-performing loans (NPL). If a real estate investor's mortgage is a NPL, it simply means the investment is not profitable. Instead of generating growth, NPL destroys savers' deposits and hinders growth.

What is your Prediction on the Chinese Economy?

In the past, China required an increase in credit expansion twice the size of her increase in nominal GDP to achieve a 10% annual GDP growth.

Last year, in 2015, it was a different story.

It took China an increase in credit expansion almost four times (i.e., $15.4 trillions) the size of her increase in nominal GDP (i.e., $4.1 trillions) to achieve a 6.9% GDP growth.

China's economy is slowing down.

The important question is: Where is the Chinese economy heading?

I have created four scenarios to show you the consequence of each policy option.

Scenario 1:

If China's increase in credit expansion remains at 15.4 trillion Yuan (i.e., $2.32 trillion USD), as in 2015, China's economy will stagnate and will experience no growth.

The Chinese government is highly unlikely to allow this outcome.

What does it mean for China to increase credit expansion at this rate?

The total credit in China is currently $21.3 trillion USD.

For China to increase in $2.32 trillion USD in the economy every year, in twelve years' time, China's total credit will be $50 Trillion USD. All these credit expansions will mean China will have the same economic condition over the next decade as in 2015.

This is a soft landing approach.

Scenario 2:

If China increases its credit exponentially every year, China's economy will continue to grow at a rate higher than 6.9%, despite a slowdown in export and an increased number of non-performing loans.

In this case, it will take China less than a decade before total credit in China hits $50 trillion. However, credit growth at this pace will cause a credit bubble we are all familiar with, in 2008, when TCMD peaked at $50 trillion USD.

This is highly likely what will happen.

Scenario 3:

The third option for China is to devaluate its currency to create a favorable environment for export.

But here is a problem.

Devaluation of RMB caused fear for local and overseas investors to exit the Chinese market before their RMB holdings lost value. This results in capital flight as more people take money out of China.

According to Goldman, the net outflow of capital in China was approximately $500 billion since October 2015.

Bloomberg estimated that, in 2015, the net capital outflow amounted to $1 trillion.

That is why there was a huge drop in China's foreign exchange reserve.

So, the option for China to devaluate RMB really depends on how well

Chinese policy makers handle the capital flights.

This is the new China we are facing, today. Thirty years of export-led growth investment-led economic model transformed China from a third world country to the second largest economy in the world.

With overcapacity and low demand from the rest of the world, the Chinese economy has little options, but to slow down or massively increase credit growth to sustain the current growth rate.

Either way, the increase in credit growth will yield a diminishing return, and the NPL will continue to increase. The Chinese economy will inevitably slow down in the decades ahead.

Final Words

Boom and bursts of asset bubbles are rarely new. What makes the current ones interesting is the dependency of one bubble upon another. The real estate bubbles we are seeing around the world today is an indirect result of decades of credit growth in China, fueled by U.S.'s running decades of trade deficit.

With all these bubbles reinforced by one mega credit bubble from China, it is no longer valid to look at the fundamental of a domestic economy. To decode a credit bubble, it becomes necessary to understand how the global economy really works.

In the new age of credit, the size of our economy is not only larger, but different. No longer is asset price only driven by demand and supply, but by unlimited credit creation. The new rules under credit driven economy rendered most of our traditional economic concepts irrelevant.

There is no wonder why many economists find the present economy defying the law of gravity.

This is a long chapter and I hope its length is worth the value. I hope by understanding the symbiotic relationship between U.S. and China, the foreign exchange market, and the role of credit growth, you have the knowledge to understand how things might play out in the coming decade.

Chapter 7

What is Wrong with Europe's Economy?

Since the financial crisis of 2008, the financial news around the world had been focusing on the debt problems of U.S. and Europe. The collapse of Lehman brothers caused banks in the West to take extreme cautions when lending. European banks that had invested heavily in the subprime mortgage were hit the hardest. To save the banks in Europe and stop them from failing, governments needed to step in and bail out banks across the European Union (EU).

However, the cost of the bailout proved to be high. Some countries in EU almost bankrupted their own government to save the banks.

As the crisis continued, banks became more dependent on the governments. Governments became accustomed to borrowing large amount to finance their budget and accumulated a lot of debt. As the debt level became too high, governments found it increasingly difficult to finance their debts. The banking crisis in the Euro Zone quickly evolved into a sovereign crisis.

All Eyes on Greece

Greece had its debt level twice the size of her economy. Since Greece owed billions to banks and financial institutions across EU, if Greece collapsed, other countries across EU would collapse like a chain reaction. The result would be another global financial crisis.

So, how did Greece accumulate that much debt in the first place?

Before Greece adopted Euro as a currency in 2001, Greece had been using a currency called drachma – a fistful of six metal sticks used as currency as early as 1100BC, and it was also a form of bullion denominated by weight.

But in 2001, Greece joined the Eurozone with many European countries and used the Euro as its currency.

The Euro has been great in facilitating trades, but nineteen countries sharing a currency has its problems.

But what caused Greece to adopt Euro as opposed to drachma?

Greece has its own story to tell.

From 1950 – 1973, Greece's economy enjoyed a period of sustained economic growth, secondary only to Japan. The drastic devaluation of drachma had attracted foreign investments and fast development of tourism. Greece GDP often exceeded 10% in the 1950. Its economy consistently outperformed other European countries.

However, Greece's economic miracle declined as the economy began to stagnate in the 1980s. The inflation rate in Greece was double digits, and it was not until 1995 before it resumed back to single-digit.

At the early stage of adopting Euro, Greece's economy actually benefited. Interest rates on loans in Greece began to fall dramatically, because the world had confidence in the Euro. Greece's citizens also benefited, because luxury goods, like BMW, suddenly became more affordable, because they adopted Euro. This encouraged the private sector to borrow. Private sector debt jumped from 59% of GDP to 129% of GDP. Trade went from balanced in 1995 to a current account deficit of 15% of GDP by 2008.

Decades of corruption and tax evasion caused a lot of economic problems. So, when the U.S.'s financial crisis happened in 2008, two of Greece's main industries – tourism and shipping – took a great hit. Eventually, Greece's depression made the news and was dragging down Europe's economy.

The Problem With Euro

Ironically, one of the biggest reasons Greece is in such bad financial shape is because of adopting Euro.

When a government issues a bond in its own currency, the markets around the world will buy that bond, based on confidence of the currency from that country. When the Greece government issues Greek debt, it issues bonds denominated in Euro. This tricked the market into loaning Greece money, because they had the wrong signal that the strength of the Euro is reflecting the health of Greece's economy. The Greek government could overpromise to its citizens at the expense of going deeper and deeper into debt.

Another problem is that when ECB buys these bonds, Euro is created and dilutes the purchasing power of all Euros, including countries in the Euro zone that are financially responsible with low debt level.

When ECB buys bonds from a deficit country like Greece, it means the rest of Europe is loaning money to the bankrupted Greek government. This is creating unfair economic burden for hard working citizens from financially responsible countries like Germany.

Countries sharing one currency, one central bank, and able to issue their own debts is doomed to fail.

European Debt Crisis

While all eyes are on Greece, Greece is not the only country that constitutes the European debt crisis. Four other European Union members, including Portugal, Italy, Ireland, and Spain, were also in serious financial trouble because of high sovereign debt. With Greece, they are commonly known as PIIGS.

Highest EU debts as a % of GDP

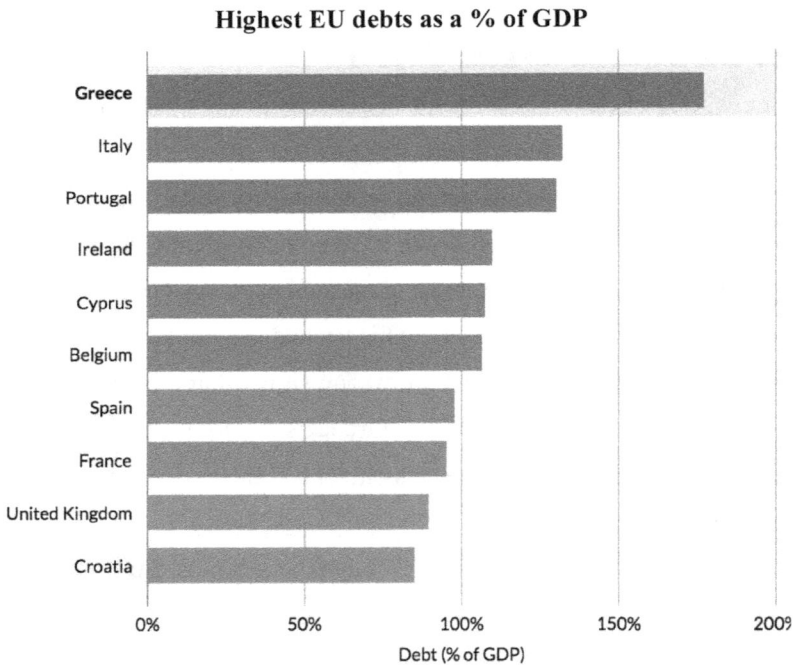

Fig 7.1: Highest EU debts as a % of GDP
Source: http://www.telegraph.co.uk/

What was the Policy Response in Europe?

"Within our mandate, the ECB is ready to do whatever it takes to preserve the euro. And believe me, it will be enough."

-Mario Draghi, President of ECB

As the European banks could not borrow money from one another or from anywhere else, Europe's banking system was on the verge of collapse.

That was when the ECB and the Eurosystem stepped in.

It is worthwhile to understand that ECB and the Eurosystem are different.

ECB is the central bank of the 19 countries that have adopted Euro, and the Eurosystem comprises ECB and the national central banks (NCB) of the 19 member states part of the Eurozone. Both ECB and the Eurosystem aim to maintain the financial stability in the Eurozone.

Although ECB is widely mentioned in the media, it does not carry out monetary policy by itself. The monetary policy of Europe is carried out by ECB with NCB.

The following page is two tables showing the balance sheet of ECB and the consolidated balance sheet of Eurosystem.

By 2015, the total asset held by Eurosystem was €2,781 billion, whereas the total assets held by ECB was €256 billion.

Eurosystem has a lot more influence than ECB.

Consolidated balance sheet of the Eurosystem as at 31 December 2015[1]

(EUR millions)[2]

ASSETS		31 December 2015	31 December 2014
1	Gold and gold receivables	338,713	343,630
2	Claims on non-euro area residents denominated in foreign currency	307,115	270,250
	2.1 Receivables from the IMF	80,384	81,298
	2.2 Balances with banks and security investments, external loans and other external assets	226,732	188,951
3	Claims on euro area residents denominated in foreign currency	31,109	27,940
4	Claims on non-euro area residents denominated in euro	20,242	18,905
	4.1 Balances with banks, security investments and loans	20,242	18,905
	4.2 Claims arising from the credit facility under ERM II	0	0
5	Lending to euro area credit institutions related to monetary policy operations denominated in euro	558,989	630,341
	5.1 Main refinancing operations	88,978	156,129
	5.2 Longer-term refinancing operations	469,543	473,285
	5.3 Fine-tuning reverse operations	0	0
	5.4 Structural reverse operations	0	0
	5.5 Marginal lending facility	468	924
	5.6 Credits related to margin calls	0	2
6	Other claims on euro area credit institutions denominated in euro	107,863	59,942
7	Securities of euro area residents denominated in euro	1,161,159	590,265
	7.1 Securities held for monetary policy purposes	803,135	217,242
	7.2 Other securities	358,023	373,022
8	General government debt denominated in euro	25,145	26,715
9	Other assets	230,810	240,252
	Total assets	2,781,145	2,208,238

Figure 7.2: Eurosystem Total Assets

Source: http://www.ecb.europa.eu

Financial statements of the ECB

Balance Sheet as at 31 December 2015

ASSETS	Note number	2015 €	2014 €
Gold and gold receivables	1	15,794,976,324	15,980,317,601
Claims on non-euro area residents denominated in foreign currency	2		
Receivables from the IMF	2.1	714,825,534	669,336,060
Balances with banks and security investments, external loans and other external assets	2.2	49,030,207,257	43,730,904,005
		49,745,032,791	44,400,240,065
Claims on euro area residents denominated in foreign currency	2.2	1,862,714,832	1,783,727,949
Other claims on euro area credit institutions denominated in euro	3	52,711,983	2,120,620
Securities of euro area residents denominated in euro	4		
Securities held for monetary policy purposes	4.1	77,808,651,858	17,787,948,367
Intra-Eurosystem claims	5		
Claims related to the allocation of euro banknotes within the Eurosystem	5.1	86,674,472,505	81,322,848,550
Other assets	6		
Tangible and intangible fixed assets	6.1	1,263,646,830	1,249,596,659
Other financial assets	6.2	20,423,917,583	20,626,359,858
Off-balance-sheet instruments revaluation differences	6.3	518,960,866	319,624,726
Accruals and prepaid expenses	6.4	1,320,068,350	725,224,031
Sundry	6.5	1,180,224,603	1,092,627,246

Figure 7.3: ECB Total Assets

Source: http://www.ecb.europa.eu

When the Europe crisis started in late 2009, the fear of contagions caused Banks to stop lending. The fundamental economic problems and the high debt level of troubled European countries (e.g., PIIGS) caused their banks to be unable to borrow on the financial market at a reasonable interest rate. Many European countries had forgotten the rules designed to make the Euro work. Their government went deeper and deeper into debt. Other European countries, even with a sound economy, founded it difficult to borrow.

To prevent a complete collapse in 2007 and 2008, the ECB aggressively provided unlimited funding at a fixed rate to the European Banks and lent money to banks that could not borrow in the financial market.

With the tension in Europe growing, in June 2009, ECB launched bond purchase programs.

The first programme launched covered bond purchase programme (CBPP1) with a nominal value of €60 Billion, which ended by 30 June 2010.

Between November 2011 and October 2012, ECB launched the covered bond purchase programme (CBPP2) with a nominal amount of €16.418 Billion.

To further control the situation, ECB finally agreed to purchase bonds issued by the Euro area government through launching the European Securities Markets Programme (SMP) in May 2010.

"We have not discuss a precise scenario for the SMP. As I often said, the SMP is neither eternal nor infinite"

-Mario Draghi, President of ECB

So, what exactly is neither eternal nor infinite SMP?

SMP is just an auction to buy bad bonds. This is similar to how the Federal Reserve buys the MBS to keep the U.S. from defaulting. ECB is buying up all the bad bonds from a troubled European member state's government, because investors are no longer willing to buy the bonds from the highly indebted government. The accumulated SMP purchased by ECB was €220 Billion.

Between 2011 to 2012, ECB announced Longer-term Refinancing Operation (LTROs) that allows banks to borrow funds from the ECB for three years at 1% interest.

"Use of the European Central Banks's three-year funding programme is expected to exceed €500 billion in February when lenders are offered their second chance to access the new long-term refinancing operation."

-Credit Suisse

So, what are LTROs?

LTROs is part of Central bank's open market operations to conduct monetary policy. Instead of maturing in three months, like normal loans do, LTROs matured in three years. This is cheap money provided to banks to borrow for a long time.

LTROs was to encourage the banks to buy the high yield sovereign debt and alleviate the funding crisis of governments.

So, the banks offered bonds to ECB for the loan and used the funds from ECB to buy government bonds with a high interest rate, earning a profit. Some of these funds were also used to stimulate the economy. The first injection was carried out in December 2011 when the banks took over €489 billion from the ECB. This is why you see the rally in the

Eurosystem total asset and the European market during this period.

In June 2014, the ECB announced the launch of Targeted Longer-Term Refinancing Operations (TLTROs). They provide finance to credit institutions for a period up to four years to stimulate bank lending to the economy and ease the funding pressure. TLRTOs are targeted operations designed to support bank lending to non-finance corporations and household sectors (i.e., except loans for households to buy homes because the ECB does not want to have a housing bubble).

Then, ECB launched the third covered bond purchase programme (CBPP3) on October 2014 and asset-backed securities purchase programme (ABSPP) on November 2014 to expand its expanded asset purchase programme (APP), such that banks could provide lending in the economy.

In March 2015, the Eurosystem launched the Public Sector Purchase Program (PSPP). This is to supplement the purchase programmes for ABS.

The total purchase of these three programs can be found in the link in the ECB website -http://www.ecb.europa.eu/mopo/implement/omo/html/index.en.html

The combined purchased amounted to €60 billion per month.

These asset purchase programmes were quantitative easing and should end at the end of March 2017.

Total Eurosystem Assets

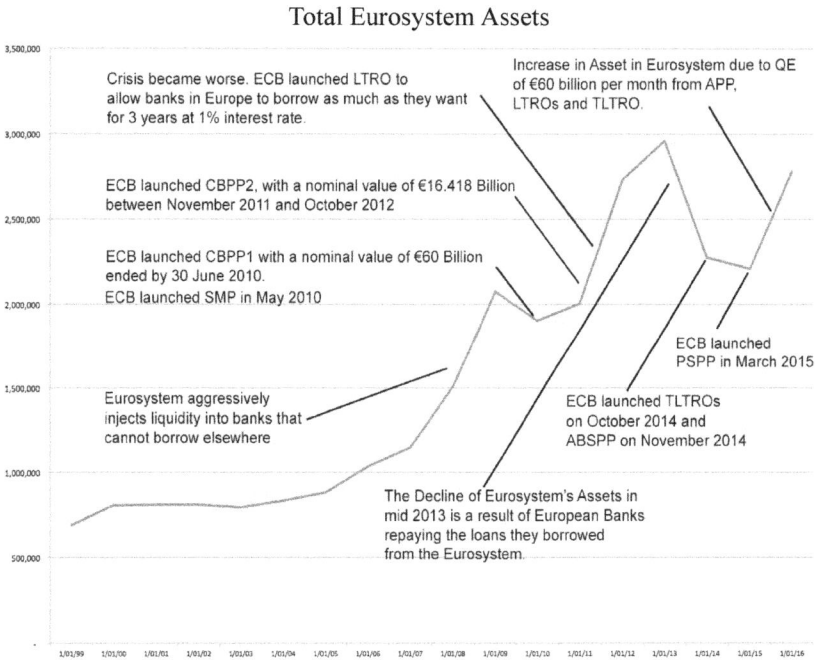

Crisis became worse. ECB launched LTRO to allow banks in Europe to borrow as much as they want for 3 years at 1% interest rate.

Increase in Asset in Eurosystem due to QE of €60 billion per month from APP, LTROs and TLTRO.

ECB launched CBPP2, with a nominal value of €16.418 Billion between November 2011 and October 2012

ECB launched CBPP1 with a nominal value of €60 Billion ended by 30 June 2010.
ECB launched SMP in May 2010

ECB launched PSPP in March 2015

Eurosystem aggressively injects liquidity into banks that cannot borrow elsewhere

ECB launched TLTROs on October 2014 and ABSPP on November 2014

The Decline of Eurosystem's Assets in mid 2013 is a result of European Banks repaying the loans they borrowed from the Eurosystem.

Figure 7.4: Total Eurosystem assets

Source: http://www.ecb.europa.eu

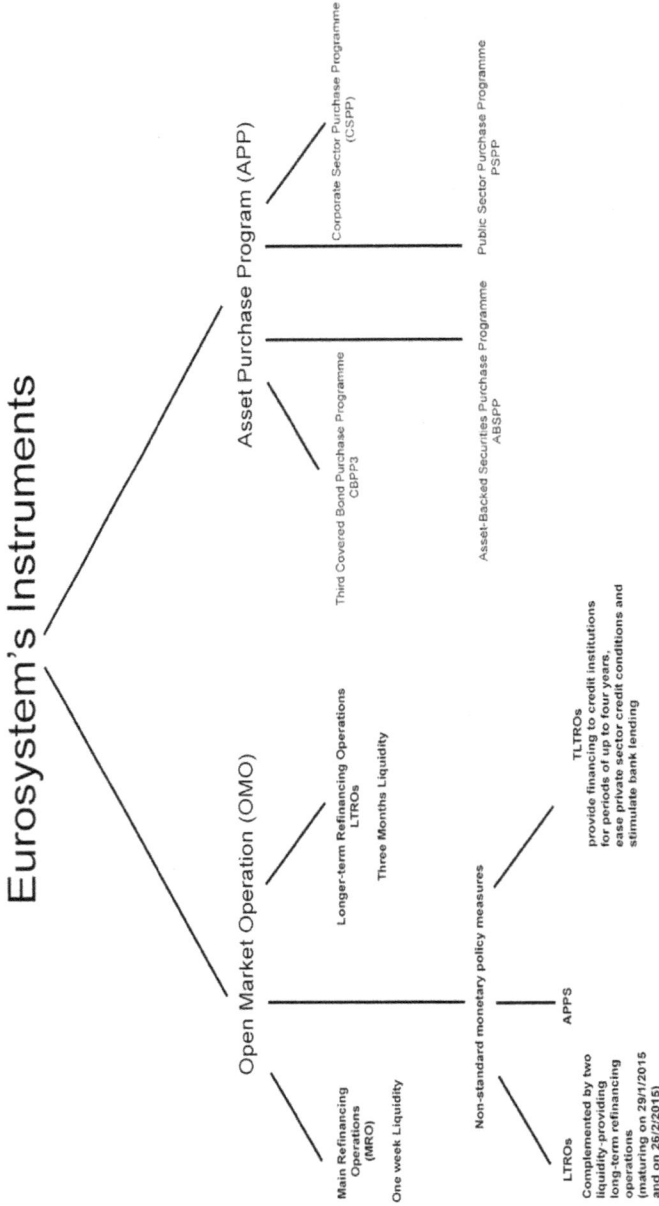

Figure 7.5 Eurosystem's Instruments
Source: http://www.ecb.europa.eu

Are More Debts the Solution to Debts?

This year is the eighth year into the European crisis, and the situation of Greece is far from resolved. Despite multiple austerity packages, tax rise, harsh spending cuts, and bailouts packages, Greece's economy had shown little to no sign of recovery. Unemployment is close to 24%.

"I don't see any progress. The economy is stagnant, the private sector devastated, the public administration underfunded and ineffective. And there is always the spectre of Grexit at the end of the tunnel."
-Local Greek Citizen,2016

"If we continue down this road, a fourth, even a fifth, bailout should be expected."
-Aristides Hatzis, associate professor of law and economics at Athens University, 2016

[**Note**: Greece received 1st bailout of €100 billion on 1st May 2010; 2nd bailout of €246 billion to supersede the 1st bailout ;3rd bailout of €86 billion by the IMF, ECB, the European Commission and the Greek government. Troika was the term referring to a decision group formed by EC, ECB and IMF.]

Italy is in no better position either. The Italian banks' non-performing loans had accumulated up to €360 billion, which is stagnating the credit growth of Italy.

Portugal's largest bank, Caixa Geral de Depósitos (CGD), is thought to need a cash injection of €4 billion to rescue it from difficulties.

So, more debt is not the solution to debts.

However, this is not the case for Ireland and Spain.

Ireland's €67 billion bailout had stabilized its banking sector, and it was the first to exit the Eurozone bailout programme. Its GDP was surging and grew 7% in Q3 2015.

Spain's €100 billion bailout package also helped its economy to rebound.

Troika's bailout packages and the Eurosystem's instruments are effective in some, but not all, countries.

Based on this fact, it might be controversial to draw a fine line on whether the solution to debts is more debts. Despite many economists disagreeing, we cannot deny that it worked – so far. In Part II of the book, I will expand more on this subject.

Why Did Euro Exist?

If Euro is doomed to fail, why did Euro exist in the first place?

For most of Europe's history, it has been at war with itself. Countries at war with each other do less business together. Europe always had trade barriers, tariffs, and different currencies. You can imagine that doing business across Europe can be a difficult task and expensive.

First, you need a fee to exchange currency. Then, you need to pay a tariff fee for trade. This stagnated economic growth.

When WWII happened, Europe was devastated.

Because the situation was so dire, the fastest way to rebuild Europe was to remove all these trade barriers and tariffs.

Then the idea of a unified Europe was born.

After that, countries in Europe banded together to achieve this goal. They brought down barriers and lowered the cost of doing business. The last barrier was the Berlin Wall.

When united Germany was ready, 27 countries signed the *Masstricht Treaty* and created the European Union.

Despite doing business being easier, there was one major obstacle – the currency.

On 1ˢᵗ January, 1999, Euro was created. Countries within the European Union discontinued their local currencies and their own monetary policies, transferring this authority to the newly formed European Central Bank (ECB).

Monetary Policies VS Fiscal Policies

Although the intention of creating the Euro was good, countries having the same monetary policies, but different fiscal problems, posed a problem that led to the European debt crisis today.

Monetary policies control the currency supply and the interest rate of borrowing; fiscal policies decide how much a government collects in taxes and how much it spends.

A government can only spend what it collects from taxes. Anything above is called deficit spending.

Before the Euro, countries like Greece paid high interest on its borrowing cost, and it was not as easy to find loans from other countries. After it joined the European Union, things worked differently. The amount Greece could borrow increased dramatically.

So, smaller countries suddenly had access to credit they never dreamed before.

Less creditable countries could borrow the same rate as productive countries, like Germany.

With this excessive credit available, the Greece government could perform deficit spending programs. Greek politicians could promise something for nothing.

That was how countries, like Greece, Portugal, and Italy, could pay down debts using more debts.

For Ireland and Spain, the cheap credit fueled a gigantic housing bubble.

The adoption of Euro also allowed countries to build factories across Europe. Spanish Banks could lend to German companies in Spain. And French businesses in Portugal could borrow from Portugal banks. This had made doing business very efficient, but all the European countries became tightly intertwined.

A debt problem for Greece became a debt problem for Europe. If Greece defaults, Spain defaults, followed by Italy, and then pretty soon it could be Germany.

"€100 Billion is put up for the Spanish banking system and 20% of the money has to come from Italy. Under the deal the Italians have to lend to the Spanish banks at 3%, but to get that money, they have to borrow on the market at 7%. It is genius, isn't it brilliant?"
-Nigel Farage (June 2012)

And that is why an exit in Greece will cause the Eurozone to fall apart.

The problem is that, despite the present Euro crisis could be settled, the fundamental problem still exists. As long as there is a mismatch in fiscal policy and monetary policy, irresponsible governments will always spend far more than they can repay to promise something for nothing at the expense of other productive countries. However, if fiscal policy matches monetary policy, the power of all countries in the European Union will be centralized - the result is United States of Europe.

In 2016, the term BREXIT became very popular after the British due to political reasons. How many more countries will join the EXIT program? What will be the fate of the Euro?

Chapter 8

Derivatives of Debts

"Derivatives are financial weapons of mass destruction."

-Warren Buffett

In the year 2000, U.S. President Bill Clinton signed a bill creating the Commodity Futures Modernization Act (CFMA). This helped to pave the way to an explosive derivative market today. Between 2000 and 2007, the derivative market grew from $100 trillion to $700 trillion. As I am writing, in 2016, the size of this complex, unregulated derivative market is $1.2 quadrillion USD, which is over 15 times the size of all GDP of the world combined.

Size of Derivative Market relative to the Rest of the World in 2015 (Trillion of US$)

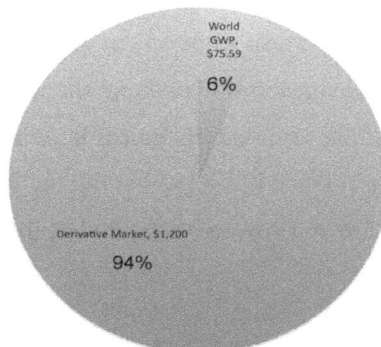

World GWP, $75.59

6%

Derivative Market, $1,200

94%

Figure 8.1: Size of Derivative Market relative to the Rest of the World in 2015 (Trillion US$)
Source: Author

What Exactly Are Derivatives?

Warren Buffett once said that derivatives are the weapons of mass destruction.

What are derivatives? How are they related to debts? Who creates them? How will they impact the financial markets? How is it related to you?

Before going into detail, let's understand what the word derivative means.

Cheese is a derivative of milk. Cheesecake is a derivative of cheese, which is a derivative of milk. The value of a derivative derives from an underlying asset. The value of cheese depends on the quality of milk. If the milk is fresh and of good quality, you will get a good quality cheese; if the milk is no good, the cheese derived from that milk will definitely be bad quality.

Before 1971, the U.S. dollar is a derivative of gold. After the Breton Wood System collapsed, the U.S. dollar is a derivative of debts.

Shares are derivatives of the U.S. dollar. Mutual funds are derivatives of shares. Options are derivatives of shares. The value of mutual funds and options derives from the value of shares, which are derivatives of U.S. dollars – the derivatives of debts.

So, the word derivative is really not that complicated.

What makes derivative appear to be so complicated in the world of finance is because the masterminds behind the financial industry purposely want to confuse you with technical jargon.

The more confusing finance is for the public, the better for them.

You will understand why I say so by the end of this chapter.

Derivatives in the World of Finance

A financial instrument is a contract or agreement that legally binds certain financial rights and obligations between two trading parties. Your mortgage with a bank is a financial instrument in which you have the right to own the property, but you also have the obligation to repay your mortgage.

A derivative in the world of finance is a financial instrument, whose value derives from its underlying asset.

One example of a derivative is a forward contract.

Suppose a U.S. based company sells machines to Germany and prices are quoted in each country's currency. So, fluctuations in € / $ might be too extreme, such that it will have a huge impact on the U.S. company's revenue.

EURO VS USD

Figure 8.2: EURO vs USD
Source: www.ecb.europa.eu

How do we eliminate this exchange rate risk?

This is where derivative comes into play.

The U.S. company can hedge the exchange rate risk by entering a foreign currency forward contract with a third party. The terms of the forward contract require both parties to lock in an agreed € / $ exchange rate in six months' time. So, the fluctuation of the € / $ will become irreverent to the U.S. company's profit or loss, because this risk is now hedged. However, the U.S. company gives up all the benefits, if the USD appreciates against the euro. This forward contract is forward rate agreement (FRA).

Unlike stocks, these forward contracts are not traded in an exchange (e.g., New York Stock Exchange), which is centralized, regulated, and publicly transparent; instead, they are traded over-the-counter (OTC) through decentralized dealer networks to save cost.

However, not all derivatives are traded over OTC. Future contracts are like forward contracts, except they are traded in an exchange.

Another popular derivative is options. Unlike forward and future contracts, where it must be executed upon agreement, an option gives the buyer the right, but not the obligation, to buy or sell an underlying asset at a specific price by a certain date.

One classic example of applying an option is the real estate market. Imagine you have found your dream house worth $500,000, but you won't have enough cash to buy it for another year. You fear the property price will continue to rise in the next year. So you negotiate a deal with the owner to give you the option to buy the house for $500,000 in one year's time by paying a $1000 option fee. This is called a call option. Within one year, you can have the option to buy this property for $500,000.

Derivatives are not only used to hedge the price of an underlying asset. In the case above, if the price of real estate far exceeded $500,000 before the option expires, your option can be sold for $5000, $10,000, or higher. This is speculation.

So, now we understand there are two applications for derivatives in the world of finance– hedging and speculation.

Hedging and speculation are the two forms of applications of derivatives in the world of finance.

No discussion of better risk management would be complete without mentioning derivatives and the technologies that spawned them and so many other changes in banking and finance. Derivatives have permitted financial risks to be unbundled in ways that have facilitated both their measurement and their management. Because risks can be unbundled, individual financial instruments can now be analyzed in terms of their common underlying risk factors, and risks can be managed on a portfolio basis. Concentrations of risk are more readily identified, and when such concentrations exceed the risk appetites of intermediaries, derivatives and other credit and interest rate risk instruments can be employed to transfer the underlying risks to other entities. As a result, not only have individual financial institutions become less vulnerable to shocks from underlying risk factors, but also the financial system as a whole has become more resilient.

-Remarks by Federal Reserve Chairman - Alan Greenspan, October 5, 2004

At the American Bankers Association Annual Convention, New York, New York

So, according to the Federal Reserve Chairman, derivatives are excellent financial instruments that can hedge against risk, don't you think?

The World's Biggest Market

The derivative market is the largest market in the world, right now.

1.   Derivatives Market

2.   Currency Market

3.   The Bond Market

4.   The Stock Market (i.e. Equity Market)

5.   The Commodities Market

6.   The Real Estate Market

The reason the derivative market is so large is because numerous derivatives are available on virtually every possible investment asset you can think of. Derivatives can be applied to stocks, commodities, real estate, bonds, and FX.

Just last year, the size of the derivative market was estimated to be $1.2 quadrillion. Anything quadrillion is very dangerous.

Why Derivatives are Weapons of Mass Destructions?

Despite the cause of the financial crisis in 2008 being due to the subprime mortgage meltdown, derivatives played a large role in the crisis. American International Group (AIG), the world's biggest insurer with $1 trillion in assets, lost $99.2 billion in 2008 because of exposure to derivatives.

Before the housing market in U.S. collapsed, U.S.'s mortgages were pooled and packaging together in the form of MBS. They were done with a financial tool, known as collateralized debt obligation (CDO), which bundles various types of debts from low risks to high risks, called tranches.

AIG saw this as an opportunity for insurance and presented an option to insure these CDO with a derivative, called credit default swap (CDS).

What are CDS?

A CDS, as its name suggests, swaps the risks of credit default from the CDS buyer to the CDS seller. The reason AIG insured these CDO with CDS is because the chance of paying out the insurance of default of CDO is highly unlikely. And they were right for a while. AIGFP, one of AIG's divisions, had their revenue rise from $737 million in 1999 to $3.2 billion in 2005 due to CDS.

However, AIG was on the wrong side of the bet as CDO defaults rose to a high level. AIG was on the brink of collapse.

Since AIG is a large international company, if AIG is allowed to collapse, many other banks and companies around the world that invest in or are insured by AIG will crumble like a house of cards. In addition, many other big financial firms, like Goldman Sachs, had $20 billion tied to AIG's business. AIG is simply too big to fail. Instead of allowing AIG to collapse, AIG received a bailout package of $85 billion from the Federal Reserve.

[**Note**: CDO is not a derivative but a security.]

The problem with CDS(s) is that they are OTC and highly unregulated. Trades are conducted privately and have zero visibility. Participants in OTC derivatives bear the risk of their trading party defaulting. This is counterparty risk.

OTC derivative transaction is a threat to the stability of the global economy.

The Rise of Shadow Banking

Financial Stability Board (FSB) is an international body that monitors and accesses the vulnerability affecting the global financial system and proposes actions needed to address them.

In 2014, the broadest measure of the shadow banking industry, referred to as the Monitoring Universe of Non-Bank Financial Intermediation (MUNFI), grew $5 trillion in 2013 to reach $75 trillion. This was 120% of the global GDP, or a quarter of the total financial assets in the world.

But what exactly is the shadow banking industry?

Below is an explanation from Bloomberg.

Shadow banking tends to take off when strict banking regulations are in place, when real interest rates and yield spreads are low and investors search for higher returns, and when there is a large institutional demand for assets........The current environment in advanced economies seems conducive to further growth of shadow banking.

Too many regulations and record low interest rates are encouraging investors to look elsewhere outside the conventional banking sector. The service that shadow banking system provides includes CDS, hedge funds, private lending, securities lending, insurance etc. Most often, shadow banks are the financial intermediates, and they do not take deposits like commercial banks; therefore, they are not subject to the same regulations. Shadow banks can be any business that offers credit-related product and services. This includes General Electric offering GE credit to have a transaction, an individual using Ford Motor Credit to buy a new car, or AIG insurance. The reason it is called shadow is because it operates outside the regular banking system and is not controlled by regulators.

The problem with shadow banking is governments around the world find it difficult to control the economy using interest rate or currency supply, which will eventually lead to systemic risk – a risk that can bring down the entire global economy.

Conspiracy of the Rich

Who are the biggest winners of the derivative bubble of 2008?

If you look at the top six performing banks in the U.S. and their asset holding, it will serve as a good indicator to tell us whom these winners are.

Top Six Largest Financial Holding Companies in U.S.

Reporting Period - quarter ended 20160331 :

Name	Net Income	Assets
	(USD, in thousands)	
JPMORGAN CHASE & CO.	5,520,000	2,423,808,000
BANK OF AMERICA CORPORATION	2,680,000	2,188,633,000
WELLS FARGO & COMPANY	5,462,000	1,849,182,000
CITIGROUP INC.	3,501,000	1,800,967,000
GOLDMAN SACHS GROUP, INC., THE	1,135,000	878,102,000
MORGAN STANLEY	1,134,000	807,497,000

Figure 8.3: Top Six Largest Financial Holding Companies in U.S.

Source: http://ibanknet.com/

The top-performing bank is JP Morgan Chase & Co with a total asset of $2.42 trillion USD. The total asset of these six financial holding companies is equal to a mind-boggling $9.9 trillion USD. This is close to China's GDP in 2014!

What is more interesting is their derivative holding.

Each year, these companies must file a 10-K as SEC filing is part of their annual report.

JP Morgan Chase & Co Total Derivative notional amount in 2014 & 2015

Notional amount of derivative contracts
The following table summarizes the notional amount of derivative contracts outstanding as of December 31, 2015 and 2014.

	Notional amounts (b)	
December 31, (in billions)	2015	2014
Interest rate contracts		
Swaps	$ 24,162	$ 29,734
Futures and forwards	5,167	10,189
Written options	3,506	3,903
Purchased options	3,896	4,259
Total interest rate contracts	36,731	48,085
Credit derivatives (a)	2,900	4,249
Foreign exchange contracts		
Cross-currency swaps	3,199	3,346
Spot, futures and forwards	5,028	4,669
Written options	690	790
Purchased options	706	780
Total foreign exchange contracts	9,623	9,585
Equity contracts		
Swaps	232	206
Futures and forwards	43	50
Written options	395	432
Purchased options	326	375
Total equity contracts	996	1,063
Commodity contracts		
Swaps	83	126
Spot, futures and forwards	99	193
Written options	115	181
Purchased options	112	180
Total commodity contracts	409	680
Total derivative notional amounts	$ 50,659	$ 63,662

(a) For more information on volumes and types of credit derivative contracts, see the Credit derivatives discussion on pages 218–220 of this Note.
(b) Represents the sum of gross long and gross short third-party notional derivative contracts.

Figure 8.4: JP Morgan Chase & Co Total Derivative notional amount in 2014 & 2015

Source: http://investor.shareholder.com/jpmorganchase

JP Morgan Chase & Co's total derivative notional amount is $50,659 trillion USD. This included everything, such as interest rate contracts, credit derivatives, foreign exchange contracts, equity contracts, and commodity contracts.

If you combined all the six financial holding companies' derivative notional amount, it is a figure equal to $238 trillion USD, which is 20% of all the existing derivative contracts in the world.

Notional Amount of Derivative Contracts of the Six Largest Banks in U.S.

September 30,2015 (in US billion)

J.P.Morgan Chase & Co	$51,352
Bank of America Corporation	$45,243
Wells Fargo & Company	$6,074
CitiGroup Inc	$53,042
Goldman Sachs Group, Inc	$51,148
Morgan Stanley	$31,054

Table 8.1: Notional Amount of Derivative Contracts of the Six Largest Banks in U.S.

Source: http://www.occ.treas.gov

With such a staggering amount of derivatives in their balance sheets, when these derivatives fail, the Federal Reserve will bail them out at the expense of the taxpayer in the name of saving the global financial market. It makes one wonder if the U.S. government is regulating the banks or if the banks are regulating the U.S. government.

But, how are these six banks allowed to accumulate such a staggering amount of derivatives at the beginning?

Fall of Glass-Steagall Act

During the Great Depression, almost 5000 banks failed, and $140 billion vaporized through bank failure. In the first 100 days of U.S. President Franklin Roosevelt's presidency in 1933, he had enacted measures to ease the financial pain of the public and to close the loopholes that fueled *the Great Depression*.

One of the statutes enacted during *the Great depression* was the

Banking Act of 1933, which is also known as *Glass-Steagall Act.*

The Banking Act of 1933 is the statute that establishes the F*ederal Deposit Insurance Corporation (FDIC)* - an independent agency created by U.S. Congress to insure deposits in commercial banks. Prior to that, if a bank failed, all the depositors' deposits would be lost. Today, each depositor is insured to at least $250,000 per insured bank.

Glass-Steagall Act was an act passed by the U.S. Congress as the *Banking Act of 1933*. The act was crucial to stopping the unprecedented bank run and restoring the public's broken confidence in the banking system.

If you recall *the Great Depression*, you will understand it was pure speculation. Ironically, it wasn't only the public speculating; the banks played a very large part in this speculation as well.

Prior to *the Great Depression*, the distinctions between commercial banks and investment banks were cloudy. Commercial banks, like J.P. Morgan & Co, could take on huge risks with depositors' money by investing bank assets and selling securities through IPO. The *Glass-Steagall Act* was a response to *the Great Depression* by creating a firewall that separates commercial banks' activities from investment banks' activities. Commercial banks can only take in deposits and lend to individuals and business; investment banks can only sell securities to investors and manage mergers and acquisitions. Commercial banks cannot operate as an investment bank.

Because of the *Glass-Steagall Act*, J.P. Morgan & Co was separated into J.P.Morgan Chase & Co (i.e., commercial bank) and Morgan Stanley (i.e., investment bank).

There are no restrictions that prevent banks from amassing its financial power in other sectors, such as underwriting insurance.

In 1956, the Congress had reinforced this firewall by extending the *Glass-Steagall Act* with the *Bank Holding Company Act*. This act was to build a firewall between banking and insurance and closed the loophole for bank holding companies to own both bank and non-banking businesses.

Despite these benefits of financial regulations from the *Glass-Steagall Act* in the U.S., other countries around the world gained comparative financial advantages, because they do not have as many regulations as the U.S.

As a result, President Bill Clinton repealed part of the *Glass-Steagall Act* through the *Gramm-Leach-Bliley Act of 1999*. This removed the barriers among commercial banks, investment banks, and insurance companies set by the *Glass-Steagall Act*.

Although it might be controversial whether the *Glass-Steagall Act* could have prevented the Financial Crisis of 2008, we cannot deny that financial deregulation and the improper use of derivatives helped to fuel the crisis from non-bank sectors, like Enron, AIG, Lehman Brothers, and Bear Sterns.

Final Words on Derivatives

Although derivatives are financial weapons of mass destruction, so is uranium 238. From uranium 238, you can build a nuclear power plant to provide electricity for a country; from uranium 238, you can also build a nuclear bomb that can devastate a country. So, the risk associated with derivatives is not the derivatives themselves; it is how people use them that decides the risk.

Some More Interesting Facts about Derivatives

Although derivatives are often referred to as a high-tech financial trading tool, it existed a long time ago.

Around 1700, the Japanese economy was largely based on rice as a medium of exchange. Back then, Samurais were not paid in yen but rice.

During that period, Japanese landlords would store the surplus of rice in warehouses and then issue vouchers to promise the delivery of rice at a future date. So, these vouchers represent the right to take delivery of a quantity of rice at a future date at a specified price. Since these vouchers become transferrable, a new market in the buying and selling of vouchers was formed. These rice vouchers were traded on the Dojima Rice Exchange near Osaka in 1730.

Dojima Rice Exchange is considered by many to be the first future (derivative) market.

PART II

HOW TO RESTORE
THE GLOBAL PROSPERITY

Chapter 9

A Seven Billion Balloon

"The test of a first-rate intelligence is the ability to hold two opposed ideas in the mind at the same time, and still retain the ability to function.""

-F Scott Fitzgerald

Before we continue with the second part of the book, I would like to share an interesting concept with you.

What do you think of the following picture?

Is it a floor or ceiling?

Figure 9.1: Optical Illusion

Or can it be both a floor and a ceiling?

Optical illusions play tricks with our mind. It tricks us into believing that something isn't true. One reason investing becomes so difficult today is because of the wealth illusion painted by our great artists in the 21st century – our mainstream and financial experts. Since a picture is worth a thousand words, what I am about to show you is one of the biggest optical illusions in the stock market no mainstream media want you to see.

Optical Illusion of the Stock Market

Below is a chart of Hong Kong Hang Send Index (^HSI), which is the stock exchange in Hong Kong. The blue line (HIS measured in HKD) is the graph we see on television broadcast by mainstream media. From December 1969 to December 2011, ^HIS had risen 132.7 times.

HONG KONG HANG SENG INDEX (^HSI) in Dollar and Value

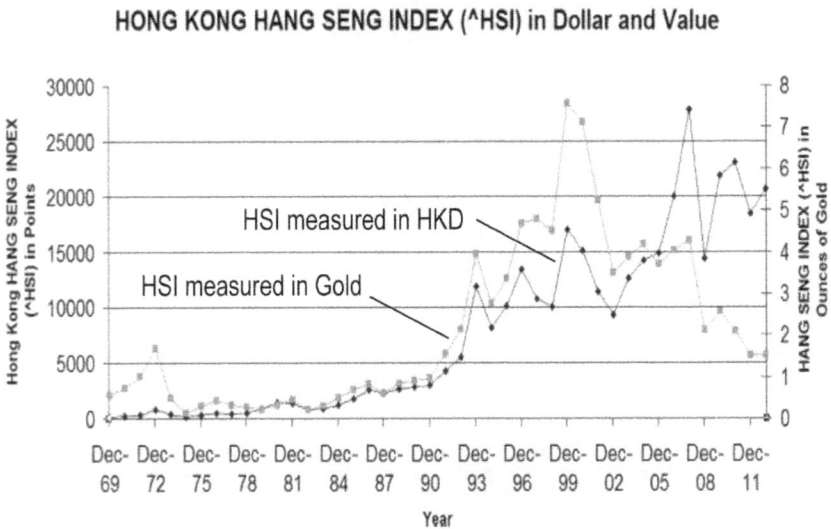

Figure 9.2: Hong Kong Hang Seng Index in dollar and Value

Source: Author

Stocks in points are much like chips in a casino. Instead of measuring the index in dollar, points are measurement units.

From 1969 until today, you will see the stock market is climbing one way – UP.

If you look at the stock exchange in your own country, I bet you will see a similar picture.

But what is wrong with this picture?

If the stock market is really a good indicator of all the wealth we generated in the economy, shouldn't we be wealthier?

The answer lies in the orange line of the graph.

The orange line measures ^HIS in ounces of gold, which is how many ounces of gold required to buy a share of ^HIS.

Historically, it took an average of two ounces of gold to buy a share of ^HSI. Since 2003, just when everyone thought the stock market was about to take off again as China entered the world trade organization (WTO), the stock market measured in gold had crashed. ^HSI measured in gold (i.e., real money) had been crashing for the entire decade!

This is telling us that a lot of true wealth was moving out of the stock market since 1999, while a lot of paper dollars were created and circulated. Does that reinforce what we learnt in the first part of the book?

But what is the point of measuring the stock market in gold?

"Money is gold, and nothing else."

-J.P. Morgan

The message behind this chart is telling us that the stock market is going up in price, while it is falling in value. If you price the stock market, not in points, which is a derivative of the paper dollar, but in other commodities, like livestock, silver, or oil, I bet you will probably get a similar pattern.

A Word of Caution

A famous American novelist, Francis Scott Fitzgerald, once said the test of first-rate intelligence is the ability to hold two opposed ideas in the mind at the same time and still retain the ability to function.

If you can allow the above example to sink in, then congratulations; you are ready for the rest of the book.

Part II of the book is about solutions on how to restore global prosperity. The solutions you will encounter might contradict your beliefs or values, but I hope you can open your mind, just like how you opened your mind to understand the optical illusion of the stock market.

One of the main problems of our school system is that it wires students to think in terms of "right" or "wrong." Ironically, things in the real world are not merely as simple as a right or wrong answer.

Let me give you some examples of the controversial statements I am referring to:

1) Real Estate will always going to go up!

2) Gold will skyrocket to $15,000 USD per ounce.

3) Australia is a different country.

4) QE will always cause inflation.

5) Getting in University will always guarantee that you have a good future.

6) Real Estate is all about demand and supply.

7) Getting a good academic grade is crucial to success.

8) Negative interest rate just doesn't make sense.

9) Taxing the rich can solve the problem of poverty.

The list can go on and on and on....

A Seven Billion Balloon

In November 2011, the world marked its birth of 7 billion humans living on earth.

Interestingly, this rapid growth in population only existed in the past century.

It may surprise you that it took the world 1800 years to reach a population of 1 billion. And it was not until 1930 when the world population hit 2 billion.

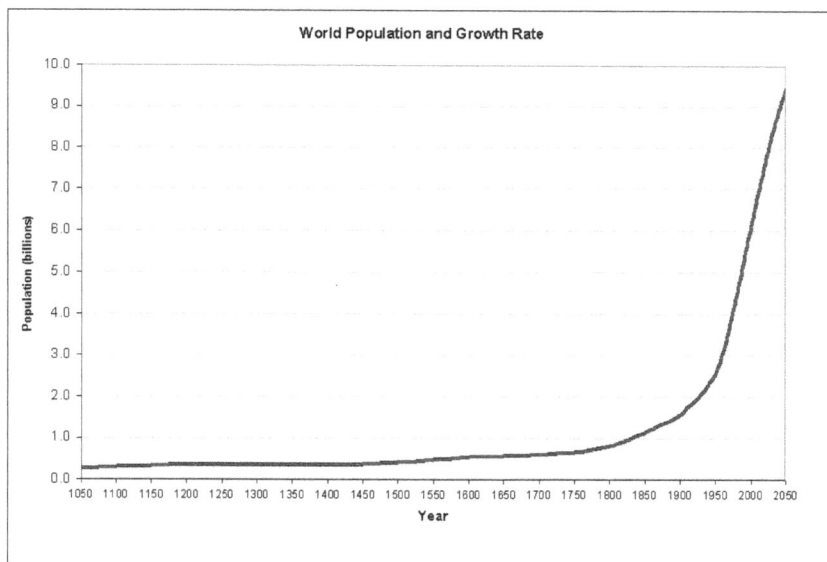

Figure 9.3: World Population Growth

Source: http://blog.dssresearch.com

If you recall your high school mathematics, this growth is called exponential growth.

What caused the world population to explode since the 20th century?

If you refer to the TCMD in earlier chapters, you will discover these two charts are almost identical to each other.

It makes one wonder if population growth is driving debt growth or debt growth is driving economic growth.

What will happen to the world population if debt reaches a point where it can no longer grow?

Chapter 10

How to Restore the Global Prosperity

"There are two and only two ways that any economy can be organized. One is by freedom and voluntary choice—the way of the market. The other is by force and dictation—the way of the State."

-Murray N. Rothbard

If I used an analogy to describe the global economy, I would picture it as a hot-air balloon being inflated by credit, instead of air. Floating on top of the bubble are all the assets like stock, property, bond, precious metals, and the world's seven billion people.

What makes this balloon different is that it is full of holes on every side, and credit keeps leaking out.

For years now, the balloon has had a tendency to sink.

And every time this balloon sinks, central banks around the world reflate it back by injecting credits into it; the harder it is trying to deflate, the harder policy makers around the world will reflate it.

The only reason the balloon is still in the air is because the government and central banks around the world are pumping in more credit to replace the credit destroyed when the private sector defaulted on the debts.

U.S.'s QE programs, China's printing of RMB by intervening its local currency, Europe's LTRO, and Japan's QE to combat deflation are some examples of the government's reflationary actions.

Lesson from the Great Depression

"I would like to say to Milton and Anna: Regarding the Great Depression. You're right, we did it. We're very sorry. But thanks to you, we won't do it again"

-Ben S. Bernanke

Ben Bernanke was the Chairman of the Federal Reserve from 2006 to 2014. His recent book, *The Courage to Act*, is his story on how the Federal Reserve arrested the contagion and prevented an economic collapse of unimaginable scale.

In 2002, Ben Bernanke made this startling admission in a speech given in honor of Milton Friedman's 90th birthday: "I would like to say to Milton and Anna: Regarding the Great Depression. You're right; we did it. We're very sorry. But thanks to you, we won't do it again."

It can be seen that Milton Friedman's view on the Great Depression played a large role on the Federal Reserve's policy response towards the financial crisis of 2008.

But what did Milton Friedman suggest? What hadn't the Federal Reserve done during the Great Depression? Why did the Federal Reserve Chairman make such a startling admission? What is the lesson of the Great Depression?

[**Note**: Milton Friedman was the great free market champion and one of the most influential economists of the past 200 years.]

In 1950, Milton Friedman and Anna Schwartz compiled historical data about U.S.'s monetary history. In Milton's book - *A Monetary History of the United States, 1867–1960*, he shared his discovery about the cause of the Great Depression that is controversial to traditional explanation about the cause of the Great Depression.

Milton's finding discovered that the Great Depression was not necessarily a direct result of the stock market crash of October 1929, over-speculation of the 20s, and speculative investment. Instead, it was a failure of government, a failure of monetary policy, and a failure of the Federal Reserve System to act with the intention of those who established it.

Basically, Milton suggested the government and the Federal Reserve should have stepped in during the Great Depression and should not have allowed the market force to rebalance the economy.

Due to the Federal Reserve's inaction, from 1929 to 1933, the total M2 money supply declined by one-third. The total number of banks went down by one-third.

Milton argues the Federal Reserve could have prevented the decline in money supply at any time. If the Federal Reserve acted sooner, the Great Depression could have been mild and ended by the middle of 1930, and it would not have been a major catastrophe for the rest of the world – famine killed millions of people in the U.S. and U.S. GDP contracted by 46% during the Great Depression

Could it be true that Milton's argument is correct? Should the government really have stepped in during such a catastrophic event? Is more debt the solution to debts? Is printing more money the lesson being learnt from the Great Depression? What ended the Great Depression?

Before criticizing Milton's argument, it is valuable to understand his logic behind it, as this might give us insights on how to restore global prosperity.

The Two Schools of Economics

"The ideas of economists and political philosophers, both when they are right and when they are wrong, are more powerful than is commonly understood. Indeed the world is ruled by little else. Practical men, who believe themselves to be quite exempt from any intellectual influence, are usually the slaves of some defunct economist."

- John Maynard Keynes

There is a century-old unsettled debate among economists whether government intervention is beneficial to an economy. They are Keynesian economics and Austrian economics.

Ludwig von Mises is one of the most influential members of the Austrian School of Economics. Austrian Economics persuasively summarized the role of credit played in the Business Cycle and how credit through fractional reserve banking created the boom. However, the banking system will eventually run out of money to lend, and the credit ceases to expand. Everything reverses like the swing of a pendulum. And a depression begins. The depression will cleanse away all the mal-investments during the boom and destroy the credit and savings that financed it initially. At some point, a new equilibrium will be attained again, and the cycle repeats.

"There is no means of avoiding the final collapse of a boom brought about by credit expansion. The alternative is only whether the crisis should come sooner as the result of voluntary abandonment of further credit expansion, or later as a final and total catastrophe of the currency system involved."

- Ludwig von Mises, 1949

Ludwig von Mises thinks a bust caused by credit expansion is inevitable.

Austrian economists proposed that interest rate is the key in business cycles. When the Federal Reserve sets interest rates lower than the market would, then credit expansion takes place, which causes an artificial boom. So by creating even more credit to combat a depression during the bust is like attempting to cure the same evil by the very means that brought it about. The underlying problem is a misdirection of production due to false interest rate signal.

John Maynard Keynes, a brilliant and intelligent academic in the 20th century, is the spearhead of Keynesian Economics. The reason our current economic curriculum is divided into two sets of economic laws - macroeconomic (i.e., for nations and government) and microeconomic (i.e., for individuals) is because of Keynesian theory.

Keynesian economists believe aggregate demand is the key in business cycles. They advocate that spending, not saving, drives economic growth. A government can smooth out of volatility of the market by expanding the money supply, running large budget deficit, and stimulating the economy with an artificially low interest rate.

It appeared that the Austrian clearly made more sense.

What will happen if we adopt the Austrian's theory to restore global prosperity?

How to Restore the Global Prosperity?

Imagine if the hot-air balloon at the beginning of this chapter is allowed to deflate by natural force, and the central banks around the world cease to pump credit in it. What do you think will happen to the 7 billion people on top?

Well, the balloon will crash to the ground.

If that balloon were close to the ground surface, the severity would be minimum. And the 7 billion inhabitants would probably survive.

This is not quite the case for our ballooned economy today – we have set the world altitude record for the highest hot air balloon flight in history.

Austrian economists, like Ludwig von Mises, proposed there is no means of avoiding the final collapse of a boom brought about by credit expansion, and abandon of further credit expansion will avoid a total catastrophic collapse. And they were right, if the world was under a classical gold standard, where gold is money and credit was tight.

To glance into the future for a possible solution on how to restore global prosperity, it is necessary to compare The Great Depression and the financial crisis of 2008.

During the Great Depression, the Federal Reserve remained inactive and allowed the market force to correct the economy. They took a different policy response during the Financial Crisis of 2008 as they expanded their balance sheet aggressively.

The Great Depression (1930)	Financial Crisis of 2008
Nominal GDP felt by 45% between 1929 and 1933 and did not recover until 1941	Nominal GDP rose 10% between 2008 and 2012
The stock market fell 87% and did not recover until 1954	The stock market fell 49% but recovered by 2013
Unemployment peaked at 25% in 1933 and 20% in 1938	Unemployment peaked at 10% in 2009 and 5% in 2016
Global trade collapse	Global trade contracted by 20% in 2009 but recovered by 2010
International banking collapsed	Bailout prevented the banks from collapsing
Depression caused WWII	No war

Table 10.1: Comparison of 1930 Great Depression and the Financial Crisis of 2008

If we adopted the Austrian approach today and allowed the free market force to act, the result could have been far worse than the Great Depression.

Debt growth results in population growth, and a collapse in debt means a collapse in population.

Now, the global economic balloon is too high in the sky. To continue global prosperity, it seems that it is impossible to take the Austrian's free market approach of volunteer collapse. Central banks around the world had worked too hard to prevent that from happening, since the financial crisis of 2008.

And this had left us one option – continue to expand the credit supply.

But can central banks and our governments around the world print our way to prosperity?

In my first book, *"Corruption of Real Money"*, I have outlined the details of the Great Depression and how the government's New Deal program was a failure. I have discussed how a wrong lesson has been learnt from the Great Depression, and the Federal Reserve's monetary policy is treating the symptom, rather than curing the disease.

That statement is true.

If the free market is allowed to work today, and bubbles around the world were allowed to deflate, the world will eventually return to equilibrium in a very unforgiving way.

This is the eighth year into the financial crisis of 2008, and the main reason the world is still experiencing slow growth today is because our credit bubble is deflating by the market force, but governments are trying to inflate the deflating bubble to maintain our level of prosperity.

Does that mean printing currency can only delay the inevitable collapse?

As a student of Austrian economics, I oppose the idea of printing currency, as it makes no sense in the context of the Austrian economics framework.

However, if Ludwig von Mises was still alive, it would be interesting for him to explain how the graph below is possible.

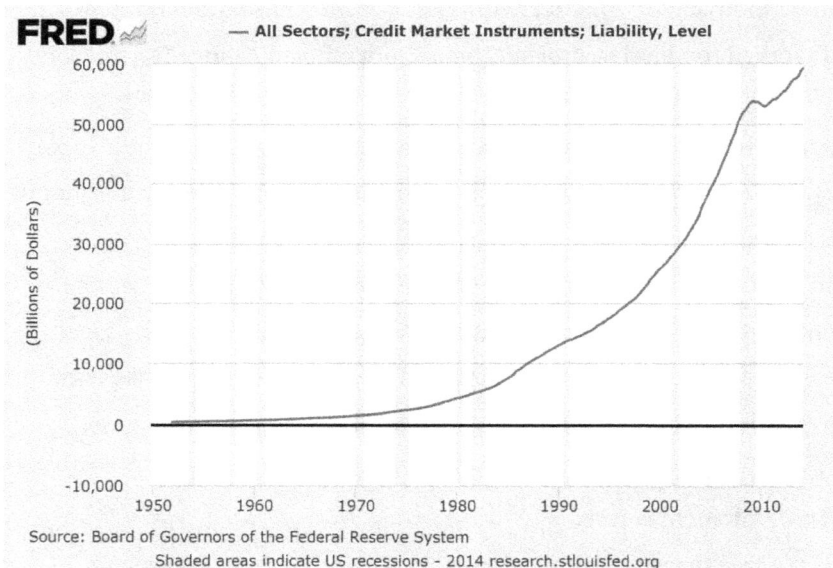

Figure 10.1: Federal Reserve - Total Credit Markte Debt (TCMD)

Our current economic system no longer works like the times of Ludwig von Mises. Mises might have been correct a century ago, but we are living in a global dollar system, where the old rules of economics are no longer applicable if governments interfere in the market.

In Mises's age, where the world was in a classical gold standard, QE programs of the scale we see today would be impossible as it would cause high, if not, hyperinflation. This did not happen in U.S. nor Europe.

One of the main reasons such massive QE programs become sustainable is because of the unprecedented force of globalization, which is highly deflationary. Instead of hiring someone in the U.S. for $200 USD, a U.S. company can hire a Chinese or Indian for $10 USD or less per day.

Instead of viewing QE as a dangerous tool, QE is a very useful monetary policy to sustain the level of prosperity in the world temporarily. Each president must incur twice as much debt when the leave the office than when he came in. And this is exactly what is happening.

Do you mean the solution to our debt problem is to incur more debts?

Yes and No. During the Great Depression, President Roosevelt's New Deal program was a failure, despite increasing state and federal expenditures on welfare from virtually nothing ($9 million) to $479 million. That government spending resulted in high inflation, as globalization was non-existent back then. So, non-productive deficit spending did more harm than good. As a result, the Great Depression resurfaced in 1937.

Wasteful government deficit spending will not help to restore global prosperity.

So, are there any examples in history where productive use of deficit spending restored the global prosperity?

If you have read *Corruption of Real Money*, I have detailed how World War II was the medicine of The Great Depression. Many people feared the world would slide back into the Great Depression after WWII. However, it did not. The miracle prosperity baby boomers enjoyed is lasting even today.

The reason is because of productive use of debt.

Here is a quote from *Corruption of Real Money*:

> *During WWII, government spending was unprecedented. Between 1940 to 1945, Federal Spending went from $9.47 billion to $72.11 billion. Military spending went from $1.66 billion to $64.53 billion. These might not sound a lot in today's dollar terms, but it was an astronomically large number during that period...*

> Source: *Corruption of Real Money pg 145*

Productive use of government deficit spending during WWII is a classic example of how a country in severe economic crisis can restore global prosperity. By spending productively on manufacturing, technology, and developing new industries, the return of that massive spending had not only lifted the U.S. out of the Great Depression, but also locked in decades of prosperity the world had never seen.

Chapter 11

A Second Look at Quantitative Easing

Before beginning this chapter, I would like to show you the chart below.

This is the U.S.'s adjusted monetary base.

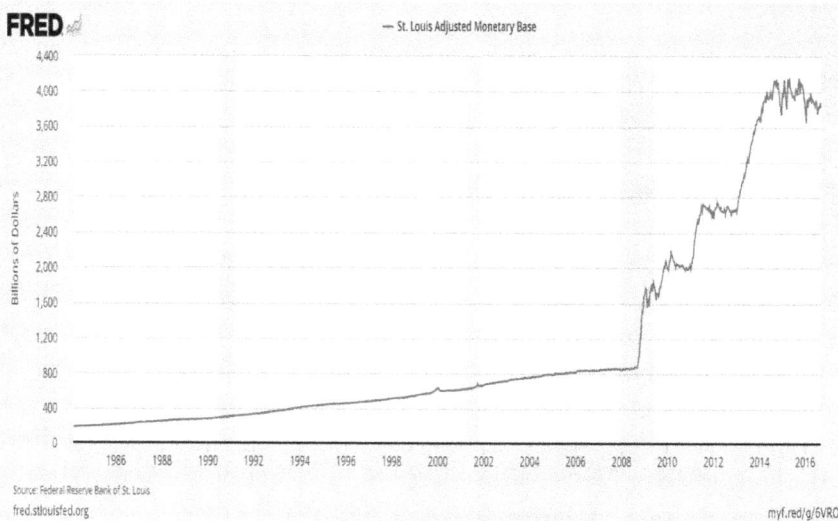

Figure 11.1: Adjusted monetary base

Source: Federal Reserve

It took 200 years from the coinage Act of 1792 until 2008 for zero monetary base to reach $850 billion USD. When the financial crisis happened in 2008, the Federal Reserve expanded the currency supply through quantitative easing to prevent the credit from contracting.

The expansion of credit from $850 billion USD to $3.82 trillion kept the world from collapsing into a Great Depression.

The Federal Reserve is adding $85 billion USD every single month, roughly 10% of the monetary base in 2008.

Next, I want to show you the TCMD again.

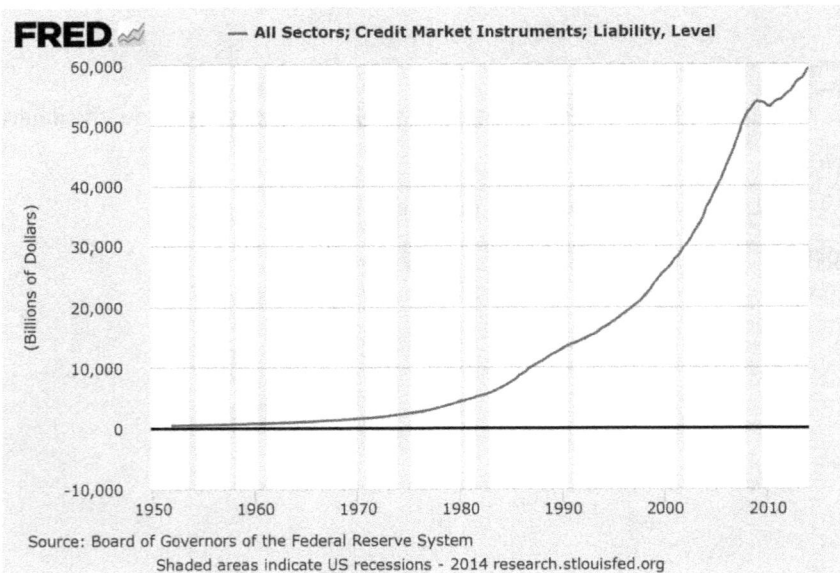

Figure 11.2: Federal Reserve - Total Credit Market Debt (TCMD)

Source: Federal Reserve

If you compare the monetary base to the TCMD, you will discover, even after the expansion of currency supply, the U.S. monetary base is only about 6.36% of the U.S. TCMD (i.e., $3.82 trillion / $60 trillion by 2016).

Monetary Inflation vs Asset Price Inflation

It is worth understanding that the Federal Reserve has no direct control of the TCMD; it can only influence it through monetary policies such as QE.

Everyone assumes QE can instantly create inflation; yet, this is not the case in reality.

There is a difference between monetary inflation and asset price inflation. What we see at the beginning of this chapter is an example of monetary inflation. Asset price might or might not follow, depending on when these currencies enter and circulate in our economy.

Most of the currency created by the Federal Reserve shored in the bank's balance sheet or is spent through deficit spending and then enters our economy fairly slowly. The Federal Reserve does that to instill public confidence in the banks and to make the bankrupted banks appear as if they are healthy.

From the graph below, you can see the excess reserve of banks was close to nothing, until the Federal Reserve printed all these excess reserves and placed them in the banks' balance sheets after the crisis of 2008.

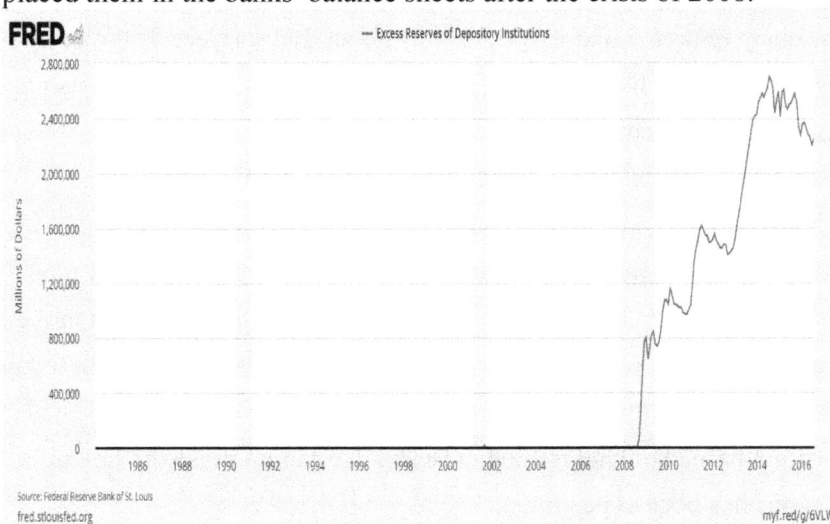

Figure 11.3: Federal Reserve – Excess Reserves of Depository Institutions

Source: Federal Reserve

Velocity of Money

Another reason QE might cause immediate asset price inflation is because of the velocity of money.

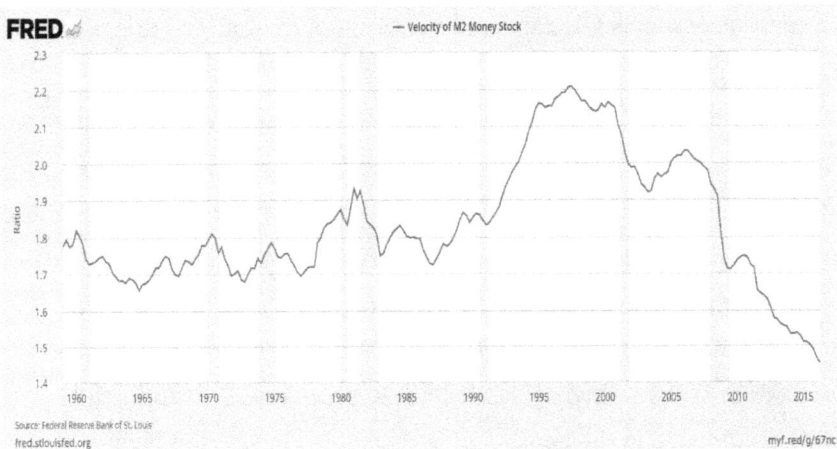

Figure 11.4: Federal Reserve – The Velocity of M2 Money Stock

Source: Federal Reserve

The velocity of money is the frequency one unit of currency is used to purchase goods and services within a given time. You can think of it as how many times a dollar is spent to buy goods and services. If the velocity of money is high, like at the beginning of 90s, there are more transactions happening in an economy.

A higher velocity of money has the same effect as an increase in currency supply.

If you examine the graph carefully, you will find the velocity of money was stable between the 1960s and 1990. After that, the velocity of money escalated, peaked in the late 90s, and then declined from 2000 until today. The slowdown in the velocity is offsetting the expansion of an adjusted monetary base. And that is another reason we cannot sense the inflation everyone has been expecting.

A Second Look at Quantitative Easing

I hope I have convinced you that the effect of QE depends largely on how it is being used.

Although the primary agenda of QE is to stimulate the economy and encourage banks to lend, its hidden agenda that is not announced is to reduce the government's deficit.

Can QE be used to reduce government debt? How is this supposed to work?

Under the dollar standard, our supply of monetary base can be expanded indefinitely. How QE behaves under the dollar standard differs greatly from the Bretton Wood system, where the credit supply is constrained.

But why is this important to understand?

It is because QE might be a solution to the debt crisis, and not a disaster, which is contradicting to many economists' beliefs.

In order to predict where the economy is going accurately, understanding the principle of sound money and the history of money is important, but insufficient. You must understand and be able to project government's monetary policies. In my opinion, applying old economic rules in the current economic climate is dangerously wrong.

In previous chapters, we understand that, if the demand of credit by the government is too high, it will cause interest rate to rise and crowd out the private sector, discourage private investment and consumption. Government cannot run high deficit, as the borrowing cost is high. This was the case where credit was tight and the supply of credit had constraints. However, it is no longer true today.

Today, with the help of QE, the supply of credit is abundant. Despite the government's large budget deficit with high demand of credit, the supply of credit through QE overwhelms the government's demand, and this pushes down the interest rate. That is why the private sector can continue to borrow and consume at this artificial low interest rate, and the government can continue to run large budget deficit.

The Federal Reserve monetizes the government debt this way.

However, what makes me believe QE is more than what it seems is the following table, extracted from the Federal Reserve 101st Annual Report in 2014.

Let me give you an analogy.

When you borrow money from your parents, theoretically, you will pay interest on your loan. You will write a loan receipt to your parents acting as your bond. Then your parents discovered you are going to college and give all the interest on your loan receipt back to you. That means you pay no interest on the money you borrow from your parents. The loan receipt you owed to your parents has been cancelled.

Do you mean the Federal Reserve creates currency and loans it to the U.S. government without charging interest?

Yes. And this is how governments around the world are cancelling their debts. When the Federal Reserve buys government bonds, it earns interest from the bonds. In 2014, the Federal Reserve's current net income amounted to $105 billion USD; Earning remittances to Treasury means the profits that the Federal Reserve earned are returned back to the Treasury, and this was $96.9 billion USD.

This is how QE is being used to reduce government debt.

This way of using QE to cancel government debt only works if the Federal Reserve keeps the government bond in its balance sheets and does not resell it back to the public.

Table 4. Income, expenses, and distribution of net earnings of the Federal Reserve Banks, 2014 and 2013		
Millions of dollars		
Item	2014	2013[1]
Current income	116,562	91,150
Loan interest income	2	6
SOMA interest income	115,933	90,503
Other current income[2]	627	641
Net expenses	10,715	9,135
Operating expenses	3,926	3,765
Reimbursements	-570	-530
Net periodic pension expense	383	617
Interest paid on depository institutions deposits and term deposits	6,862	5,223
Interest expense on securities sold under agreements to repurchase	112	60
Other expenses	2	0
Current net income	105,847	82,015
Net additions to (deductions from) current net income	-2,718	-1,029
Federal agency and government-sponsored enterprise mortgage-backed securities	81	51
Foreign currency translation losses	-2,907	-1,257
Net income (loss) from consolidated VIEs	110	181
Other deductions	-2	-4
Assessments by the Board of Governors	1,864	1,845
For Board expenditures	590	580
For currency costs	711	702
For Consumer Financial Protection Bureau costs[3]	563	563
Net income before providing for remittances to the Treasury	101,265	79,141
Earnings remittances to the Treasury	96,902	79,633
Net income (loss)	4,363	-492
Other comprehensive (loss) gain	-1,612	2,289
Comprehensive income	2,751	1,797
Total distribution of net income	99,653	81,430
Dividends on capital stock	1,686	1,650
Transfer to surplus and change in accumulated other comprehensive income	1,065	147
Earnings remittances to the Treasury	96,902	79,633

[1] Certain amounts relating to 2013 have been reclassified to conform to the current-year presentation.

[2] Includes income from priced services, compensation received for services provided, and securities lending fees.

[3] The Board of Governors assesses the Reserve Banks to fund the operations of the Consumer Financial Protection Bureau.

Figure 11.5: Federal Reserve Income, expense and distribution of net earnings

Source: Federal Reserve

Ending Japan's Debt Crisis

The Federal Reserve is not the only central bank cancelling the national debt this way.

For years, Japan has been renowned for having the world's largest government debt. Its public debt exceeded one quadrillion yen in 2013 and was more than twice its annual GDP.

To combat Japan's deflating economy in the past 26 years, Japan had been launching QE programs, and their target was to keep the inflation close to 2%.

The first QE was launched in March 2001. However, as you can see, the bank of Japan (BOJ)'s QE 1 appeared to have little to no impact on the inflation. (i.e., ~ 0 and 1%). Apart from that, it had also driven the interest rate to near zero for a long period, but failed to get the economy moving. After 5 years of the QE experiment, in 2006, Japan tapered the QE program. Nikkei dropped by 20%. The inflation rate went from positive to -3%.

Japanese Monetary Base and Price Level (CPI)

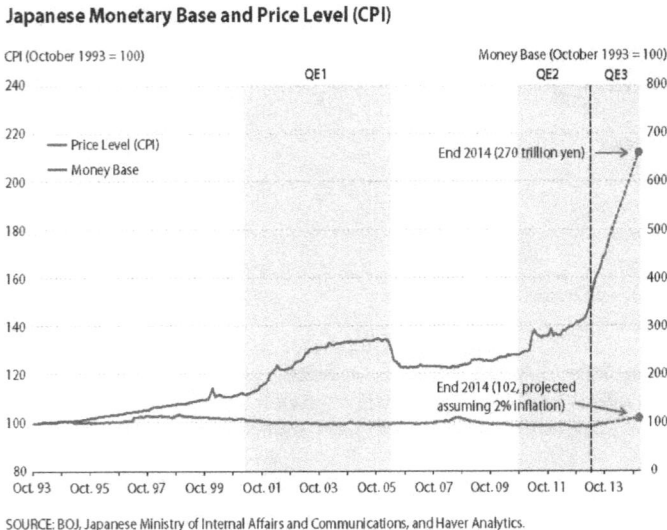

SOURCE: BOJ, Japanese Ministry of Internal Affairs and Communications, and Haver Analytics.

Figure 11.6: Bank of Japan's QE Program

Inflation Expectations in Japan

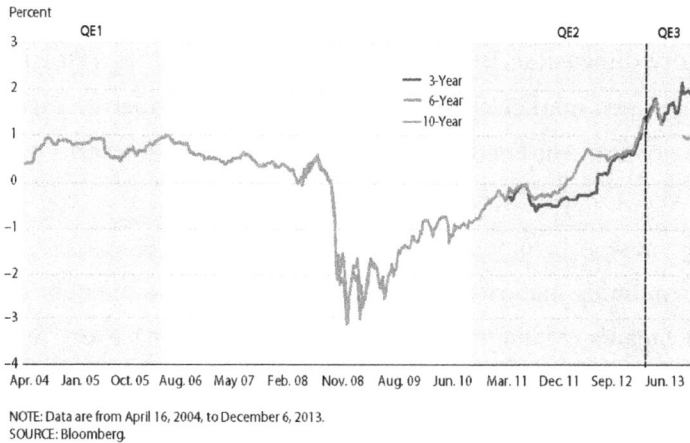

NOTE: Data are from April 16, 2004, to December 6, 2013.
SOURCE: Bloomberg.

Figure 11.7: Impact of BOJ's QE

So why didn't QE work in Japan? Is it possible that BOJ wasn't aggressive enough to expand its bond-buying program – then dropped it? Or is QE only a disaster?

Let's fast forward and have a look at what is happening today.

In Q4 2014, Japan shocked the financial market through increasing its size of QE program.

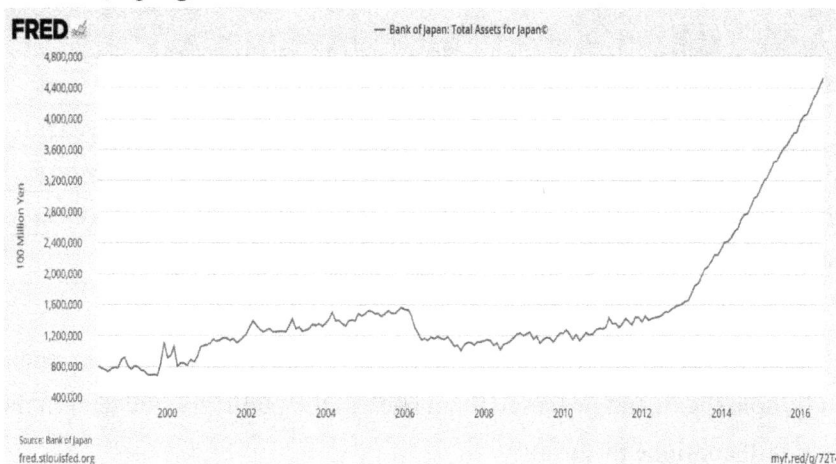

Figure 11.8: Bank of Japan Total Assets

Source: Federal Reserve

Quantitative and Qualitative Easing (QQE) is one of the latest monetary policies launched by BOJ to reach its price stability target of 2%. Regarding the quantity dimension, BOJ increased the size of QE to ¥80 trillion per year in the open market operation; in quality dimension, they purchased Japanese government bond at a pace of ¥80 trillion per year. That is why you can see a sharp increase in total asset of BOJ. Because of QQE, BOJ's Japanese government debt holding went from 10% to 35%. And the average remaining maturity of BOJ's purchase is approximately 13 years.

All of Japan's existing government debt is shrinking every month and could be cancelled.

[**Note**: Negative interest rate is the other monetary policy implemented by BOJ, apart from QQE]

Global Debt Cancellation

Public debts are acquired aggressively by central banks around the world through QE.

	Per Month	USD per month	Total Public Debt	Years to Cancel all public Debt
BOE	£8.75 billion	$11.4 billion	$2,084 billion	~ 16 years
BOJ	¥6.67 trillion	$66.7 billion	$10,460 billion	~ 13 years
ECB	€80 billion	$90.4 billion	$10,660 billion	~ 10 years
The Fed	$85 billion	$85.0 billion	$13,620 billion	~ 13 years
Total		$253.5 billion		

Table 11.1: Global QE

If the central banks around the world continue to buy back government bonds, hold them, and not resell them back to the public, public debt in the world will continue to shrink.

But Can Debt Be Cancelled that Easily...

Based on everything we have been taught about economics, central banks using QE to cancel government debt seems strange and should not work. After all, there is no such thing as free lunch.

However, our economy changed.

In the past, when globalization had not happened, if the U.S. government runs large deficit and the Federal Reserve prints currency at a rapid pace, the economy would be over-stimulated. The constraint of the Bretton Wood system would have prevented the U.S. from running a large trade deficit. If we looked back what had happened during the Vietnam war and Johnson's Great Program, such massive spending caused double digit inflation. This was typically how the economy worked when our dollars were backed by gold.

If you are trying to understand it in a traditional economic perspective, which is no longer applicable today, it is an absurd idea that the Federal Reserve prints over $3.5 trillion USD to buy government bonds.

Such massive printing of currency to finance government deficit would have already caused hyperinflation.

However, it has not.

Globalization, the dollar standard, and excessive capacity offset the massive effect of QE, and that is why it allows the Federal Reserve, BOJ, ECB, and BOE to print a massive amount of currency – at no cost.

But Why Won't the Central Banks Just Write all the Debt off?

When the governments pay interest to the central banks for their bond purchase, and when the central banks return these profits to the government while holding the bonds, the overall result is that the central banks are offsetting the interest the government paid on those government bonds owned by the central banks.

It is a debt cancellation in disguise.

Writing off these government debts will make the overall government to GDP ratio lower. Yet, I think central banks are saving this trick until the next economic crisis happens.

Be Prepared for Massive Global QE

Based on historic monetary policies since 2008, it is highly probable that governments worldwide will continue to do whatever it takes to keep the global economic bubble inflated through QE programs.

The world's credit growth is too weak to support economic growth, and China's economic bubble is deflating; consequently, the threat of deflation is high.

Be prepared for massive global QE to combat the force of deflation.

Chapter 12

International Minimum Wage

"Raising the minimum wage isn't just pro-worker; it's pro-economic growth."

-F Scott Fitzgerald

One of the fundamental reasons the world is facing such imbalance today is because of globalization.

Globalization makes it possible for many U.S. companies to shift their manufacturing base to developing countries. Instead of paying a U.S. employee $200 a day, there is an abundant supply of cheap labor willing to work for less than $10 per day. This created a scenario where developed companies are shipping their manufacturing jobs to developing countries, but people who earn a minimum wage in China cannot afford to buy the product they created.

But when did that begin to happen?

When the Bretton Wood system broke down, trade between nations no longer had to balance. Countries could print their currencies to manipulate their value to make export more competitive. Due to high competition, U.S. businesses relocated their factories to countries like China to drive down their wage expense and push up the profit margin. They push pressure on the idea of free trade.

No one was paying attention to the devaluation of the RMB.

From the early 80s to 1994, China devaluated its currency dramatically until it became the most competitive manufacturing base in the world.

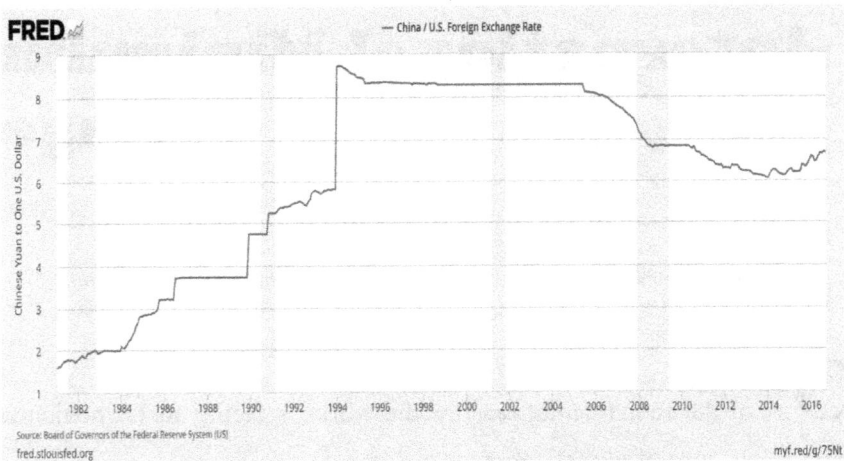

Figure 12.1: China / U.S. Foreign Exchange Rate

Source: Federal Reserve

That was when trade between China and the U.S. became hugely imbalanced.

Because of this flaw, China continues to be savers and exporters, and U.S. continues to be consumers and importers. Over the past three decades, a symbiotic relationship between China and U.S. formed. The $4 trillion dollars' worth of foreign exchange reserve accumulated by China's trade surplus with the U.S. transformed China to become the second largest economy in the world.

U.S. Interest Rate is Hijacked

Below is a chart showing the 10-year U.S. government bond yield. If you recall Chapter 3, we left off with a question on what determines the interest rate. And after understanding the entire picture of the global economy, you will realize that the U.S. interest rate is not solely set by the Federal Reserve, like many people believe.

The U.S. interest rate is largely influenced by China.

But how?

10 Year U.S. Government Bond Yield (Long Term Interest Rate)

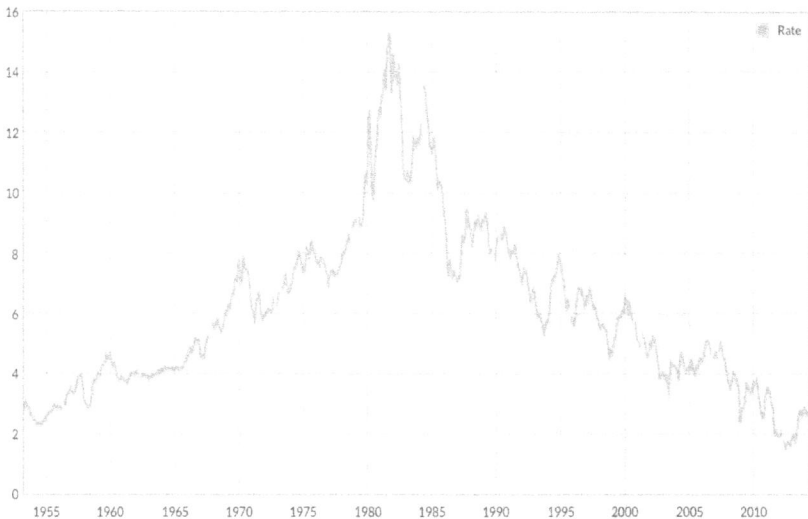

Figure 12.2: 10 Year U.S. Government Bond Yield

Source: Federal Reserve

When China exports cheap Chinese goods to the U.S., it exports deflation and pushes down the price of goods. To combat deflation and keep inflation rates close to 2%, U.S. must drive the interest rate down. Apart from that, China is the largest holder of U.S. Treasury bills, notes, and bonds. Out of the $4 trillion in these securities held by foreign countries, the amount China held accounts for $1.24 trillion. By accumulating so many government bonds, China played a leading role in pushing down the U.S. bond yield.

The reason, I believe, U.S.'s interest rate might remain low in the long-term is because of the China-U.S. symbiotic relationship. If U.S. does a **major** interest rate hike, the RMB will need to rise to maintain a close relationship with the dollar. However, a rising RMB will hurt the already weakened Chinese economy. To avoid that, China will retaliate by further depreciating its currency and exporting deflation to U.S.

That is why I think the U.S. interest rate is hijacked.

[**Note**: A small basis point in the U.S. interest rate hike is unlikely to hurt the China-U.S. relationship. So a small hike in interest rate is possible, but not a major rate hike.]

The Global Economy Knot

Excessive credit creation fueled by the U.S. trade deficit caused an imbalance in supply and demand; wage differentials between developed countries and underdeveloped countries are so great it will only encourage the imbalance of trade to persist.

Today, we are reaching a breaking point, where unemployment in developed countries, like U.S., is increasing, and the low wage workers, constituting a large proportion of the population in China, cannot afford the product they create.

This is the consequence of prolonged trade imbalance, which most economists believe is not a bad thing.

In order to permanently restore global prosperity, the balance of trade MUST be restored. The West must manufacture, invent, and produce more than they consume.

But how can we achieve that?

Consider, if the U.S. trade deficit contracts, millions of Chinese workers will lose their jobs. A shrink in U.S.'s import would cause a shrink in China's import, which would cause heavy damage to export led growth countries around the world. This is exactly what happened when U.S. shrank its import and export since the financial crisis of 2008.

If the U.S. trade deficit continues, the global imbalance will get worse until it is unsustainable– and we have reached this point already in 2016. Global demand is too weak to absorb the excessive supply. And the problem of overcapacity in the world is fueling the threat of deflation.

How do we arrange the global economy in such a way that Western countries can produce goods that the world needs, and at the same time, mass population in the developing countries can avoid massive unemployment or potentially benefit?

Before arriving at a solution, it is worth noting that it is too late to allow the free market to correct, because the cost outweighs its benefit for both the creditor nations and the debtor nations. If free market is allowed to work, and global trade is to balance in a way, like in the Breton Wood System, it could mean a massive correction in USD/ RMB. RMB will appreciate and Chinese will get even wealthier with the increase in purchasing power of RMB. U.S. will suffer decades of recessions. Since all the world currencies are pegged to the USD, the world will face a new great depression. This is a possible scenario that is unlikely to happen with the present of governments' fiscal and monetary policies.

But is it possible to restore trade imbalance not by free market?

International Minimum Wage

No solution is perfect. There is a plus and minus to everything.

One less destructive way to restore the trade imbalance is by massively increasing the international minimum wage.

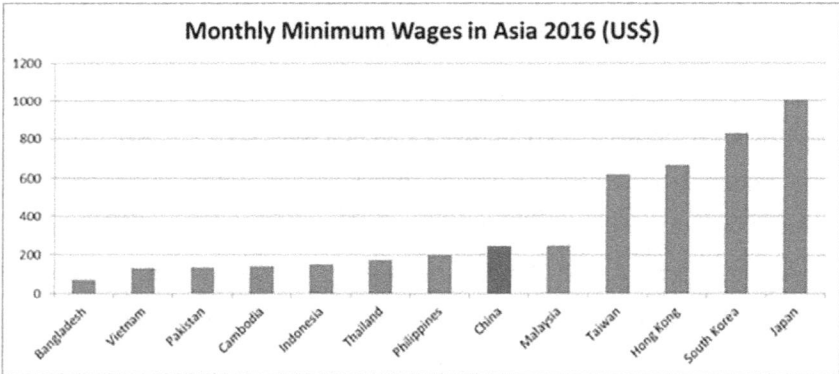

Figure 12.3: Monthly Minimum Wages in Asia in 2016
(The equivalent monthly rates are calculated on the basis of a 160 hour working month.)

Source: www.clb.org

The benefit of raising the international minimum is that third world countries will have an immediate effect that boosts the aggregate demand of the world. Take China as an example; instead of having a minimum wage of $200 per month, we could increase it to $250 per month. That way, we can shrink the gap of income polarization and create a wealth effect for low wage earners. Increasing international minimum wage is better than appreciating the value of RMB, because it only directly benefits the group of people who need a living wage.

For the West, an increase in international minimum wage alleviates the deflationary pressure caused by globalization. Instead of having a manufacturing base in China or Thailand, western companies can relocate them back in their home country. As this trend continues, jobs will return to the West.

However, massively raising the international minimum is not without challenges and drawback.

First, who will pay for the increase in minimum wages?

Wages must come from employers.

Is it even realistic for wages to triple, while businesses stagnate around the world?

It sounds ridiculous.

But an increase in the minimum wage is the only long-term solution to restore the balance of trade, where the benefits outweigh the cost among other alternatives.

In the age of fiat currency, it is not entirely impossible to use non-conventional ways to resolve global imbalance. After all, the origin of the U.S. trade imbalance was because our money is no longer backed by gold.

For that reason, I propose the following framework:

1)   An incremental, controlled amount of QE in developing countries. That QE package is funded by the government or through the help of IMF if necessary. QE will boost the purchasing power of 70% of the population living below poverty and stimulate the aggregate demand in the world. The reason this QE is incremental and controlled is to avoid high inflation or hyperinflation as these currencies will be spent in the economy. The amount of QE should be controlled such that it will not cause inflation to

rise over 2%.

This QE is only available to workers employed and earning a minimum wage.

2)   Reindustrialize the West. The U.S. government will relax tax law for start-ups, businesses, and manufacturing and technology industries (e.g. nanotechnology). If necessary, government will fund these new industries through budget deficit or QE. The goal is to invent the type of products demanded and affordable by the rest of the world. These types of products should be sophisticated, so they are not cost effective to plagiarize or counterfeit.

Despite the conditions not listed above and other risks involved, this is one of the least destructive ways to restore the balance of trade without a deflationary collapse. During the process, people working at a minimum wage will be greatly benefited.

Similar to how government spending ended the Great Depression in WWII, the world is in a war of imbalance today. If governments around the world can globally coordinate and spend diligently, I believe the global economic unbalance can be resolved, and once again, we can lock in decades of prosperity.

Chapter 13

Final Words

A person who has 20/10 vision can see twice as far away. I hope this book can provide you with such vision in the age of paper currency. More importantly, I hope you enjoy reading it.

Legacy of Debt is a phrase used by former British Prime Minister David Cameron, when he opposed to pass "Legacy of Debt" to our children. In a traditional sense, it means to reduce government budget deficit to restore global prosperity for our generation.

Free market approaches might correct global imbalance, but the price of extreme deflation far outweighs the benefits.

As the global deflationary pressures around the world intensify, and central banks around the world are printing massive amounts of currency to combat deflation, I am taking an alternative approach by embracing the use of the legacy of debt to restore global prosperity permanently.

Before closing this book, I wish to thank you for taking the time to read this book.

I truly believe that intelligence is the ability to hold two opposed ideas in the mind at the same time and still retain the ability to function. I hope the case I presented in this book can give you the whole picture about the current state of the global economy and ideas of what could be possible to restore global imbalance.

Last, I wish you all good luck.

Make use of this 20/10 vision.

The global economic crisis is far from over.

Recommended Readings

To further enhance your financial diligent

Economy

Man Economy and State with Power and Market (**Murray N. Rothbard**)

America's Great Depression (**Murray N. Rothbard**)

Crash Proof (**Peter D. Schiff**)

Free to Choose (**Milton Friedman and Rose Friedman**)

The Dollar Crisis (**Richard Duncan**)

Corruption of Capitalism (**Richard Duncan**)

Human Action (**Ludwig Von Mises**)

Monetary History and Money

Gold (**Nathan Lewis**)

A Primer on Money, Banking and Gold (**Peter L. Bernstein**)

Guide to Investing in Gold and Silver (**Michael Maloney**)

A Monetary History of the United States, 1857-1960 (**Milton Friedman**)

The Federal Reserve

End the Fed (**Ron Paul**)

The Creature of Jekyll Island (**G. Edward Griffin**)

The Case against the Fed (**Murray N. Rothbard**)

About the Author

Marco Chu Kwan Ching
Author, Investor

I began my profession as an electrical engineer in TOSHIBA after graduating from *The University of New South Wales* (UNSW) in 2009. I had a small web design business for indexing restaurants. I was firmly sitting on the dream of most undergraduates- a job and a part time business. With the collapse of the global economy in 2008, I first noticed how the effects of the financial crisis unfolded. I experienced the accelerating inflation rapidly eroding our wealth. I witnessed the foreclosures of businesses, income polarization, the interventions of the Government monetary policies. Even with little life experience on these subjects, I know something is not right. The current financial system is developing cracks. This sparked my interest in studying monetary history and the global economy. I set out to research the answers myself.

What I found shocked me to my core. The root of all the problems lie within our philosophy of money. The definition of money is flawed. Currency is not money. The original idea of money being a container to store the value of our labor, time, ideas, and talents are replaced by debts. Money, rather than being a store of value, becomes a plan to transfer our wealth away from us. My mission is to educate as many people as possible about these findings, so they are armed with the right knowledge to protect themselves and their family from this corrupt monetary system. That's why I am willing to give up my time to work on the material that now appears in the *Legacy of Debt*.

Thank you for Reading!

Thank you for reading this book! I know you could have picked from a dozens of books about this subject, but you took a chance with mine and I appreciate it.

Lastly, I just have one small request,

If you believe that this book is worth sharing, would you take a few seconds to let your friends know about it too? If you love my work, please feel free to leave a positive feedback on Amazon and Goodreads.

My contact:
https://www.facebook.com/marco.chu.10
https://www.goodreads.com/author/show/15944678.Marco_Chu_Kwan_Ching

Corruption of Real Money Facebook Page
https://www.facebook.com/CorruptionOfRealMoney/

Corruption of Real Money Twitter Page
https://twitter.com/CorruptionofMon

Goodreads Page
https://www.goodreads.com/book/show/32502564-legacy-of-debt

Corruption of Real Money Website
http://www.corruptionofrealmoney.com

***

Book Series by Marco Chu Kwan Ching

1 **Corruption of Real Money** **(Monetary History and Global Economy)**
http://www.corruptionofrealmoney.com

2 **Terrorlands (Children's Horror Fiction)**
http://www.terrorlands.com/

www.ingramcontent.com/pod-product-compliance
Lightning Source LLC
Chambersburg PA
CBHW022106210326
41520CB00045B/236